Thatcher Stole My Trousers

Alexei Sayle

BLOOMSBURY CIRCUS

LONDON · OXFORD · NEW YORK · NEW DELHI · SYDNEY

Bloomsbury Circus
An imprint of Bloomsbury Publishing Plc

50 Bedford Square
London
WC1B 3DP
UK

1385 Broadway
New York
NY 10018
USA

www.bloomsbury.com

First published in Great Britain 2016

British Library Cataloguing-in-Publication Data
A catalogue record for this book is available from the British Library.

Library of Congress Cataloguing-in-Publication data has been applied for.

ISBN: HB: 978-1-4088-6453-1
TPB: 978-1-4088-6456-2
ePub: 978-1-4088-6455-5

4 6 8 10 9 7 5

Typeset by Newgen Knowledge Works (P) Ltd., Chennai, India
Printed and bound in Great Britain by CPI Group (UK) Ltd, Croydon CR0 4YY

MIX
Paper from
responsible sources
FSC® C020471
FSC
www.fsc.org

For Linda

The twentieth-century philosopher George Santayana once wrote, 'History is a pack of lies . . . told by people who weren't there.' I at least was there.

Contents

Eric's Last Day

All his working life my father was a railwayman. Through his older brothers Joe Sayle got a job on the old Cheshire Lines Committee at the age of sixteen in the year before the General Strike and remained in the railway industry until he retired due to ill health in the late 1960s. The railways became so woven into our daily life that alongside Communism, trains became our family credo. There weren't many problems we thought couldn't be solved either by the violent overthrow of capitalism or by getting on a train.

In September 1971 I climbed aboard the sleek jet-plane-like carriage of a blue-and-grey InterCity train that waited imperceptibly humming at the platform of Liverpool's Lime Street Station embarking on the most important journey of my life. I settled myself into a plastic, foam and metal seat facing a wide table, gauzy orange curtains hanging at the window. In the buffet car all the food came from a department of British Rail called 'Travellers Fayre', the spelling of 'Fayre' implying that your food would be cooked by the Knights Templar and served to you by capering jesters, which indeed it often was.

In a piece of almost Soviet centralisation, from the Highlands to Cornwall every single item of refreshment in the buffet car was distributed via a central depot in the Midlands so that all produce on the railways was stale days before it reached the customer.

After a few minutes the journey towards the capital began with a surge of electricity and as we emerged from the sandstone tunnels that led out of Lime Street Station I was able to get a good view of a piece of graffiti which had recently appeared scrawled in paint on the wall by the side of the track, a missive which greeted each and every traveller coming from the South. It read in big black letters, 'FUCK OFF ALL COCKNEYS'. This message remained untouched for the next twenty years, despite its being passed by endless maintenance crews whose only action from time to time seemed to be to give it a fresh lick of paint.

This rail journey to London was almost as routine for me as the bus ride to school or the ferry crossing over the River Mersey. Being the son of a railwayman meant I was entitled to free or reduced-price train travel right across Europe, so when I was a child I'd frequently taken the four-hour journey with my parents to the capital, to march alongside them on political demonstrations or to accompany Joe to Trades Union Congresses at Southern seaside resorts, or as the first leg of the Continental rail trips we took every summer, firstly to France, Belgium and Holland and then later further east to the Communist countries of Czechoslovakia and Hungary. Later as a teenager I'd ridden the train on my own, visiting older friends in the capital, attending art exhibitions at the Tate or the ICA or at the beginning of several doomed

European hitch-hiking holidays which inevitably ended with me getting on a train in some European capital and fleeing back home.

This particular journey though felt different. Because I was leaving Liverpool for good and moving permanently to London, any return trips would be as a visitor. The next day would be my first as a student of painting at Chelsea School of Art. Being accepted to study at such a prestigious institution seemed proof to me that I was, as I'd always suspected, a truly talented and exceptional individual. Once the letter arrived containing my acceptance I would say to people back home in Liverpool, 'Yeah, I'm going to live in London, man, and I'll be like studying at like only the best painting college in the country. There were like fifteen thousand applicants for twenty places but I got the slot, man.'

It had been my strong desire to get away from home, to live in London, for as long as I could remember. There was a boutique called Neil's Place on Mount Pleasant in Liverpool where it was said the clothes sold there 'came from London'. That they were as hideous as anybody else's clothes was irrelevant, they 'came from London' and that meant Neil was rich enough to own a rather lovely British sports car styled by Bertone called a Gordon-Keeble, which was always parked ostentatiously outside his shop.

I wanted to move to the capital despite the fact that Liverpool was a city where for its size there was an extraordinary amount going on – music, art shows, poetry, football – but it still couldn't match London. I would read in the papers about all the rock gigs, exhibitions and plays in the capital and was awestruck. I didn't actually want to go to any of them, I just wanted to live in a place where they were on, where others took on the burden of seeing them all. London was the spot where everything was, and more importantly it was the place where my mother wasn't.

Because they were Communists and mixed in the same radical circles as I did, my parents had recently started turning up in the same pubs and attending the same late-night parties as me. It was not a good idea to have your mother relating anecdotes about your potty training to girls you wanted to get off with.

I wanted to move even though recently I'd achieved a great ideological victory over my mother Molly. Molly had suddenly noticed on Mother's Day other children and teenagers in the street coming to visit their mothers, bringing them chocolates and flowers and cooking them breakfast in bed. Angered by the fact that I had done nothing, she started yelling, 'You never do anything for me! Why don't you do something like the other children in the street for your mother on Mother's Day, bring me flowers or clock radios!'

'But, Molly,' I replied calmly, 'you expressly told me when I was a child that Mother's Day was a capitalist conspiracy thought up by the floral industrial complex and the fascist greetings-card monoploy to steal the hard-earned cash of the working classes.'

'Fuck off, Lexi,' she said.

Yet though it was my strongest wish to leave home and go to college I was also scared. On the bookshelves in our front room in Valley Road, Liverpool, amongst the serious and mostly wrong volumes from the Left Book Club, there were several optimistic novels of social progress such as Winifred

Holtby's *South Riding*. In *South Riding* the uplifting conclusion is that the bright working-class girl manages to throw off her proletarian past and, fighting against great odds, gain a place at university. What the novel doesn't mention is the bright girl's sense of dislocation, her feeling that she will never again be part of any tribe, neither the one she has left nor the one she is going towards, that she has made a terrible mistake, will be lonely for the rest of her life and people in London will laugh at the provincial cut of her trousers. The bright girl's fears in *South Riding* would have been compounded if she'd chosen to begin her new life sharing a damp cellar with a load of Arabs.

Rather than staying in the college's reasonably priced hall of residence in Battersea I'd chosen to take up the offer of a place in the flat of a friend who was already living in London. This turned out to be a foolish choice. As far back as I could remember, and becoming more pronounced once I got to my teenage years, my inclination was to make important life decisions based not upon what was sensible or right or appropriate but rather on what I thought might sound impressive to some imaginary people who lived inside my head. These people encouraged me to make a lot of mistakes.

Queen's Gate, South Kensington, was a long, tree-lined boulevard of Italianate stucco mansions, running from Old Brompton Road at its southern end to the gates of Hyde Park on Kensington Gore. Many of the houses were embassies or palatial homes but Number 99, though distinguished by a loggia supported by cast-iron pillars which ran along the whole of the first floor, was a decaying wreck, and 99B, the basement, was a warren of empty, dank rooms with only an outside toilet in a brickwork cubicle under the road. Just one of these rooms was occupied by my friend from Liverpool. He was a Palestinian electronics engineer called Wassim Abdullah, who had recently got a job in London and had rented the room from the Pole who owned the entire house. I hadn't really paid much attention when he'd told me about the place and offered me somewhere to stay, deafened as I was by a fantasy of independence. The imaginary people in my head were particularly impressed by the fact that Queen's Gate was only a few minutes' walk from my college. When I reached my new home late at night, clutching my one suitcase and my slim folder of art work, Wassim informed me that the space where I was assigned to sleep was a patch of floor at the foot of his bed. He occupied the bed itself with one or sometimes two girlfriends while the stretches of floor down the sides were usually taken up by other Arabs.

The room turned out to contain many hazards both hygienic and environmental. Apart from poisoning by the various moulds and decomposing foodstuffs that were scattered about, there was also a serious danger of electrocution. Rather than buy a conventional alarm clock Wassim had built his own digital version, highly advanced for the period, which, while wildly inaccurate as a timepiece, irresistibly drew mice out from all the dank corners of the basement to creep up close, hypnotised by this sinister humming black box squatting on the floor. Then from a few centimetres away the clock would kill the rodents with a flash of the electricity that was constantly leaking from its faulty innards. Every morning there would be a small pile of furry corpses beside the clock which you had to step over to get to the gruesome outside lavatory while ensuring that you didn't get an unpleasant shock yourself. Rather than to a bell or a buzzing noise, Wassim had rigged the alarm to a car headlight on a cardboard tube suspended from the ceiling. To wake him up the headlight would shine directly into his face, and a record player with a version of the Maoist Peking opera *The East Is Red* on the turntable would start to play. All this blazed and squawked into life every morning some time between 6 a.m. and 9.15.

So, awake hours before it was necessary, I walked through unfamiliar streets into Chelsea for my first day of higher education.

The School of Art was a white, mosaic-tiled cube with a large bronze Henry Moore statue out front in the courtyard. The hard-edged modernist block bore no relation to the other buildings on Manresa Road, which were odd-looking two- and three-storey brick cottages. I found these houses unsettling because it was impossible to tell when they had been built – it could have been any time between about 1790 and last week. In Liverpool everything looked exactly like it was supposed to look while here in London things seemed to shift and squirm.

Passing one of these houses at the north end of the street I noticed a policeman stationed at its white-painted rustic gate. Later I learned that this was because the house belonged to an MP named Margaret Thatcher who had recently been appointed Secretary of State for Education and Science and was therefore technically in charge of my schooling. Most government ministers did not have a policeman at their gate but this Thatcher woman had a way of getting on people's nerves.

My first day at college was lonely and confusing, my spirits only lifting when next to me in the canteen queue during the morning break I found someone I'd known slightly from Southport Art School, where I'd just completed a two-year foundation course. In fact I had met him only once when he'd come to pay a visit the previous term, acting the successful returnee from the big city. His name was Eric, and a fellow student in my year said to him, 'Oh Alexei's got into Chelsea for next term.'

He replied dismissively, 'They're taking anybody these days.' And I said, 'Fuck off, Eric.'

It was a measure of my desperation that, eagerly pushing next to him, I now said, 'Hi, Eric, man, remember me? Alexei from Southport? We had a nice chat about how you'd look out for me when I came here.'

'Oh yeah . . . hi, man . . .' he replied in a confused fashion. I noticed that Eric was very pale, there was a thin sheen of sweat on his face and he seemed to have chosen for his breakfast two tea bags laid on a slice of bacon and smeared with jam. 'Actually, man . . .' he said, 'I don't feel too . . .' and so saying Eric passed out, pulling his tray on top of him as he fell.

Nobody else seemed interested in this figure lying on the floor covered in tea bags and bacon so I went to get the only other person I knew, my supervising lecturer who I'd been introduced to just that morning. This man, an important and celebrated abstract expressionist painter, was extremely annoyed at having to take a student with a bleeding head wound and his agitated friend to Fulham's St Stephen's Hospital in his brand-new, bright yellow Alfa Romeo Giulietta.

Eric was wheeled off on a trolley while me and the lecturer sat and waited in uneasy silence until finally a nurse came to us and said, 'Well Eric should be OK though from the look of things he's suffering from a bad case of pleurisy . . .' and here she stared hard at me and her voice became stern, 'but also, judging by the marks on his arm, for a long time your friend has been a heavy drug-user.' I saw the celebrated abstract expressionist looking at me thoughtfully. Though Eric was a mere casual acquaintance, someone who I had never spoken more than a few words to, from my very first day of college all the staff thought that I too was a junkie.

It's a Sort of . . .

Eric did not return the next day or any day after that, and following its shaky start my first term continued to be difficult. Just before the Christmas break I received a letter from the head of the painting department informing me that my performance and attendance had been poor and in a couple of months I would have to go before something called the painting council. If my work then didn't measure up I'd be told to leave.

I knew I hadn't been working very hard but didn't consider this floundering to be entirely my fault. There were a number of factors that were making my life at college tough. Firstly there was the problem of the visiting lecturers. Among all the leading art schools there existed a custom of hiring practising painters and sculptors as visiting lecturers. This was basically a way of subsidising artists by paying them a fee in return for which they would pop into the college a few days a term to talk to the students, to let them see what a real artist looked like. In theory there was nothing bad about this practice but unfortunately most of these painters and sculptors resented having their time taken up, had no commitment to education and possessed no teacher training. I would be sitting in my space, having just worked up a bit of conviction over what I was doing, when some gangly man in a leather jacket would come along, take one look at my painting and say, 'No! no! no! That's completely wrong what you've done, it couldn't be more wide of the mark if you'd actually tried to produce the worst art in the history of the world ever. You see the mistake you're making is . . .Oh is that the time? I'm off now, see you again in six months. Good luck with your terrible painting!'

Secondly there was the problem of the talking. One of my difficulties was that I couldn't talk a good painting and in the art world talking a good painting seemed to be much more important than actually painting a good painting. In the twentieth century art had become so much about the internal thoughts of the artist, intellectual ideas of randomness and accident, real or faked incompetence and naivety, that nobody could be sure any more what was good art and what wasn't. The painters and sculptors who succeeded were the ones who gave the most convincing explanations of what their work was about. If you talked a good painting your work would then be taken up by 'the three Cs' – four if you included cunts. The first C was the critic, who would write you up in the papers and magazines; the second C the art gallery curator who would put your work in important shows; the third the collector who would buy your art to put on their walls or in their gardens making you rich in the process.

But the talking came first. The most frequent phrase I would hear being used by my fellow students was 'It's a sort of . . .'. As in 'It's a sort of evocation of the decline of the

Habsburg Empire.' This being said of a pile of fire extinguishers covered in glue and nailed to a stuffed donkey.

My problem was that I had gone to art school because it was my only chance of higher education, since I'd passed only four O levels, and because I was good at painting and drawing, but I had never truly been able to say what my work was about. My pictures were all copied from photographs, vaguely political in theme and done with thin washes of oil paint heavily diluted with white spirit applied with very stiff brushstrokes that seemed to tear at the canvas. Several of the lecturers asked me if I was perhaps imitating Turner's watercolours or Goya in his later years, but the truth was that I had spent the allowance the college gave me for materials on drink, and so I diluted the few tubes of oil paint I owned with turps simply to make them go a lot further. Similarly the visible strokes came from the fact that I used brushes other students had thrown in the bin because they were worn down to stumps. When they weren't looking I fished them out again. More than that I had only the vaguest idea what my pictures were about and so could offer no convincing explanation.

The problem of the visiting lecturers might have been surmountable if some tutor had taken me in hand and eased me through my early months, but during the upheavals amongst students in Paris in 1968 a notion had arisen that for the staff of any educational institution to actually try and do something called 'teaching' was hierarchical, hegemonist and probably imperialist as well. The staff at Chelsea took to this hypothesis with enthusiasm and so even if you wanted to be demotivated by a practising artist it was often quite hard to find one. The best person to ask where the teaching staff of the art school had got to was the policeman stationed outside Margaret Thatcher's house. He'd usually be able to tell you whether they were in a pub on the corner of the Fulham Road called the Queen's Elm, a wine bar on the King's Road called the Loose Rein or the Chelsea Arts Club, which was in the next street.

Yet though I was unhappy there I really didn't want to be thrown out of college. To be ejected and forced to return to Liverpool would have felt like the most enormous catastrophe. The people in my home town could be very cutting and sarcastic, especially to somebody who had gone around loudly bragging about what a special person they were to have gained a place at Chelsea School of Art – the very institution that was now kicking them out.

Fortunately, though my painting wasn't going well, I had begun making short, sort of funny films with a fellow student from Southport called Alan Hodge who was studying graphics at Saint Martin's School of Art on Charing Cross Road right in the heart of the West End. We produced these little movies using a Soviet-made clockwork 8mm camera.

On the day of my interview in front of the painting council I showed my and Alan's films alongside the few scrawny paintings I had managed to produce – though I made no mention of the fact that the 8mm movies were part of a joint project. One short featured me playing the part of a very bad magician, standing on a rickety table in a garden performing all kinds of inept tricks, some of them done with crude stop-camera techniques that Alan had pioneered. The bogus and insincere performer I portrayed was surrounded by an enthralled, hysterical and dumb audience who rapturously applauded and cried out for more following his every clumsy sleight of hand and badly performed trick – I think the film might have been a satire on art criticism.

As I looked around the painting council in the flickering light of the projector I saw that this panel of men who were judging me were arranged in precisely the same kind of semi-circle as the idiotic audience in the film, and being only a few years older than the students in the movie were dressed in exactly the same style.

Afterwards, as I waited nervously outside the principal's office, my supervisor, the man I hadn't spoken to since we'd been in the A&E department at St Stephen's Hospital on the day that Eric collapsed, came up to me and said, 'That was us, wasn't it?'

'How do you mean?' I replied, playing for time.

'The idiots in the audience, that was us, wasn't it? The staff here at Chelsea, the painting council?'

In reality it wasn't directly about them but rather it was about all authority figures in art, but that didn't stop me saying, 'Yeah, man. It was like totally and completely about you lot.'

'Well,' he said, 'it was great. We've decided you can stay here for the next two years. Also . . .' And here a softer tone crept into his voice. 'I'm glad to see you've kicked the H.'

Along with the relief that flooded through me there was a sense both of resentment of and admiration for those who ran the college. What a wonderful and humane institution, I thought to myself, that's prepared to give someone their life back owing to the fact that they have cruelly mocked, pilloried and satirised that same institution. But on another level, I still thought they were a pretentious bunch of wankers.

A Long Way to Go for a Chocolate Bar

One thing that unsettled me about Chelsea School of Art was that it was so full of posh kids. This was something I had not anticipated. I don't know who I'd thought would be a student at an art college in Chelsea – after all this was not an academy of social work or a mining institute – but it had simply never occurred to me that there would be so many offspring of the bourgeoisie. This was a particular problem for me as a practising Communist and as the child of Communists because we believed that these kids and their parents were responsible for every single bad thing that happened in the world. The speeches our leaders made, the articles that were printed in our newspapers and the books of Communist theory that we studied all railed against the ruling class and the bourgeoisie and the terrible crimes they committed. But in coming face to face with our enemy I realised that up until that point I hadn't truly believed that they existed. The rich had just seemed like some remote malevolent entity, a kind of distant bogey class, something to frighten the proletariat with. My dad would say to me, 'If you don't eat your greens then that representative of the kulaks [i.e., the land-owning rural bourgeoisie who extract surplus value from the honest toil of the peasant class] who lives under the stairs will come and get you.' But here they were attending lectures or in the adjacent studio space and they seemed perfectly nice with the most lovely manners.

Something else I observed about the children of the wealthy was that they all seemed to know each other. Not necessarily literally, but there was a web of private school or parental connection which meant that each rich kid would always have a strong link to the next rich kid.

'Do you know Arbutus Splodge?' one would ask another.

'No, I don't think so.'

'He did prep at St Malegrewe's.'

'My brother did prep at St Malegrewe's.'

'Well he'll know Arbutus Splodge then.'

'Why do you ask?'

'I've heard he's having a turkey sandwiches and champagne party.'

'Well in that case I'll get my brother to procure us an invite.'

These children of the wealthy were very different to the students at my previous college in Southport. None of them were rich, indeed it was only in that brief era of education for everybody that they could have got to an art school at all. There was a boy we called Nightshift because his appearance was so dishevelled and untidy he always looked like he'd just come off a nocturnal stretch at an iron foundry or a badly run abattoir. There was another whose only piece of artistic equipment was a half-inch painter-and-decorator's brush that he used for everything, including life-drawing, calligraphy, watercolour landscapes and graphics.

I had one friend at Southport who was on probation for some minor crime and therefore his local authority decided not to give him a grant or pay his fees. Faced with the prospect of starving he stole a huge box of a KitKat rival Bar Six from the pavilion of a tennis club and lived on them for a year. Sometimes if I fancied a chocolate bar I'd get the train to Southport making full use of my free train pass and go to his bedsit for a Bar Six rather than pay for one myself in a shop. Yet this boy later on became head of department at an art school himself.

In such company it wasn't hard for me to quickly become one of the cool kids at college. I was the only student there who came from Liverpool. The others in my group were either from the small seaside town of Southport itself or from villages in the hinterland built on the rich black Lancashire soil that always smelled of cabbages, so I was, in effect, the hip dude from the big city. That wasn't going to happen at Chelsea.

One day in the first term I was in an art history class and the lecturer put up a slide of a Van Gogh painting. Behind me I heard a girl in my year say, 'Oh yes, I know that painting, the original's in the hall of our apartment in Rome.' And I thought: Fucking hell, it's not even in the living room, it's in the hall where they keep the coats! Though my idea of a hall and her idea of a hall might have been different.

I had only known one child of the wealthy before. She was a pretty, rich girl, a student at Liverpool University, who'd joined the Maoist party, known as the Communist Party of Britain (Marxist–Leninist), that I was a member of before I went to Chelsea. This girl appeared to have been so crippled by guilt over her parents' wealth that after a few months she'd given up her university course to go and work on the production line in a factory. At the same time she had begun an affair with an obnoxious, loud-mouthed, married dock-worker who was one of a gang who used to stand by the door in the pub we all drank in. This guy didn't even know how lucky he was to have a pretty, rich girl work out her parental issues on him, instead he assumed that there was something about his repellent alcoholic personality that was intrinsically attractive to young women.

There was another guy who drank in the same pub called Harry Jackson who worked as a bus driver. One night Harry arranged to go for a drink with the rich girl but when he turned up wearing a suit she was really disappointed because she'd wanted him to be wearing his corporation bus driver's uniform, so she would be seen out and about with a true proletarian.

Of course this girl got on very well with my mother, constantly flattering Molly, saying what an inspiration she was to all women, and in return my mother really liked her and told me on several occasions that she wished that this girl was her child rather than me.

The guilt this girl felt over being rich would have appeared alien to the affluent kids at Chelsea who seemed to have a sunny and untroubled attitude to the many advantages their parents' money gave them.

The War on Britain's Roads

One of the reasons for my poor college attendance was that during my first year in London I kept going back to Liverpool to visit my new girlfriend – indeed I was on Merseyside so often that a lot of people didn't realise I'd moved to London. Linda and me had met in the summer just before I was due to go to Chelsea. Her best friend from school, Dorothy, had been going out with my best friend from school, Cliff Cocker. The four of us had met for a drink in the Philharmonic pub. During the evening I kept slipping off to use the phone, leading Linda to suspect I was calling my girlfriend, when in fact I was ringing my mother, keeping her updated on whether I was coming home or not. Then after the pub closed at 10.30 we went to the Masque, a late-night coffee bar, reached via a rickety set of stairs, above a record shop called Probe Records in the studenty area of Liverpool. In order to have somewhere to go after the pubs closed you were forced to endure folk music, readings of their work by the third-best Mersey beat poets and milky coffee served in shallow Pyrex cups that ensured it was cold before you could drink it.

In order to entertain my audience of two pretty girls, I brought out my best material. In 1968 at the age of sixteen I'd tried to spend the summer alone in Paris sleeping under the bridges of the Seine. The city was only just recovering from the student riots which had brought down the government so the authorities were extremely edgy. One example of this edginess was that I had managed to get myself arrested, driven to the outskirts of town in a police van and told never to come back. As usual, since my solo holidays always ended in failure, I wandered about aimlessly until a railway station appeared and I took the train back to Liverpool. Over the years I'd worked this slender story into an epic, Homeric narrative of adventure and danger, which I always told girls as soon as I could because it really seemed to impress them. But when I tried to tell it to Linda in the Masque she just laughed at me and said I'd behaved like an idiot. On the other hand she told me she could get the same bus as me home even though I knew it was out of her way and when I asked her if she'd go out with me again she said yes.

Linda had studied English at Bangor University in North Wales for three years before becoming a teacher, and was currently working at a boys' secondary modern school in Hoylake on the Wirral. She had attended Bangor because after passing her A levels she had gone on holiday, hitch-hiking around Europe with a couple of girlfriends, and told her parents to choose her university for her: anywhere as long as it wasn't Liverpool. Wanting to keep their only daughter as close as possible Linda's mum and dad had used a wooden ruler and an old atlas to measure, in inches, the nearest university town to Liverpool and had chosen Bangor in North Wales, not realising that though it might have been near on paper, it was in a whole other country where many spoke a different language, there were two large river estuaries to be skirted and a narrow coastline fringed by mountains to be travelled down, so it took her over six hours to get there on the bus.

It was a relief, though not a surprise, to learn that Linda was interested in left-wing politics – you could not really go out with someone if they weren't. People would say, 'I met this girl, she was really good-looking and her dad imported denim of a previously unknown style and quality from the West Coast of the United States, but she couldn't differentiate between the various factions involved in the liberation struggle in the Western Sahara so I finished with her.'

Only a few months after we met we spent our first New Year's Eve together, wandering around the bombsites and derelict buildings of Liverpool, carrying a bucket and brush pasting up posters for a showing of a Maoist film, *Taking Tiger Mountain by Strategy*, in a room above a pub, and Linda soon joined the Merseyside Branch of the Communist Party of Britain (Marxist–Leninist). Unlike me, whose radicalism had been inherited from my parents like a dukedom, Linda was much more serious and practical in her approach to politics. When she'd been younger, about ten or eleven, she had gone through a phase of religious fanaticism. After making extensive comparisons she decided the Church that was nearest to the word of God, as revealed through the Bible, was the Baptist, conveniently located down the road in the People's Church of Everton. This was a very strict Protestant group that allowed no make-up, alcohol or pop music and was in every way very austere: they would sing hymns and nature rambles were allowed, though they spent most of their time in prayer.

At the age of fifteen she was taking O level religious education but when she compared the life of Jesus as told in the Synoptic Gospels, Matthew, Mark and Luke, she found that they differed greatly in their accounts, which made her think: If this is the word of God how can there be any contradictions? So she left.

Now she was a Maoist. Lin Piao, who at one point had been Mao Tse-tung's successor and official best friend, had suddenly fled China after supposedly plotting to depose the Great Leader, but his plane had been shot down. According to reports in Western newspapers the Chinese authorities had been alerted to his defection by his daughter. Linda's dad asked her, 'Would you turn your father in?'

'Yes, if I thought you were an enemy of the revolution,' she replied. 'After all, don't you think, Dad,' she continued, 'that it's better that one man dies if it saves ten thousand?'

'His own daughter,' Linda's father kept repeating in a hurt and wondering tone.

My girlfriend was happy enough to introduce me to her parents early on in our relationship. When I first went to their flat, picking her up on the way to a meeting, I wore my best clothes, my dad's railway overcoat tied up with string and some huge green flares my mother had made in her trademark style with one leg much shorter than the other, both of which I felt complemented my long, uncombed, greasy black hair and beard. After I'd gone, Linda's mother burst into tears because she thought her daughter was going out with a forty-year-old tramp. Linda's dad, Pat, was a very shy man who didn't say much. In fact the only one he'd open up to was their cat. Sometimes the family would listen at the door as he told their pet about his day or how he planned to move to Guernsey and open a sweet shop.

The only time Pat became voluble was when showing visitors the hot-water boiler and central heating system, which was located in a cupboard in the kitchen of their flat. He had an interest in the central heating because he was a pipe-fitter welder. Everyone got a look at the boiler including Linda's schoolmates, and of course me, though Linda's dad didn't really expect me to be interested, seeing as he thought I lived in a cardboard box. All in all we both felt things had gone quite well.

On the other hand I managed to keep Linda from meeting Molly my mother for as long as possible, but one winter's afternoon my luck finally ran out.

If I was back from college in London, I would be waiting when Linda got off the train from Hoylake at Liverpool Central Station. That day we decided to walk through the entrance to Lewis's department store, which led directly off the station concourse. There was a Luis Buñuel film that year which had been a surprise hit in the cinema called *The Discreet Charm of the Bourgeoisie*. In the sense that you could definitely say it was about anything, the movie concerned a group of upper-middle-class people attempting – despite continual interruptions – to dine together. In one scene one of them enters a secret cubicle as if they are visiting the lavatory but instead they shamefully and hurriedly eat a meal. That was the way food and dining were regarded in Liverpool in the early 1970s, as an ignominious and unseemly practice. One of the few places where eating was celebrated was the Food

Hall of Lewis's. We liked to walk through the marble-lined hall between the chiller cabinets full of pies, cakes and sliced meats.

That day in a corner by the biscuit counter I suddenly became aware of a crowd of shoppers clustered around some-body who, though they couldn't be seen, could easily be located by their screaming, sobbing and crying out in great distress.

'My God!' Linda said. 'It sounds like there's a woman over there who's having some kind of breakdown.' She appeared to be planning to slow down, possibly to offer help, but I had already recognised the sound of the screaming, sobbing and crying out in great distress from its usual place in the living room of our house.

I said to Linda, 'That's my mother, just keep walking.' Unfortunately my girlfriend, not having met Molly before, was appalled at my callousness and insisted we go over to offer assistance. Pushing through the press of people, we came upon my mother at the centre of a circle of disturbed and horrified onlookers, her eyes raw with weeping, her clothes in disarray from where she had been tearing at them and her red hair sticking straight up in the air.

'They've robbed me, Lexi!' she shouted, not at all surprised to see me amongst the crowd. 'They've stolen from me and they won't do anything about it!'

When she'd calmed down a little Molly explained between anguished sobs that a shop assistant had short-changed her by ten shillings, and that was why she was making such a scene. She screamed at the woman until a manager appeared and offered my mother a £5 gift voucher by way of apology. When we got home the missing banknote was found in Molly's purse.

Linda insisted on getting the bus back to our house with my mother. As the three of us walked from the stop on Oakfield Road towards our house a car suddenly swerved across from the opposite lane into oncoming traffic and its male driver yelled at Molly, 'Fuck you, you old bat!'

With equal fury my mother screamed at the departing vehicle, 'No, fuck you, you fucking fuck!'

What shocked Linda was not just the verbal assault, but the way in which my mother afterwards instantly reverted to her previous calm demeanour.

Linda asked my mother, 'Molly, why was that driver swearing and trying to kill you?'

Molly professed to have no idea, except, as she said, 'You'll find, Linda, that owning a car makes people act like capitalists and all capitalists think nothing of driving at fifty miles an hour on the pavement shouting swear words.' This wasn't the explanation.

When a child, especially an only child, leaves home it can be extremely traumatic and parents react in a variety of ways; some become obsessed with grandchildren, others take to the bottle and a few become lollipop ladies. The School Crossing Patrol was an organisation of old people rather like the Second World War Home Guard or the *Volkssturm*. They were not armed with First World War .303 Lee-Enfields or Panzerfausts, instead their weapon was a round orange, red and white sign mounted on a four-foot long pole which read, 'Stop Children Crossing'. With this pole they were supposed to shepherd children across the road from their school gates or help them traverse busy junctions in safety. Molly's post was a busy corner at the intersection of nearby Breck Road and Oakfield Road. Dressed in a police cap with a glossy peak, a silver Liver bird badge at its centre, the strap drawn tight under her chin, and a shiny white plastic mac, she was supposed solely to help local schoolchildren get over the road, but she saw it more as an opportunity to conduct her own private war on motorists, a war as ferocious in its way as that being waged by the Vietcong against the forces of US imperialism. She was, at the same time as being a lollipop lady, secretary of the Merseyside Medical Aid for Vietnam Committee and perhaps some of the stories of armed struggle she had heard had seeped into her consciousness. A lot of Communists, like my mother, never approved of automobiles – couldn't see the point of a car unless it was dark green, armoured and had a big red star painted on the front.

Like the unhappy American Marines 'in country', the drivers of Anfield never knew when or where Molly was going to strike next. It was an accepted convention that a lollipop lady pretty much stuck to the corner that they had been assigned, but my mother had given herself a more roving brief so that a motorist might be in their car half a mile away from the junction with no schoolchildren in sight when Molly would leap out waving her lollipop at their windscreen, forcing them to scream to a halt. A minority chose to swerve around her swearing, but this was only a temporary victory since Molly knew that unless they wanted to take a long detour the drivers had to come back the next day and then she'd be waiting for them.

It's Under the Hat when You're Ready

Linda and I came from very similar backgrounds, in fact in purely Marxist terms her family outranked mine, since while my dad as a railway guard was only semi-skilled and in a service industry, her father was a skilled worker, a pipe-fitter welder involved in the construction of power plants and factories, which made him a true proletarian. Linda and her family had only recently been rehoused to a brand-new tower block maybe half a mile from where I lived in Anfield. Before then they had occupied a Victorian house on nearby Seacome Street off Scotland Road, but in 1967 the whole district had been swept away so thoroughly that there was more left of Hiroshima than there was of Linda's old neighbourhood.

Their high-rise was called Marwood Tower and I had passed it many times on the bus going into town before I knew she lived there. In front of their block was a children's playground I'd often noticed because it was said to be 'award-winning'. I assumed that the body which had given the playground its award was the Society for Promoting the Injury of Children by Encouraging them to Play on Lethal Structures, so dangerous and scary did the twisted bits of rusty metal scattered in front of the flats seem. Fatal injuries had only been avoided by the fact that, as far as I could tell, no children had ever tried to play on this bleak windy triangle of land at the junction of three major roads.

Where I came from in Anfield was early-twentieth-century working-class terraced housing, and growing up there I had felt, not exactly that the area was prosperous but that there had been a definite sense of security. All the houses were neat and all the men had jobs they went off to every morning. Where Linda had grown up, Seacome Street, it had been much poorer. Their house hadn't been fitted with electricity until she was six and it never possessed an indoor toilet. There had also been a more Dickensian, or perhaps Hogarthian, quality to the inhabitants of her area compared to the dull solidity of the people of Anfield. She told me of a family from her old street who on a Monday morning following the weekend, after the husband's wages had run out, would pawn their cat. The wife would carry this ferocious tortoiseshell tom to the pawn shop. Then every night on her way back from school Linda would see it sitting happily in the shop window until Thursday came around and it would be redeemed.

But attitudes on Scotland Road were also harder, more entrenched into a kind of working-class prejudice against anybody trying to gain a world outside the narrow boundaries of a few streets. Linda had been the first child in the whole neighbourhood to go to a grammar school and she had faced a lot of resentment, yet the same girls who taunted Linda when she came home in her school uniform would play with her in the street once she'd changed into her ordinary clothes.

It was not that a lot of the other kids in her neighbourhood lacked intelligence, just that access to the better schools was fixed in favour of children from richer areas, so the majority of youngsters from working-class neighbourhoods were excluded. Getting to a grammar school was conditional on passing the eleven-plus exam, itself based on the work of an 'educational-ist' called Cyril Burt who, after his death, was shown to have been faking his research results, rather like a sort of educational Donald Crowhurst – the yachtsman who in 1969 had pretended to sail around the world, while he was in fact bobbing about in the middle of the Atlantic, sending false radio reports of his position, before throwing himself overboard.

Linda's parents were much more conventional than Molly and Joe and they suffered a great deal of anxiety over what the neighbours might think, whereas mine, particularly my mother, did not share these concerns. Indeed my mother and father revelled in their difference, their unconventionality.

Linda's mum and dad also had a fear of stepping outside the narrow confines of people who were exactly the same as them. Her mother had one anecdote that illustrated the dangers of mixing with those who were different. When she'd worked in a factory Linda's mother's best friend had been a pretty girl called Nellie who one day accepted the offer of a date from a man who was a clerk in the factory's office, and therefore somebody who was several rungs above her on the social scale.

They had arranged to go to the cinema, the clerk bought the tickets and then after they'd settled in their seats and the lights began to go down he'd turned to Nellie and whispered, 'It's under the hat when you're ready.'

CRUEL SHOES

In the early 1970s many in Britain still lived from day to day in great pain, distress and discomfort. The great majority of this pain, distress and discomfort was caused by their shoes. The idea that footwear should be comfortable was not one that was prevalent back then and the situation was made worse by the fact that nearly everyone's shoes were made by a single, gigantic, lazy and inefficient monopoly called the British Shoe Corporation. You could buy your shoes in a multitude of different shops with names like Freeman, Hardy and Willis, Saxone, Trueform, Bertie, Dolcis, Manfield, or Curtess, thinking they were separate entities, when in fact they were all the same, all just fronts for the British Shoe Corporation.

This might have gone some way to explaining why the young assistants would disappear for such a long time when they said they'd look in the back of the shop for a shoe in your size. I began to wonder if perhaps all the BSC shoes in Liverpool were stored in a single depot connected by underground tunnels to each of their stores and the assistant would have to walk several miles, or travel by light electric railway, to get you a pair of suede Chelsea boots in a size 10. This lack of competition also meant that the shoes were very badly made and often broke, sometimes throwing you to the ground or twisting your ankle. For some reason British Shoe Corporation shoes often seemed to have a large piece of jagged metal as part of the inner sole that regularly snapped, stabbing you in the foot and increasing the enormous pain your footwear already gave you in normal day-to-day use.

For our first proper date I had told Linda I wanted to take her to a Chinese restaurant, so she dressed up and I too wore my best clothes – my blue velvet jacket, white sailor trousers that buttoned up the front and a pair of blue-and-white 'co-respondent' shoes with three-inch-high stacked cork soles. In fact, the Chinese restaurant was really just a chip shop halfway between my house in Anfield and her parents' flat off Scotland Road, which had a shabby side room with linoleum on the floor and a couple of wonky dining tables for people to eat off. Linda, who had dined at considerably better places, was very kind not to mention how crappy it was. Or perhaps she was put off by the blood seeping into my socks as I limped painfully into the restaurant. Though it was only a few hundred yards from our house to the chip shop, by the time I got there my shoes had so cut up my feet that they were bleeding profusely. I had planned to walk Linda home but in fact, when I stood, the pain was so great that I couldn't move without her support and so, looking like a victim of some overdressed war, I hobbled home leaning on the shoulder of my girlfriend.

The Popular Front for the
Liberation of Finchley

After Christmas Wassim, having had enough of living in a
dingy vault in South Kensington, found us a much nicer flat
to rent in the north London suburb of Finchley. Unlike our
former dreary basement this was a large, light-filled apartment, formed from the top half of a semi-detached house,
halfway down a pleasant, tree-lined avenue that led off the
high street.

I had no idea why he took me with him when he moved. It
can only have been the Arabic obligation to provide hospitality, since apart from paying my portion of the rent more or
less regularly I did not contribute anything else to the life of
that flat.

The apartment came with a third bedroom, so Wassim
advertised for flatmates in the London newspaper the *Evening
Standard*. Almost the first to respond were a pair of pretty,
twenty-year-old French girls who worked as secretaries in
central London. Unsurprisingly every other applicant was

told to fuck off and they got the room. Wassim, like all the other Arabs I'd met, had always tended towards a nocturnal lifestyle, and having two young French girls to run around tickling all night didn't help him get any rest, so often the only sleep he got was on the tube going into work. Sometimes in the middle of the night I would emerge from my bedroom dressed in striped flannel pyjamas and shout at them, 'Can you keep the noise down, please! You know I have to be in college by lunchtime.'

Wassim was a persistent and prolific shoplifter, something I pretended I was fine with (in Liverpool I'd heard shop-lifting referred to as 'affirmative shopping'). In fact it made me uncomfortable but I kept my mouth shut because of the free food. Wassim's way of shoplifting meant that all the food in our apartment needed to be flat so it fitted under the big coat he wore when he went foraging in the local supermarkets. This in turn meant the fridge in the kitchen was crammed with large amounts of sliced ham, wafers of smoked salmon and slivers of cheese but there was nothing to put it on. I suppose I could have bought some bread or a packet of crackers with my own money, but that thought never occurred to me.

Even amongst a people whose hospitality verged on the demented Wassim was considered extremely hospitable, and soon our apartment turned into a social centre for young Arab men living in or passing through London.

One weekend the flat became the location for the Annual General Congress of an organisation known as PFLOAG – the Popular Front for the Liberation of the Occupied Arab Gulf. PFLOAG was a Marxist revolutionary group that hoped to stir up revolt in the Sultanate of Oman mostly by smoking, staying up all night and reading foreign newspapers in cafés.

The first I knew about the conference was when I got up on a Saturday morning to fix myself some slices of breakfast but couldn't get into the kitchen because it was full of Arabs who'd formed a breakaway caucus and were in the middle of drafting a resolution of no confidence in the executive, who were at that moment running around the living room tickling the French girls.

In late spring, a little while after the PFLOAG congress and perhaps not unrelated to it, our flat was raided by the Metropolitan Police Special Branch. The assault party consisted of a group of plain-clothed officers, accompanied by dogs and their handlers, plus a large squad of uniformed police, some of them armed with big old-fashioned .38 Webley revolvers. The usual tactic with these swoops was to bash down the door early in the morning and then run in shouting and yelling. The thinking behind this was that everybody in the apartment was supposed to be asleep and would therefore be disorientated and compliant when the assault group burst in. But when they charged into our place at 5 a.m. all the people in the flat except for me – Wassim, the French girls, the other Arabs and their friends – were still wide awake, playing cards, cooking food or making strange electrical devices, and it was the Special Branch, the uniformed officers and their dogs, who ended up confused and disorientated and who, after a desultory and distracted search, left without finding whatever it was that they were looking for. Though the French girls did make the unhappy police officers some cinnamon pancakes to take away with them.

Most of the Arabs were just a blur of chequered shirts, moustaches, flared trousers and loud opinions, but there was one I particularly remember: he was slightly older and more melancholy than the rest, his hands twisted into claws from torture in an Israeli prison. One night he told me of his time in a training camp in the Libyan Desert. Along with the Palestinians there were fighters from armed groups drawn from all over the world.

He told me, 'We pretended the groups from Europe were oppressed. Though really we couldn't see what they were complaining about, compared to what the rest of us were suffering in our homelands.' The people who truly baffled him were the guerrillas from the factional wars going on in the Horn of Africa. 'They would boast,' he said, '"When we took the city the first thing we did was set fire to the hospital, then we blew up the reservoir and finally we rocketed the telephone exchange," and I would say to them, "But didn't you need the hospital and the reservoir and the telephone exchange for your people?" "No . . . no!" they replied. "Those things were all built by the government, they had to be destroyed!"'

'And what happened next ?' I would ask.

'"Oh," they said, "everybody got typhoid from polluted water, which they couldn't be treated for because the hospital wasn't there any more and we weren't able to phone anybody for help because we'd burnt down the telephone exchange, but at least we destroyed the things the government built! Then the government forces came back and killed everybody, except those of us who weren't too weak from typhoid to run away."'

Years later when I heard about Live Aid I suspected it was not the simple solution to famine that it seemed to be because of that conversation. The Marxist fighters from the Horn of Africa he'd described, the callous revolutionaries who would blow up a hospital just because it was built by their enemies, had in the intervening years seized power in Ethiopia. I was certain if they were given £150 million raised by the concert then they would just use it to pursue their wars and very little of it would go to the starving. Which was what happened.

One winter evening, since there was nobody else around, Wassim and I tried to have a night out in our neighbourhood. Finchley was an old-fashioned place: at 5 p.m. as the men and women came home from their work, trudging up the slope out of the tube station that resembled a rural halt, all the shops in the high street would be closing, the butcher, the greengrocer and the baker locking their doors and pulling down the blinds, gleefully turning away customers. Those men and women and their families then cowered in their houses until the next day and it was time to go to work again. So it was just the two of us driving around in his old battered beige Ford Consul looking for a place to have a drink. Wassim drove up and down to Liverpool in this car and picked up a summons from every constabulary along the entire route of the M1 and M6. Sometimes the beige-crested envelopes that dropped onto our doormat a few weeks after each of his trips north would be addressed to Wassim Abdullah but sometimes the recipient was one Abdullah Wassim, depending on which name my flatmate had given the police.

We must have looked like an odd couple: a neat Levantine man dressed in a short-sleeved shirt with a row of pens in his top pocket and a bearded, long-haired youth wearing a railwayman's overcoat. The first few pubs we tried fell silent as we entered. We finally found one in East Finchley that had been built in the 1960s as a tall cylindrical structure with a conical tiled roof. Inside under the high ceiling there was a scattering of thatched circular huts set on different levels in which drinkers sat sipping gassy beer. It was like a Bronze Age village that sold lager and peanuts.

Wassim seemed to like it and after a couple of pints of Red Barrel he began to reminisce about his childhood. Before they had been forced to flee by the Zionists, his father had been a tax collector, a mid-level official of the Ottoman Empire. After the Nakba, the catastrophe, they moved with thousands of other refugees to Beirut, a city of French colonial elegance on a curving bay, with a large Christian population amongst whom they could feel relatively safe.

On a Sunday the entire family would visit one of the city's many cinemas. He told me that his idea of what British people were like had been radically affected by watching films starring the demented Cockney nuisance Norman Wisdom, movies that were very popular in the Lebanon. Wassim said that until he saw films such as *Trouble in Store*, *The Square Peg*, *On the Beat* and *A Stitch in Time* he had always considered the British, who, along with the French, had held an iron grip on their region since the ending of the First World War, as coldblooded aristocrats – masterful, calculating and all-powerful. Once they had witnessed Wisdom's gumpy alter-ego Norman Pitkin in action they formed a completely different view. I thought, as he told me this, that the sudden collapse of the British Empire, the loss of India, Arabia, Africa and the West Indies within the space of twenty years, could be explained by the widespread viewing of Norman Wisdom movies.

These young Arab men who came to our flat in Finchley were the product of a struggle which had, unnoticed by most of the world, been going on for a generation and was now suddenly centre stage. Some had been born in camps, many had already lost brothers, sisters, aunts, uncles or cousins to death squads or in the armed struggle. There was a widely held belief in left-wing circles that to be caught up in a revolutionary conflict such as theirs was the best sort of life that you could wish for, to be oppressed made you noble and serious and a much better person than those of us in the West with our comfortable existences free of day-to-day terrors. However, after spending time with them, though I still loved their energy and generosity, it seemed to me that witnessing the horrors and suffering the traumas had not made them grow into something heroic and noble at all, instead had kept them in a kind of emotional refugee camp where everything was half-built and unfinished. In my experience there was a childish, hysterical quality to these young Arabs. Compared to me or my fellow students at Chelsea they appeared gullible and naive and desperate to believe in something, anything that would show them that despite what they had experienced the world made sense, that one day they would achieve some kind of justice.

Still, there was something about their constant laughter, their intelligence and enthusiasm for life which could sometimes make me feel grey and dull by comparison.

And they found me totally perplexing. None of the Arabs who came to our flat appeared to have much time for art or literature, which they thought of as irrelevant and dissolute in a time when everybody's energies should be directed to the practical problems of the anti-colonialist struggle.

'So you paint pictures?' they would ask me.

'Yes.'

'Do your pictures highlight the suffering of the downtrodden masses under the heel of the imperial oppressor?'

'No, not really, no. They're murky paintings of people sort of running about a bit.'

'And you make films?'

'Yes.'

'Are your films documentaries about the expropriation and murder of the Palestinian people?'

'No, not really, no. They're just sort of funny and mostly about how pretentious art is.'

'Funny. How does it aid the revolution, you trying to be funny?'

At the same time, they could seem awfully sophisticated in a way that made me jealous. For example, all of them knew their way around London much better than I did and from what they said when they rolled into our flat at 4 a.m., smelling either of dope or plastic explosive, they were also familiar with the back streets, palaces and plazas of Rome, Paris, Beirut, Berlin and New York. And unlike me or anybody else I knew, each of them spoke a dazzling number of languages fluently.

One Saturday as I was popping out to the tiny old-fashioned newsagent and sweet shop in Finchley Central

I asked Wassim if he wanted a paper. 'Yes,' he said. 'Can you get me a *Frankfurter Allgemeine Zeitung*? I find their political coverage is so much better than *El País* or *Svenska Dagbladet*.'

The Way We Was

By the early 1970s the golden age of cinemas was long past. Going to see a movie often meant sitting in a dirty, cavernous and dank space with only a smattering of other people. Most cinemas, like the majority of shoe shops, were run by one of two massive monopolies: lazy, complacent and slow-moving organisations with no respect for the historic buildings they owned and no regard for their customers. You got the very clear sense that nobody in Odeon or ABC had any love for movies, which they found it an inconvenience to have to show.

If there had been anything else to do people would have done it, but on the TV there were only three channels to watch, there was almost nowhere to get a cup of coffee once night fell and, though I spent a lot of time in pubs, there was a limit to how long you wanted to stand crammed in a corner having to yell above the noise. Pubs, like the cinemas and the shoe shops, were generally owned by a giant corporation, staffed by managers who were shuffled from place to place like minor colonial officials, and often furnished by somebody in an office hundreds of miles away so they had the atmosphere and personality of a room where you were taken by the border police if your passport details didn't quite add up. The beer in pubs, apart from the few where they eccentrically hung on to non-keg beer drawn by hand pumps, was either a gaseous yellow lager, a metallic-tasting orange bitter or a mysterious dark brown liquid called 'The Mild'.

One day when she was still at school Linda's dad said to her, 'You're sixteen now, Linda. You'll soon become a woman.'

Oh Christ, she thought, what's he going to say?

'And I've only got one piece of advice to give you as my daughter: Don't drink The Mild.'

If by some accident your local was a friendly and cosy place, this did not make you feel relaxed, rather it gave you a permanent sense of dread because you knew at any moment that your pub could be, probably would be, what was known as 'done up'. All the separate snug little bars would be knocked into one giant draughty room, the comfortable chairs would be swapped for vinyl toadstools and the subdued lighting replaced with bright neon more appropriate to a motorway tunnel. I used to think of the process of destruction as a pub being 'dunne uppye' because often a genuine Victorian pub would be remade as a completely fake Victorian pub. This process often featured the writing of nonsense on the outside walls and windows of the boozer in curly script like 'Hot Pyes To Dyne On', 'Ryche Soupes' and 'Fynest Oysters'. Sometimes I would go into one of the places and ask the man or woman behind the bar if I could have half a dozen 'Fyne Oysters' only to be met with complete bafflement. It wasn't much of a victory.

And, where we grew up, you were lucky not to get punched by the barman or barmaid, because Liverpool was a fighting town where on the weekend even the St John's Ambulance men were looking for a brawl. So it was always a bit intimidating going into the centre. I never in all the time I lived there got into a scrap, but that was more down to my slow-wittedness than anything else. For example, me and Linda were in the centre late one afternoon, and I was wearing flared trousers and my Second World War sheepskin flying jacket. A couple of hard-looking men came up to me and said, 'What time is it, greebo?' ('Greebo' was a contemptuous, insulting term meaning 'greaser'.).

'It's a quarter past six,' I replied and walked on, only realising they'd been insulting me a month and a half later.

Even without the potential for violence, it was depressing enough going into town because Liverpool City Council were forging ahead with their efforts to make all of the city look terrible. Having demolished everything between our house in Anfield and the river, leaving square-miles of nothing but rubble, they'd now started on the centre. The council had recently decided to sandblast the industrial-revolution-era grime off the few old buildings that remained standing following their brutal 1960s redevelopment. The contractor chosen for this task, presumably some relative of one of the councillors, used a water jet that was far too powerful so that now the stone figures adorning the council buildings had had their noses and limbs blasted off and there appeared to be a row of lepers lined up along the parapet of the municipal chambers and the law courts.

So, although in local movie houses you were treated like the chain-gang prisoners being taken to the picture show in

Sullivan's Travels, it was still nice to go and sit in the relative peace and quiet of the cinema from time to time and watch a film.

One evening, me and Linda went to the Astoria on Walton Road for the screening of an American movie with a limited release called *Dynamite Chicken*. This was a film partly funded by John Lennon and Yoko Ono, which was probably why it was on in Liverpool. It featured mainly music acts such as Joan Baez, Leonard Cohen, Jimi Hendrix, Muddy Waters and Sha Na Na but it was a young black man who didn't sing or play a musical instrument who really caught my attention. In between the bands he just sat and told stories, tales of his childhood growing up in a whorehouse, plus he performed an extended fantasy about what a black vampire might be like. The credits informed us that the name of this young man was Richard Pryor. Until then I'd only ever seen British stand-ups who cracked racist or misogynistic gags in an insincere and false manner but here was somebody who told authentic stories drawn from their own life, tales that were political and hip and wildly original. Seeing Richard Pryor was like finding a beautiful room in your house that you hadn't known was there. But I didn't know what to do with that room so I just shut the door and walked away.

The Maoist group spent a lot of time together, attending meetings, selling the Party newspaper outside Central Station or going to the pub, only once did we organise a group outing to the commercial cinema. And it was not some French language classic or Russian masterpiece that we were going to see, but a Hollywood film called *The Way We Were*. So eager were we to watch this movie that we trouped along on the opening night. Clearly others had had the same idea because when our little group got to the Odeon on London Road it was completely packed. The audience though was not the usual crowd of couples and office workers but instead Merseyside's entire left-wing community. This was because the film starred the two biggest names in Hollywood – Barbra Streisand and Robert Redford – and, amazingly, its subject matter was just how bloody great Communists were. In it Barbra Streisand plays Katie Morosky, a Jew and a Marxist, and Robert Redford is Hubbell Gardiner, a wealthy and handsome fellow student of Katie's at Harvard University. Unlike most people, Hubbell finds Katie's left-wing carrying-on delightful: he is captivated by her strident yelling, charmed by her aggressive leaflet-handing-out and enchanted by her endless moaning about injustice. The entire radical audience in that cinema on London Road were similarly captivated. Trotskyists cheered and embraced their erstwhile Anarchist enemies at the point when Katie turns her back on her affluent California lifestyle – due to the rise of McCarthyism – to return to the struggle, while granite-faced Stalinists wept when the couple split up because Katie finally understands that Hubbell is a weak and unreliable man.

All the comrades thought the hero of the film was Katie, the unbending, shrill, committed revolutionary, but secretly I felt a lot of sympathy for Hubbell, who ends up in LA as a writer of popular TV sitcoms. The movie makes it clear that this is supposed to be the most terrible fate imaginable but really it didn't seem that bad to me. I thought: How awful could it be, working on TV comedies in Hollywood? Never suspecting that years later I would find out that it could indeed be pretty terrible.

It was remarkable what strange films got shown in the mainstream cinema, movies such as *Lisztomania* directed by Ken Russell, featuring the lead singer of The Who, Roger Daltrey, as Franz Liszt and Ringo Starr as the Pope. Admittedly Russell had had a couple of hits, *Women in Love* and *Tommy*, but like a lot of Russell's work *Lisztomania* was a self-indulgent mess, and as the film progressed, the cinema we were watching it in gradually emptied out until only a few people remained. During a scene in which Wagner, as a sort of cross between Frankenstein and Hitler, wanders up a railway track using a guitar that is also a machine gun to mow down Jews, a man stormed up the aisle towards the back of the cinema then turned and shouted in a thick German accent, 'You are all crazy to be watching ziss!'

One weekend, when she was visiting me in London, Linda and I went to the Odeon in Leicester Square to see the newly released Sylvester Stallone movie *Rocky*. Before the lights went down I noticed in the audience a few rows behind me a mournful-looking, slightly pop-eyed, balding man with a droopy moustache. I whispered to Linda, 'You see that man in the fifth row, I think it's Walid Jumblatt, leader of the Druze militia from the Chouf Mountains of the Lebanon.'

'You're always saying that,' she replied.

'Yes,' I hissed, 'but this time I'm certain.' The Druze sect were much in the news because they were one of the factions fighting in the Lebanese civil war, which, over the next ten years, would tear the country apart. I paid close attention to coverage of the conflict on the TV news because I was always hoping to catch a glimpse of one of the young Arab men who used to come to our flat in Finchley. Then I'd be able to say,

'Hey, isn't that Ahmed manning the .50 machine gun at the PLO roadblock?' Which I thought would make me seem awfully sophisticated to whoever I was talking to.

After the film finished I approached the man with the moustache and said to him, 'Excuse me, are you Walid Jumblatt, leader of the Druze militia from the Chouf Mountains of the Lebanon?'

'Yes I am,' he said.

'What did you think of the film then?' I asked after a pause.

'It was all right,' he replied.

The Cut-price Dude of Liverpool 8

After I'd known Linda for a while I felt I had to tell her about my career as a drug dealer. At the age of sixteen, still at school and obsessed with the idea of forging myself some kind of hipster identity, I'd noticed in the pubs, coffee bars and drinking clubs where I spent my evenings that the person with the coolest aura seemed to be the guy selling the dope. He would suddenly appear, then glide about as if on wheels, speaking to his clients in intimate whispers, all the time hanging over him this romantic, lawless, outsider mystique, and everybody always seemed really pleased to see him.

I was not alone in thinking that drug dealers were the epitome of all that was trendy and hip in the late 1960s. In the film *Easy Rider* the two heroes, role models for a generation, make the money for their doomed motorcycle trip to New Orleans, in time for Mardi Gras, from a massive cocaine score. The drugs are hidden in the Stars and Stripes petrol tank of Fonda's bike. This was not seen as a bad thing. Indeed the influence of this outlaw drug movie was so far-reaching that the children's bicycle the Raleigh Chopper with its enormous chromed handlebars, tiny front wheel and two kilograms of white powder hidden in the frame was clearly based on the Harley-Davidson hard-tail Hydra-Glide motorcycles ridden by Peter Fonda and Dennis Hopper in the film.

Also and conclusively, everybody, except maybe the police and the government, knew for certain that the effects of drugs, especially marijuana, acid and cocaine, were entirely beneficial with no downside whatsoever.

I really wanted to gain some of the allure of the drug dealer for myself. My feeling was that I had the clothes and the long hair but the only things I didn't have were the cheap drugs. From watching movies such as *Easy Rider*, *The French Connection* and *The Man with the Golden Arm* I understood that one important, indeed crucial, aspect of being a proper drug peddler was that you had to have access to reasonably priced narcotics. You got these narcotics from a connection further up the chain who sold you your product at wholesale prices, and you made a profit from the difference between the price you paid and what you charged your clients. It was simple Marxist economics really. My only problem was that I didn't have this connection with a wholesaler, didn't know how to go about getting one and in fact didn't want to since I suspected that the people further up the chain might be very frightening indeed.

Then it struck me that if I didn't care about making a profit or indeed if I didn't mind sustaining a small loss then I would be able to sell marijuana or acid at the same price, or maybe even cheaper, than anybody else on the scene. So what I did was, I would buy drugs at the ordinary street price, usually from some guy in Southport that my friends back in Liverpool knew nothing about, then I'd sell these drugs to people in Liverpool, in the Maoist group I was a member of or friends from school, at a price about fifteen per cent less than I had paid. I didn't think Karl Marx in any of his works, not even his *Grundrisse*, whose subject matter included production, distribution, exchange, alienation, surplus value, labour, capitalism, the rise of technology and automation, pre-capitalist forms of social organisation, and the preconditions for a Communist revolution, covered my particular form of capitalist exploitation, which contradicted every known form of Marxist thought since the retailer – me – was in effect extracting surplus value from himself. Nevertheless when customers asked me how I got my drugs so cheap I'd just look all mysterious and say, 'Hey, I'm like connected with The Man. Know what I mean, dude?'

And they'd nod and say, 'Yeah, I understand, man . . . cool.'

When I told Linda about my cut-price drug dealing, expecting her to be impressed and maybe even a bit horrified at my lawlessness, she said it was the saddest thing she'd ever heard. I replied, 'Yeah, sad if you like having lots of great friends who cost you less than £3 a week.' But over time I began to suspect that she might be right.

In the Bleak Midsummer

At the end of my first year at Chelsea, not having anything else to do and not being invited by some Sebastian Flyte to stay at his stately home, I'd returned to Liverpool for the summer holidays. Nothing much had changed. Molly had always had a combative relationship with her neighbours but this situation seemed to be getting worse. There had been a family next door at Number 7 Valley Road by the name of Blundell. According to Molly they had wanted our house for their own daughter to live in and my mother had always felt that because of this they bitterly resented us, though as far as I could see they displayed no animosity towards the Sayles and were always perfectly nice when we met. The same could not be said of Molly's behaviour towards them. The two houses shared a water pipe, so the neighbours next door were able, if they so wished, to interfere with the flow to our home. My mother was convinced that they turned off our supply from time to time. In fact she was certain that when I was a baby they somehow knew when she was preparing a bottle of formula and would choose that exact moment to strike. One of my first memories is of my mother at the kitchen window screaming at the Blundells over the backyard wall that her child was dying of hunger because they had cut off our water supply.

Eventually the Blundells moved out and, though it wasn't in her nature to do so, Molly might have regretted how she'd treated them because the man who moved in was an ex-paratrooper and amateur-radio enthusiast. He put up on his roof a huge antenna that Molly was convinced interfered with our TV reception. One morning when I was home from college that summer I heard from my bedroom my mother screaming at this trained killer over the backyard wall, 'Now you're for it. My son's back from college and he's going to sort you out!'

You had to wonder, what was her motive for saying this? Did she truly think I would be able to somehow fight this burly man whose job was hurting people, or on a subconscious level did she really want to see me badly beaten up?

Anyway I refused to leave my room, but in the end Molly triumphed over the paratrooper because he soon had a heart attack, which meant he was forced to move out of Valley Road and into sheltered accommodation.

Over that first summer holidays I had one of my few friends from college come and visit me in Liverpool. His name was David Pearce. In fact I had two friends at Chelsea and they were both called David. The other was David Wagstaffe. He lived at home with his parents in Leytonstone so had more money than the rest of us. He always seemed to have a full packet of twenty Rothmans King Size cigarettes, clean clothes and enough money to pay not only for his main dish at lunch in the canteen but a pudding as well.

Even though I was desperate for friends, my instinct was always such that if I saw a weakness in a person I couldn't resist niggling at it. So I encouraged everybody to call David Wagstaffe 'Waggy' as a nickname, a ploy that worked pretty well. I would also constantly cadge cigarettes off him, partly because I wanted the cigarettes but also because I knew it annoyed him.

One day in the canteen I had got my own spoon and was stealing half of his pudding when he suddenly shouted, 'You think I'm your friend but I hate you, you think I like you but I don't, I really, really, hate you.' It was a sign of how desperate we all were for mates that he didn't stop sitting with me at lunch and I didn't stop stealing his pudding.

David Pearce was from the small Shropshire town of Craven Arms and he was gay, always dressed in the same outfit of black Lewis Leathers motorbike jacket, black T-shirt and tight narrow jeans. Since the Sayles had always been big on conspicuous tolerance of persecuted minorities my mother Molly was delighted to have a gay person staying with us. 'Lexi, what would your gay friend like for his breakfast?' she would shout up the stairs. Or, 'Lexi, where are you and your gay friend going to go this afternoon? Are you going to go somewhere fucking gay?' My mother had never shown such benign interest in my movements before.

In fact, though Molly's conspicuous tolerance would have once marked her out in our neighbourhood as somebody different and distinct, it was now commonplace. Returning after being away for a year it struck me that something felt unfamiliar, although it took me a little time to figure out what it was.

Eventually it became clear to me that our community had undergone a radical shift while I'd been at art school. In Anfield and other working-class districts there had occurred a convulsion. It was as if one night at the beginning of the 1970s there'd been a massive meeting at which everybody had agreed to completely change their attitude to more or less everything. Up until that moment girls who got pregnant were sent off to terrible institutions run by cruel nuns and their children put up for adoption, unhappy and loveless marriages were regarded as the norm since divorced people were inevitably shunned and refused service in shops, homosexuality was considered an outright evil and the few black people in the neighbourhood were discriminated against in a thousand different ways.

Now the entire population of Liverpool 4 had decided they were done with all that nonsense. From now on everybody was going to do exactly as they wanted and nobody was going to stop them and nobody was going to judge them.

The positive part of this was that people no longer had their lives ruined simply for being different. The negative aspect was that everybody felt free to indulge in whatever took their fancy. Vices, many of which had formerly belonged only to the upper classes or the intelligentsia, now appeared in north Liverpool for the first time. Drink, drugs and bizarre sexual practices were the most common excesses but the worst vice – do-it-yourself – wasn't far behind. Overnight people suddenly began enthusiastically knocking their houses about, so I would walk down our street, Valley Road, wondering what fresh horror would have appeared since the day before. In the past there had been a harmony and a uniformity to our neighbourhood of terraced houses which was now totally destroyed by the efforts of the inhabitants. Within a year many bay windows were hacked back to give the houses a flat front – because for some reason people wanted to make where they lived smaller – internal walls were demolished – meaning that upstairs floors sagged – and bizarre stone cladding was glued to the front walls enabling all kinds of corrosive mould to collect beneath. Most of this work was badly done and the materials used cheap and nasty. Also people seemed to think that in replacing their traditional wooden windows with poor quality metal double-glazing they'd done enough home improvement for a decade or two so totally neglected every other aspect of their dwelling. They stopped sweeping the step or washing their windows and began leaving rubbish bags and bits of motorcycle in the front area so that the rawness of the aluminum frames only served to highlight the peeling paint, dirty steps and crumbling brickwork.

What Is this Place You've Brought Me to, Roger?

My second year at Chelsea began with me moving into a flat all by myself. Sharing with Wassim and the French girls in Finchley had taught me that I wasn't suited to living with other people; if I couldn't be happy there I was better off alone. The flat had formerly belonged to a fellow member of the Communist Party of Britain (Marxist–Leninist) called Daphne who was moving to Sheffield and was in an area of London known as North Kensington. I had once read in a magazine that in Paris there is an inhabited island in the centre of the Seine called the Île St-Louis. Many of those who lived in the seventeenth-century townhouses never left their area from one year to the next and when they did they would tell their neighbours that they were 'going into Paris' or 'visiting the mainland'. North Kensington was, at least in my mind, a similar sort of island. My new home was set in a triangle about a mile wide at its base, the southern coast being formed by a branch of the tube's Metropolitan Line running in a channel between Hammersmith Broadway in the west and the City in the east. Its eastern edge was defined by eight tracks of the Great Western Railway Line coming out of Paddington Station, this too in a deep cutting. This eastern border was particularly wide because parallel with the eight trails of silver railtrack there also ran the Grand Union Canal, which was spanned by only one ancient stone footbridge connecting the island with the Harrow Road, north-west London and beyond. The western coast of my neighbourhood was more psychological than physical, being the Portobello Road with its busy market, beyond which rose big rich houses on leafy avenues utterly different to the crowded, seething tenements on my atoll. Another way to look at it is that my area resembled the tiny, pulsating, oppressed enclave which had been created five years before: North Kensington was the Gaza Strip of Notting Hill Gate.

If you wanted to get to my house by tube you took the Underground to Westbourne Park Station then, climbing the steps, turned right down the Great Western Road taking the first right again into Tavistock Crescent. In a narrow gap between an Irish navvies' pub and a row of flat-fronted Georgian houses were some steep iron treads leading upwards to a grey metal footbridge entirely covered by a curved roof of wire-mesh. This bridge crossed back over the Metropolitan Line and brought you finally to the island of North Kensington and to the house I lived in: Number 10 Wornington Road, London W10.

The houses in Wornington Road were large Victorian dwellings that had fallen into a state of grave disrepair, mostly painted in a shade of brown paint that no longer existed (probably because it had been called something like 'Wog

Brown') and seemed completely unchanged since some time before the Second World War. In contrast to the houses, the modern world lay right at the end of the road, cutting the sky in two. The Westway A40 extension rose on its concrete legs where the streets ended and though you couldn't see the cars because they were so high up, there was a constant hum and muted swishing noise as J. G. Ballard and The Clash rode in and out of town.

I occupied the ground floor of Number 10, comprising what had been the front living room before the house had been divided up, and was now my living room/bedroom and a back portion which was the kitchen. The house, even by the standards of the street, was extremely shabby. I did not have my own bathroom but shared one, down some stairs on a half-landing, with the Spanish family who lived in the basement and who only came up once a week on a Sunday for a bath. The separate toilet up on the first-floor mezzanine was for the use of me and the woman upstairs, an alcoholic called Mrs Hotchkiss. Only half hidden under the grubby stair carpet leading to this toilet there lay the bottom half of a set of false teeth which nobody ever bothered to remove.

One evening I came home from college to find Mrs Hotchkiss lying drunk at the foot of the stairs. She blearily looked up and said, 'What is this place you've brought me to, Roger?' From then on when I was in some frightening or mystifying place I would often find myself thinking: What is this place you've brought me to, Roger?

On the corner of the street facing the Westway there was a little general store run by a West Indian with gold teeth known to everyone as 'Daddy'. This crowded little emporium amongst other things sold paraffin for the heaters many people used to keep their houses warm. These stoves, shaped a little like Abraham Lincoln's top hat, seemed to issue dampness and heat in almost equal measure and frequently toppled over, causing many fires. If you didn't pay for what you'd bought with the exact money Daddy never gave you any change but instead would dump a handful of cheap sweets in your outstretched palms, a big threatening smile on his face daring you to challenge him.

Luckily there were other shopping opportunities. At the top of Wornington Road there was a street called Golborne Road which had a number of little shops and Portuguese bakeries. There was also a smattering of working men's cafés which served spaghetti bolognese accompanied by chips and sliced bread and butter. Looming over this street was a gigantic block of flats called Trellick Tower. When he first came round David Pearce dubbed it Clockwork Orange Towers. The architect was the famous brutalist Ernö Goldfinger. To prove it wasn't the concrete hell-hole it clearly was, Goldfinger took over one of his own flats for a month and threw champagne parties for the other residents, then he decamped back to the Georgian mansion he normally occupied.

On Golborne Road there was also a little Londis supermarket where I would buy eggs so small I think they must have been laid by lizards and things called 'bacon bits' which were sort of fatty stumps of bacon that nobody else wanted. Using these ingredients I would sometimes cook myself what I fondly thought of as a Spanish omelette.

About fifteen minutes' walk south from Wornington Road towards Bayswater there was a narrow street called Westbourne

Grove which had on it these amazing things – a number of Arab- or Pakistani-owned supermarkets that were open for twenty-four hours a day! Nothing then in Britain was open for twenty-four hours a day, not even Heathrow Airport, which shut at 5 p.m. on weekdays and on Wednesday afternoons for half-day closing and staff training. Sometimes when she was staying with me, me and Linda would walk to one of these supermarkets at 3 a.m. just to buy a tiny tin of soup. This was how we felt London, the heart of the nation, should be but rarely was. Mysterious, exciting, exotic, its glistening streets lit by garish neon signs, populated by shady characters drawn from all over the world who thought there was nothing intrinsically wrong with selling you minestrone in the middle of the night.

One weekend in August the people of North Kensington, or at least the West Indian ones, held this thing called 'Carnival'. There were floats and bands, sound systems and costumed dancers and the whole parade actually came down our street but I didn't fancy all that noise and commotion so I stayed in Liverpool.

Mountain Wrongholdism

I sometimes thought that the worst thing that Marx and Engels had written was that the destruction of capitalism and the triumph of the working class was inevitable. If it was inevitable, this spread the subconscious message that really Communists didn't have to do anything much because the world they wished for was going to come along anyway. They didn't have to adapt themselves in any way to how society was changing, so their ideas, the graphic style of their newspapers, the language they spoke remained locked in the nineteenth century, while they just sort of hung around waiting for capitalism to collapse.

On the other hand if you didn't look too closely it was easy to imagine that the triumph of Communism *was* nearly upon us. The theory of Marxism–Leninism straddled the earth and appeared day by day to be growing. The two largest and most populous nations on the planet, the Soviet Union and the People's Republic of China, were ruled by competing Marxist philosophies. All of Eastern Europe formed part of the Soviet Empire. Communist North Vietnam was about to defeat the world's biggest and best equipped military complex, the USA. Other countries in South Asia, Cambodia, Laos and North Korea, were solidly Marxist. Ninety miles off the coast of Miami, Cuba bravely challenged the hegemony of the US on its own back patio. Communist Parties in India, Italy, France, the Middle East, the Balkans and most other parts of the world exerted huge influence. In South America Maoist guerrilla groups such as the Sendero Luminoso daily conducted kidnappings and robberies with the support of a large portion of the populace. But at home in the UK despite ideas of socialism and libertarianism being at the forefront of contemporary thought, the notion of a society led by a democratic-centralist Communist Party, whose ideas were based firmly in a true and pure interpretation of the teachings of Marx, Engels, Lenin and Stalin, was still having difficulty breaking out from its core of a few hundred activists, and one of the principal reasons for that resided at the Bellman Bookshop, 155 Fortess Road, Tufnell Park, London NW5, the national headquarters of the Communist Party of Britain (Marxist–Leninist).

Left-wing organisations had only about twelve words to draw their names from, including 'workers', 'revolutionary', 'front', 'party', 'Marxist', 'Communist', 'socialist' and 'Leninist', so each group was a permutation of these terms. There was the Workers' Revolutionary Front, the Socialist Revolutionary Party, the Front Socialist Revolutionary League Front and the Communist Workers' Group Front Party League Party. In Liverpool I had originally been a member of a Maoist cell that early on called itself the Merseyside Marxist–Leninist Group, later it had folded into the Communist Party of Britain (Marxist–Leninist), becoming its Liverpool branch. When I moved to London I automatically became a member of the central London branch which met at the Party's headquarters, the Bellman Bookshop.

In the few hours when it bothered to open, potential customers at the Bellman Bookshop were met with astonishing hostility and aggression. The problem with the shop was that a lot of members of the Party, particularly the ones who were favoured with the role of manning the shop, were socially inept, angry and resentful individuals, the sort who were drawn to radical politics because they had a grievance with the world and were looking to get their own back. If, say, a young apprentice or a medical student came in, interested in Marxism but still with a few doubts, which they expressed via a number of intelligent but sincere questions, their enquiries would be met with querulous replies: 'Why do you want to know this?' 'Who told you to ask that?' 'Are you a police spy?' Soon they would flee from the dark and dusty interior, all interest in Marxism–Leninism extinguished as they resolved instead to join the Liberal Party.

It always struck me as odd, this obsession members of the Party had that inquisitive strangers might be police spies. Surely, I thought, if there were infiltrators in our organisation then they would have learnt beforehand how to blend in, to act like the rest of them, to dress badly and distrust laughter and not draw suspicion to themselves, to quietly and diligently work their way into a position of influence. If there were any police spies in our group then they would be on the central committee. Which turned out to be the case. In fact the only people who truly took us little left-wing groups seriously, who bought into our fantasies of seizing power in the name of the proletariat, were the various arms of state security such as MI5, MI6 and the Metropolitan Police Special Branch.

It transpired that not only was every one of the revolutionary parties riddled with undercover Special Branch, agents from the intelligence services and part-time police informers (all of them unknown to each other), so were all the central committees of the left-wing trade unions. These men and a few women, in order to maintain their radical credentials, to seem more revolutionary than their non-spy colleagues, needed to pursue highly confrontational policies (though often the people they were trying to impress were other police spies). Therefore a lot of the militant trade union tactics and revolutionary nonsense, thought of as typical of the era – confrontational strikes, pointless occupations, massive and impractical wage demands, petulant walk-outs – were in fact the work of the security services and Her Majesty's Constabulary. Maybe the Arts Council, the Royal Institute of British Architects and the National Theatre were also riddled with police agents, which would go a long way to explaining their avant-garde and seemingly incomprehensible output.

And the senior London members of the CPB (M–L) weren't much nicer to actual members of the Party, especially if they came from Liverpool. The people at the top were always suspicious of comrades from Merseyside. We were thought to have too independent a spirit, to be unwilling to unconditionally accept whatever message was handed down from the central committee. The Mao-inspired term they used when referring to members of the Merseyside branch was 'mountain strongholdism'.

The leader and founder of our party was Reg Birch, who was also general secretary of the Engineers' Union. Reg was a little man, an angry, self-taught intellectual whose pronouncements were often gibberish, but which many in the Party and the broader trade union movement treated as containing profound wisdom. So well was he thought of in left-wing circles that Reg became the first and last Maoist member of the then immensely powerful general council of the Trades Union Congress – the TUC.

In the 1950s, Reg had found Khrushchev's post-Stalin Soviet Union too easy-going and tolerant, so instead he expressed strong pro-Chinese sympathies, and for these he was expelled from the Communist Party of Great Britain. He sorted out that problem by founding his own party following the Maoist line. From then on, Reg was often either in the Irish pub – the Boston – over the road from the Bellman Bookshop, drinking with navvies, or in Tirana, the capital of Albania, drinking with the President Enver Hoxha. Of all the many little Maoist parties in the UK that competed for Communist China's favour and sponsorship we were definitely their preferred choice. The journalist Terry Pattinson was on a visit to Shanghai in 1979 when a Chinese building worker asked him, 'Do you know Reg Birch of the Engineers' Union in England? We are told he will be Prime Minister, after your revolution.'

Reg was a typical revolutionary in that all he really cared about was the revolution, which, he said with relish, would be 'ugly, protracted and bloody'. Like many in radical politics it was chaos that he really wished for: unhappy with happiness, he wished for havoc instead. He had only a vague idea of what the subsequent workers' paradise would look like and indeed I had the sneaking suspicion there was a good chance that if somebody like Reg ever gained power in Britain then turmoil would be permanent.

Not all the members were such misfits. The co-founder of the Communist Party of Britain (Marxist–Leninist), Bill Ash, was a much more interesting and sympathetic character. He was a man who embodied the nobility, decency and bravery of those who were attracted to left-wing ideas and practice in the 1930s. He was cool too, tall and handsome with a languid Texan charm, and it was said he was one of the models for Steve McQueen's character in the film *The Great Escape*. At the beginning of the Second World War Bill had walked over the bridge to Canada and enlisted in the Royal Canadian Air Force, something that cost him his US citizenship. Shot down over the Channel in his Spitfire in 1942 and captured by the Germans he was then imprisoned in Stalag Luft III from which he constantly tried to escape. Bill was actually in 'the cooler', being punished for a previous break-out, when his comrades made what came to be known as 'the Great Escape', and so he avoided being shot on capture on the direct orders of Hitler.

After the war Bill got an MBE, was awarded British citizenship and read PPE at Oxford. He then joined the BBC. Fuck knows what he was doing in our party. He was brave, handsome and didn't seem mad at all.

Bill's wife, an Indian woman called Ranjana, was much closer to the model of a proper Marxist–Leninist: humourless and steely-eyed, she was our foreign affairs expert. One Saturday a group of four of us, including Ranjana, who was dressed in a sari, went to Southall in west London for a meeting with the

Indian Workers' Association, a Maoist group we were hoping would merge with our party.

It was a weird experience for me, visiting an English suburb which was identical to every other – 1930s semis interspersed with parades of local shops – apart from the fact that all the inhabitants were from the subcontinent of India and the shops overflowed with mangoes and bright red peppers, sacks of rice and two-gallon drums of clarified butter. We were crammed, the four of us from the CPB (M–L) and about ten Indian men, into a front room already overflowing with ornate furniture, brass ornaments and red flags adorned with hammers and sickles. I wasn't paying much attention to what was being said, being more focused on all the exotic snacks laid out before us. I had never seen samosas, pakoras, mango chutney, raita and bhajis before and was cramming as many of them as I could into my mouth when one of the Indian comrades, who resembled an illustration of a 'wily Pathan' from one of the comics I used to read when I was a kid, asked Ranjana with a glint in his eye, 'Comrade Ranjana – you say that the Chinese government is the friend of the revolutionary working class.'

'That is correct, comrade,' said Ranjana.

'Well then can you please tell us in that case why the Chinese government is selling guns to the Indian government and the Indian government then uses these guns to kill the Naxalites [an Indian Maoist armed group]?'

Of course the truth was that China had its own pragmatic foreign policy objectives, which sometimes included supporting troublesome guerrilla groups on the territory of their rivals and sometimes didn't, but Ranjana couldn't say anything so nuanced, since Communism only ever entertained a narrative that was simple and heroic. Instead Ranjana thought about this tricky question for a minute then finally she said, 'Comrades, the Chinese sell the guns to the Indian government so that the Naxalites are able to steal them!'

Apart from a few engineers Reg brought with him, a lot of the Party members were young men and women, either students or professionals in teaching or the social services. I would look enviously at the nubile females listening rapt to Reg's tortured, mangled pronouncements and think that if you were a gnarly old bloke who smelt of fags then starting your own party was a really good way to get young people to revere you. In the normal world there was no way in which these young and pretty twenty-five-year-olds would pay any attention to somebody as weird and creepy as Reg Birch, but here in the sphere of radical politics his fans were as devoted as if he'd been a fashionable Cockney photographer or the handsome lead singer of a pop group.

The one thing I did for the Party was use my free travel pass for the tube that I got as the son of a railwayman to go every Friday night to a lithograph place in Walthamstow and pick up the printing plates for the Party's terrible newspaper and deliver them to the bookshop. They never showed any gratitude.

Apart from that I tried to arrive as late as possible at the weekly branch meetings of the CPB (M–L) held at the Bellman Bookshop and would always position myself right at the back near the door. Unfortunately this tactic, designed to not get me noticed, carried a certain amount of risk. Seated at the rear on the outer fringes of the meeting I would suddenly hear the door crashing open behind me, followed by the sound of somebody knocking over a dusty pile of Lenin's *What Is to Be Done?* This would be Reg returning drunk from the Boston or after some trade union meeting or back from Albania. Everybody would turn towards the noise and our chairman, ignoring the agenda, would then launch into a Fidel Castro-style, two-hour-long declamatory speech about whatever was on his mind, leaning on the back of my chair and in effect using me as a pulpit. All the while, as the members looked in my direction, I had to appear to be fascinated by what he was saying as our leader's spit rained gently down on my head.

But if those meetings in London were difficult, when I returned to Liverpool to see Linda I would attend my old branch and that too was problematic because my mother had become a Maoist and joined the Party. In the last year when I'd still been in Liverpool we'd begun holding the CPB (M–L) meetings at our house in Valley Road. I think this was because some of the members in the north end of the city resented having to travel to the south to our leader's flat in Liverpool 8 so our house in Anfield was midway. Throughout the meeting Molly would lurk outside the door with a tray of biscuits trying to eavesdrop on our secrets. Once I left Liverpool to go to Chelsea, my mother crossed the threshold.

Of all the weird things Molly had done over the years this was in many ways the oddest though it has to be said she was also better at being a member of a political party than I had ever been. Not in the sense of bringing about any of the aims of the organisation but rather in the day-to-day conspiring and undermining that people in that kind of group went in for. The leader of the Merseyside branch was a guy called

Ian Williams, a tall redhead who had once been a Liverpool University student but had been expelled for political activity and now worked on the buses with Harry Jackson. Ian absolutely hated my mother and was driven almost as crazy by her as I was. The feeling was mutual but Molly, being adept at manipulation, proved very good at making alliances with others in the branch who also didn't like Ian – those such as his very bitter ex-girlfriend who he'd left for the rich girl with the bourgeois-guilt issues. The leadership in London were also wary of Ian Williams because of his suspected mountain strongholdism and pretty soon Reg Birch was hearing my mother's name spoken of with approval though he still didn't know who I was even though he'd been using me as a pulpit for over a year.

Wet Shed in Autumn Number 2

When I was about twelve years old my father began to fall ill, fading slowly but inexorably over the following years. Little was known about Alzheimer's in those days or it may have been that in fact Joe had had a series of small strokes but either way our GP could offer little help or advice. It would be easy to date my mother's eccentric behaviour from Joe's decline but the truth was more that my father had been a restraining influence on Molly and that no longer existed.

My mother was not good at allaying the fears of her son. The anxiety all this generated in me was so overpowering that, rather than focusing on Joe's failing health, I switched to worrying about the state of Britain's ailing manufacturing sector.

All through my teens I would obsessively count UK-made cars versus foreign cars on the roads, and I was constantly rootling behind machinery such as photocopiers and vending machines to study the little metal plaques that told you where they had been manufactured so that I was often mistaken for a poorly qualified, badly dressed and ill-equipped maintenance technician.

Of course all my efforts were in vain and British industry, like my dad, continued to decline. I saw all around me how young consumers, when they purchased, say, a car, had no intention of buying British. After all, what young and fashionable person would want to drive the Wolseleys and Humbers their parents had owned when they could have a colourful and funky Citroën 2CV or a cute and clever Fiat 127? Cars with style, practicality and reliability.

I had a really strong feeling that the population's shopping choices meant some really crucial shift was occurring, something that as political people we Marxists should look into. I thought about bringing the subject of consumer choices up several times at meetings of the Party along with a number other matters that were on my mind (like I wanted to talk about the terrible things people in Anfield were doing to their houses and how that might affect the way the working class would respond to our message of world revolution). I also would have liked to ask why Labour councils hated small shopkeepers: I'd observed in Anfield how local shops were disappearing and when the little shops went the life seemed to go out of a neighbourhood. It seemed to me in fact that Liverpool's Labour council tried to put every obstacle it could in the paths of small businesses, continually hiking their business rates and not replacing the broken pavement outside their shops.

I never did mention any of these things though because I knew what the response would be: that none of these matters were of concern to a revolutionary organisation. As far as my comrades were concerned the business of our party was the big bombastic stuff, strikes at home and overseas, the anti-imperialist struggle, the China v. Russia split, the electrification of the People's Socialist Republic of Albania driven by the Marxist–Leninist thought of President Enver Hoxha.

I didn't argue but secretly I wondered why they were so reluctant to consider these matters. Though they were supposedly revolutionaries the focus of my comrades was in fact very narrow. Part of it was that, in our theology, capitalism was on the edge of collapse so any evidence that it was revitalising itself by finding new markets and new ways of selling stuff contradicted this, and we couldn't deal with contradictions. They could not acknowledge that this new consumer society was happening even though a lot of them were a part of it.

Throughout the second year at Chelsea my attendance at CPB (M–L) meetings became less and less frequent. Reducing my political activism gave me more time to not concentrate on my art. I stopped painting altogether and decided that my future might lie in film. This might have had something to do with the woman who taught film part-time at Chelsea being the one teacher who took an interest in my work so that she became an unlikely mother and indeed father figure for me. She was called Anne Rees-Mogg, was in her late forties, tall and thin with a boyish figure, and though she was posh she was nice to me. One incredible thing was that Anne's brother was the editor of *The Times* and, not at all understanding how the media worked, I assumed that by my getting to know her she would at some point have a quiet word with William, who on a slow news day would run a headline on the front page of his paper saying something like 'Fantastic new student found at art school. "Fuzzy paintings and odd films will change the world," say experts.'

Anne involved herself to a greater degree than the rest of the staff with her students, particularly the boys whom she collected so that we formed an odd little troupe, wandering around accompanied by the ticking sound of our clockwork cameras. She was happy to help her students and would drive us anywhere we wanted to go in her brown Ford Escort estate. The only problem was she never changed up out of third gear so we travelled everywhere at thirty miles an hour in a cloud of smoke and disintegrating clutch.

Anne lived in a big square house in Wandsworth and hers was the only home of a staff member at Chelsea I was ever invited to. This was the first occasion I'd been in somebody's house where they'd had the time, money and taste to think about its interior. She had collected a large number of enamelled French advertising signs which covered the walls of her kitchen and dining room and everywhere there were tiny bits of glass: antique bottle stoppers, bits of chandelier, tiny mirrors so that the light pouring in from her garden sparkled all around the room.

For lunch Anne gave us mussels cooked in white wine served in stainless-steel bowls with French bread, salad and French wine with a label like a medieval scroll. This was what I imagined being a student in London would be like, sitting with your tutor on a sunny afternoon in a room that resembled a 1930s Marseilles railway-station waiting room. It just seemed such a shame that the sort of movies Anne was involved in were so terrible.

These films, the prevalent kind of movies at art schools, were not concerned with any notions of entertainment or popularity. They had no plot, no perceivable artistry, some-times even no actual imagery; in fact nothing you could enjoy in a conventional sense, the most you could hope for was some blurry female nudity. As part of Anne's little group of boys I would sometimes be taken to a place in Primrose Hill called the Film-makers' Co-op which was based in an abandoned warehouse beside the Regent's Canal. On a dark, gloomy road curving round to a narrow bridge, the film-makers had made their home in the dilapidated, dripping interior of the build-ing, while others lived in hulking, dark green, ex-German Army border-patrol trucks parked permanently outside. At night you could see them sitting cross-legged in the backs of their vehicles eating brown rice from a bowl with chopsticks.

There existed a similar hierarchy at the Film-makers' Co-op to that in the CPB (M–L): a leader, acolytes and me being secretly appalled but not saying anything. And just like the CPB (M–L) the one thing that was conspicuous by its absence was humour.

There was also a Bellman Bookshop-style welcome for all when we got there. The audience would sit on mattresses laid around the floor and watch films that had been made by the artists of the co-op. When watching these works it often seemed to me that it would be much less unpleasant to be sitting in an empty blank room doing nothing for two hours. One of the worst things about them was what I dubbed the 'Coming Back Problem'. You would sit on your sticky mattress for half an hour watching grainy footage of a man walking across a field, up a hill, along a rocky path and finally he'd get to the top and you'd think to yourself: Well at least that's over. But then ever so slowly the man would turn and a clammy fear would grasp your heart as the terrifying realisation dawned. Oh Christ! you would think. He's going to come back! And he would. In real time the man would walk all the way back down the rocky path, down the hill and back across the sodding field.

The star of avant-garde film-making at Chelsea was a handsome, blond-haired young man called Richard who was in the year above me. The art movies Richard made were mostly stop-frame films (where a frame was taken say every second rather than the twenty-four frames per second of the normal movie). These films were of a tree or a cave and went on for hours. After he graduated I met his girlfriend on the King's Road. 'How's Richard?' I asked.

'Not good,' she replied. 'After he finished his ninety-minute film *Wet Shed in Autumn Number 2* he realised he would never make anything as important, moving or artistically significant ever again and so in despair he became a hopeless alcoholic.'

I had once had a conversation with Richard after I'd returned from a Vietnam demonstration in Sheffield where I'd got drunk on the strong ale they made for the steelworkers.

'Oh,' he said, 'my dad was in steel.'

'What?' I asked. 'He worked in a steelworks?'

'No, he owned one,' Richard replied.

Also at Chelsea we had a whole new kind of art to look at, an art form which had appeared in the 1970s, the first entirely new category to be created since the invention of the still camera in the nineteenth century. It was called performance art and it was a bit like theatre in that it was a real person or persons doing stuff in front of you but it also resembled the avant-garde films at the Film-makers' Co-op in that it was without any obvious sense or meaning. The first example of performance art was created in 1971 by an artist Chris Burden in a work entitled *Shoot*. In this piece, displaying a remarkable commitment to his art, Burden had himself shot in his left arm by an assistant. Also in 1971 a man called Vito Acconci performed a piece at a gallery in New York called *Seedbed* in which he lay hidden underneath a ramp masturbating with people walking above him while he muttered into a microphone his fantasies about the gallery visitors, which were then broadcast over a loudspeaker to those same gallery visitors.

We never had anything as controversial as somebody getting themselves shot or wanking at Chelsea but one time we sat in a studio for several hours watching a man from a group called Reindeer Werk tie splints on his arms and legs with bandages then try and pour himself a cup of tea from a teapot, spilling it all over himself. The thing was, I often found performance art very funny but you definitely weren't allowed to laugh at it.

I was told that Reindeer Werk were really popular in Poland. My fellow students just accepted this fact, but with my knowledge of the workings of the governments of Eastern Europe, where nothing happened without the intervention of the state, I wondered what the reason for this popularity was. Did the people in Poland find Reindeer Werk really brilliant and petition their government for them to see more of a man pouring tea all over himself, or did the Politburo of the Communist Party of Poland allocate funds and subsidise their work as an example of Western decadence? Or was going to see Reindeer Werk perhaps actually a punishment for dissidents and would they march these poor people at gunpoint into performances, to punish them for their disloyalty to Marxist–Leninist thought?

One Saturday morning for some reason I went into college. It wasn't like me to attend at the weekend, or indeed to go in very much during the week, maybe I'd remembered that I'd left half a sandwich in my locker. Hearing strange rustling noises in the deserted foyer I went downstairs and discovered a student from the sculpture department dragging several large tree branches heavy with leaves around behind him.

'What are you doing?' I asked.

'Performance art,' he answered.

'But there's nobody here to see it,' I said.

'Exactly,' he replied.

Molly Cooks a Chicken

To celebrate me getting my own place I decided to throw a dinner party: the guests were Anne Rees-Mogg and the two Davids. I knew I couldn't serve my Spanish omelette made out of bacon stumps and lizard eggs at a dinner party but didn't know how to cook anything else, so my mother, using the free rail pass she was entitled to as the wife of a railway-man, travelled down to London with a chicken, cooked it and some vegetables in the hideous greasy old oven I had in the flat, then before my guests arrived she went back to Liverpool.

Unfortunately, allowing her to do this meant that from that point on Molly would just turn up at my flat, unannounced and without a chicken. That was the problem with the Sayles: because we got free rail travel you never knew when we were going to appear at your door. There was a couple I knew from Southport who were now at Maidstone College of Art and they told me that they were on a special starvation diet just to try to stop me coming to visit them all the time (it didn't work, I just brought my own sandwiches).

The reason Molly kept coming to London was that she was running away from my father. My mother's response to my father's illness had always been a complicated one. A few months before, the road users of north Liverpool finally got their own back on Molly, though it was a young man on a bicycle, not a motorist, who knocked her down. I knew nothing about Molly's accident until I got a phone call from one of the neighbours in Valley Road explaining that Joe had come knocking at their door in a state of great agitation asking if they knew where his wife had gone. They took him in and somehow managed to find out that my mother had been taken to hospital where for some reason she was refusing to let anybody tell her husband where she was. By the time I got up to Liverpool Joe was very upset and confused but he pathetically rushed to hug Molly when me and Linda took him to the hospital.

When she went shopping she would often leave him outside a store and then be surprised to emerge and find that he had wandered off. There would then follow a protracted search with much hysterical shouting and crying before he was found. One New Year's Eve, Joe went missing and we spent the entire night wandering the streets looking for him. When he finally ambled home in the early hours of the morning he'd clearly been at a party because he was drunk and had a paper hat askew on his head, but he couldn't tell us where.

There was a type of jumper popular at the time made of heavy ribbed fake wool that needed a variety of belts, zips and buttons to be done up in order to secure it. My mother bought one of these for Joe even though the poor man would spend hours trying to do it up, baffled by all the various fastenings.

One lunchtime, Molly appeared at my flat in North Kensington. If I'd been at college she would probably have shown up there, so it was just as well I hadn't gone in. To keep her occupied I took her for a walk around the neighbourhood. My mother and I wandered through the market on the Portobello Road then turned towards Bayswater with me pointing out points of interest like my bus stop. As we walked along a street called Chepstow Villas with me intending to show her the twenty-four-hour supermarkets of Westbourne Grove Molly suddenly said, 'I know some people who live here,' and before I could stop her she ran over the road to hammer on one of the front doors. After a few seconds it was answered by a sleepy-looking Oriental man. The brass plaque by the entrance read, 'Legation of the People's Republic of North Vietnam'.

'Oh hello, Molly,' the man said, giving me the feeling that this might not be the first time she had appeared unannounced at the legation. Because of her work for Medical Aid for Vietnam my mother was well known to many of the diplomats from the North.

We were shown into the front room and after a little while the military attaché, a man who had been one of the heroes of the great Battle of Dien Bien Phu, when the Vietnamese had decimated the French colonial forces, entered wearing his full dress uniform with row after row of shiny medals at his breast and made painful small talk with us for half an hour. I imagined he'd rather be back in the jungle being napalmed than doing this but he undertook his task with great dignity.

A little while later, in April 1975, Saigon the capital of the South was captured by the North Vietnamese Army and that long war finally ended. North and South Vietnam were reunified the following year and our old friends from Chepstow Villas took over the former South Vietnamese Embassy, a huge mansion in Wimbledon. To celebrate re-unification they held a massive party to which the Sayle family was invited. Everybody from the left in Britain was there and as you entered the massive ballroom there was a man in a frock coat who announced your name. He called, 'Mr and Mrs Sayle and Mrs Sayle,' which was me, Linda and Molly. Molly descended the stairs and, going straight over to the Ambassador, elbowing Tony Benn out of the way, she pulled a canvas bag from her pocket. 'There's twelve pounds' worth of twenty-pence pieces there,' she said as she tried to press it into his hands, 'that we collected for Medical Aid on Merseyside.'

'No, no, Molly,' the Ambassador said. 'Not now.'

At the victory party the food was a revelation. There were Vietnamese salad rolls of rice noodle stuffed with lemon grass and coriander, little deep-fried parcels of minced pork, and sweet sugar cane coated with prawns. It was a little-known benefit of being involved in revolutionary politics – the high quality of the snacks – and also a bit of a waste, since a lot of left-wing people had no time for the sensual pleasures of eating.

The Bobo Comes to the Aid of the Resistance

As well as giving access to high-quality snacks, being a revolutionary Marxist meant opportunities for travel. In the summer break between my second and third years at art school, me and Linda undertook a very risky sort of holiday along with our friend and comrade from the CPB (M–L) Christine Walker. We intended to travel overland to Greece. Chris had recently bought a white Simca van, a vehicle that was based on the Simca 1100 hatchback, but if you bought it in commercial vehicle form with no rear seats or windows you avoided paying purchase tax.

Being young and political we couldn't just have a holiday for the sake of relaxation and travel, it had to have a higher purpose. In this case it was provided by a young Greek doctor called Sotiris who was working on Merseyside and was close to our Maoist party. Greece at that time was ruled by a fascist military junta and Sotiris was living in exile due to his activities back home which would certainly have got him imprisoned and maybe executed. When he heard we were thinking of going to

Greece, he asked if we would deliver a package from him to the resistance movement. All the time we travelled across France, Germany, Austria and Yugoslavia this plain brown-paper package about the size of a box with an Easter egg in it sat amongst our belongings, like a ticking time bomb, which it may well have been for all we knew. Though it could just as well have been a tin of Uncle Joe's Mint Balls, a kind of sweet manufactured in Everton and unobtainable in Greece.

We were supposed to take turns sitting in the passenger seat but whenever I got in the dark back of the van I would develop very convenient symptoms of travel sickness, so Linda found herself for most of the journey crammed in the rear of the Simca with very little view of the fields of northern France, the Alps or the ancient towns of Austria. Neither me nor Linda could drive so we were not aware of how tiring it could be; we assumed it was no more exhausting than being a passenger. Often late in the afternoons Chris would start talking nonsense and her movements would become erratic, at which point we would make her stop in the nearest town where we would force coffee down her. Then we would walk her around, occasionally punching her in the arm, until she started making a bit more sense, at which point we would force her back to the wheel of the Simca and make her drive for a couple more hours.

We never spoke about the package but I felt terrified at the Greek border as soldiers performed a perfunctory search of our van and the relief afterwards when they let us proceed was dizzying. After a few minutes though my spirits plummeted again. I thought to myself that this must be the way proper revolutionaries feel all the time – absolutely petrified, knowing that any moment, with just some little slip, they could find themselves thrown into prison and tortured. This was supposed to be what us Maoists wanted our lives to be like but having had just a few minutes of it, I didn't think it seemed like a lot of fun.

Eventually we arrived in Athens where we handed over our package in a pre-arranged meeting at a café in the Plaka. Then we went to stay with Sotiris's mother and sister at their apartment in central Athens.

The Greeks, like the Arabs, had a tremendous tradition of hospitality and apparently it was considered extremely lucky to have a male foreigner in your home, especially one as chubby as me. They told us that such a person was known as 'the Bobo' and it was important to feed him continually with food and drink. Sotiris's mother seemed to get through a five-litre can of olive oil most days which meant her cooking was extremely rich. Her moussaka had the specific gravity of lead and they kept making me drink over-proof ouzo at nine in the morning so that I spent my days in a bloated, alcoholic fug. Neither the mother nor the sister spoke English but there was a thirteen-year-old girl also staying with them who was the daughter of a Greek chip-shop owner in Liverpool and was fluent in both Greek and English.

Unfortunately this girl was a very wilful young lady who frequently abused her power as our only translator. We would be out in the centre of Athens and we would say to the girl, 'Tell Sotiris's sister we would like to visit the big shops to buy souvenirs.'

The girl would briefly talk in Greek to the sister then turning to us she would say, 'Sotiris's sister told me that's not possible because the shops are all closed and she instead wants us to go to a bowling alley.'

This was clearly untrue as we could see the big stores all around us with their lights blazing away and shoppers pouring in and out of their doors with no sign of them closing. We were not allowed to protest too much though because dangerously for us the wilful teenager had somehow become aware of our anti-government activities so if we disagreed with her too much she would start edging towards a policeman with a malevolent look in her eyes.

This Levantine hospitality thing turned out in many ways just to be a form of bullying. Chris was desperate to get a tan but when we went to the seaside the mother and sister made her sit with a big hat on such as would be worn by a donkey and then they coated her in yoghurt so that Chris sat in a circle of darkness sobbing.

In the end we slipped out one morning while everybody was sleeping and headed back towards Britain in our little white van.

This early morning escape sealed my enchantment with motor cars, which had been growing since we had left Liverpool. All the transcontinental trips I had taken before had been with my parents and had been aboard trains so I felt a little disloyal for falling so madly in love with cars, especially since drivers were still regularly trying to kill my mother and also I couldn't drive. But on the other hand that was part of the enchantment, you just got in this little white box, Chris did some incomprehensible stuff with her feet and the steering wheel and the gear stick and a few days later we were back home; it really was unbelievable.

SYMPATHY IN GRIFFITH HOUSE

My mother was never thirsty, she was always 'terribly dehy-drated' and this catastrophising went double for me. Molly was inclined to see anything even mildly bad that happened to her only son as a cataclysm. If I trod on something and got a minor cut to my sole she would immediately start screaming that the foot would have to be amputated. I had to a slightly lesser degree inherited this hysterical pessimism so there was no one more surprised than me when my second year at Chelsea turned out to be a considerable improvement on the first. The new intake of students seemed a lot less posh and a lot more Northern than the year above so that I began to form a solid core of friends.

They were mostly a little bit younger than me which in itself was a fresh experience since, having had long hair and a beard from the age of fourteen, I had almost always been friends with people who were older. One evening when we were still getting to know each other a big group arranged to meet in a new kind of place, an all-you-can-eat-buffet restaurant in Kensington. When I was a child in Liverpool, working-class families such as ours did not eat out frequently but when we did, at the

Bon Marché department store or a Kardomah Café, there was always a tremendous lack of generosity in both the service and the cuisine. The staff would grudgingly dole out tiny portions of food as if us diners were survivors of a shipwreck who were now crammed into a lifeboat under the baking sun with rescue not expected to arrive for weeks. You always had the feeling while dining in a British restaurant in the 1950s or 1960s that if you tried to get more than your meagre rations the head waiter was going to shoot you with a revolver.

Entering the place in Kensington I was overexcited and nervous at the thought of having a night out with my new friends. I did not notice the coat stand by the door was already vastly overloaded and without thinking took my jacket off and flung it on top of the heap of clothing already hanging there. The weight of my coat proved to be the final straw, causing the coat stand with a creaking sound to topple like a giant redwood tree: I watched in horror as it seemed to tumble in slow motion, finally crashing down onto a table around which six or seven diners were seated. This table proved not to be a table at all but an unsecured circle of chipboard resting on a trestle so the whole thing, with all the group's food on it, tipped up and flew through the air, fortunately without hitting anyone. For a second I was paralysed with fear: in any restaurant, especially back in Liverpool, at the very least I would have had to pay for seven people's dinners and would still in all likelihood have got beaten up, but with a rush of gratitude I suddenly realised that in this place and this place alone I only needed to say to the people at the table, 'Look, I'm very sorry about that but you can see that the coat stand was overloaded and anyway you can just go and help yourselves to more food.' Which is what they all did. From that moment I was in love with all-you-can-eat buffets.

A fair few of these friends came up to Liverpool for the party when in 1974 Linda and I got married. We had decided to wed almost as an affectation. All the couples we knew were living together while marriage was considered to be old-fashioned and possibly fascist so we thought we'd be different. It was only slowly as the date approached that we came to realise that marriage was actually a huge commitment not to be taken lightly or done as a fashion statement. So by the time of the ceremony at the registry office in Brougham Terrace in Liverpool me and Linda were very solemn and a bit intimidated by the weight of the event.

After the ceremony, we, our parents, Linda's brother Jimmy and Chris Walker went to the Berni Inn in town for a steak lunch. Somebody, probably one of Linda's parents unsure of themselves in a restaurant, asked the waitress what she'd recommend for a suitable wine to accompany low-quality beef, a badly burnt tomato and frozen peas. The woman, big and beefy herself with a towering beehive hairdo, thought for a few seconds then replied, 'Well . . . they say the rosé's very good.'

We wondered who exactly 'they' were. Perhaps, we thought, a group of worthies – philosophers, lawmakers, playwrights and politicians who met in convocation to decide what was good and bad in the world, to pronounce accordingly and to ensure that life was free from upset. If that was the case then they'd really taken their eye off the ball recently because things seemed to be going to hell in a hell-cart. First of all there was the OAPEC oil embargo begun by the major oil-producing countries in response to American involvement in the 1973 Yom Kippur War between Israel, Egypt and Syria. The major victims were Canada, Japan, the Netherlands, the United Kingdom and the US. Flying and boating was banned on Sundays and the speed limit was reduced to fifty-six miles an hour, supposedly the most efficient speed to drive at but which meant a trip to Liverpool took seven hours. Then there were the high rates of inflation so people's wages didn't keep pace with the cost of things, meaning there were a lot of strikes and work-to-rules, culminating in the three-day week in which electricity was rationed to three days a week, so we had to buy our wedding clothes by candlelight. And to add to that there was a stock market crash when the FT 30 lost 73 per cent and a secondary banking crisis forced the Bank of England to bail out a number of lenders, so perhaps 'they' should have been thinking about other things rather than what wine went with substandard grilled meats in a cellar in North-West England.

Linda moved her belongings into the horrible little flat in North Kensington. She did her best to try and cheer up the gloomy apartment but really it was impossible.

Slowly the group I was part of at Chelsea became the dominant faction within the college. By my third year my friend Roberta Gordon-Smith was elected as president of the Students' Union and I was voted in as her vice-president. My landslide victory came after I made a passionate speech about how I was going to bring about greater political involvement within the college. Subsequently I behaved like the worst Communist official in that I did nothing apart from pilfer the Student Union funds.

For my graduation show my films were projected every afternoon in the lecture theatre and my work, mostly scripts for the films, was on display for two weeks, and every day I would check my space to see if there was a note that had been left for me by a film producer or somebody from the BBC, but there wasn't. I left Chelsea with a 2.1 Diploma in Art and Design. The diploma itself was a gigantic piece of parchment, much embellished with seals, coats of arms and calligraphy, as large as the placards protestors carried on demonstrations: the size perhaps trying to make up for its complete uselessness.

My plan was that I would probably go to film school after Chelsea since I couldn't see anything else I wanted to do, but I had left it too late to apply that year so decided I'd have a year off and make my application in the spring of 1975. Until then I had to find work.

A lot of people I knew would have signed on the dole but I'd always been uncomfortable with claiming benefits. I'd done it a couple of times after leaving school but hated the sitting for hours in the smoky hall, the indifference of the employment exchange staff and the handing over of money in return for you doing nothing. Some were great abusers of the welfare system seeing it as a kind of payback for the rapacious nature of the British Empire or some other self-serving excuse but I always felt I should work if it was possible to do so.

The first place I went looking for employment was an edifice called Griffith House. This building was the main recruitment centre for the lower echelons of London Underground. Anybody who wanted to be a maintenance worker, station cleaner or tube train driver would first present themselves at the blank redbrick block spanning the Metropolitan Line just off the Marylebone Road. As soon as she'd moved to London Linda had found herself an administrative job with London Transport at their headquarters in St James's, and according to what she'd heard the men who worked at Griffith House were famous for displaying an extra-ordinary level of unpleasantness towards prospective employees.

I had decided to apply for a job as a booking-office clerk, which meant that along with fifty other potential recruits I was required to sit a simple mathematics test. The bitter old man who was in charge grumpily handed out our examination papers and then barked at us to start then yelled at us again to stop thirty minutes later. After we had finished and handed back the papers he went over our results with us one by one.

When he came to me he held my paper in his hand and in a voice that was almost tender he said to me, 'I'm awful sorry, son, but you've done terribly badly in this test.' Clearly my marks were so poor and my answers to the simple questions so stupid that they had melted his angry old heart. 'Have you thought of being a tube train guard?' he asked. 'You don't need maths for that.'

'No, you're all right,' I replied, realising a job behind the Plexiglas wasn't for me. 'I think I'll look somewhere else.'

The somewhere else I looked was the Manpower Employment Agency who'd pretty much take anybody. I signed on with them and they immediately found me work. Every morning at 6.30 a.m. I would cycle to Notting Hill Gate and from there in a minibus a group of about eight of us would be driven to a factory owned by Lucas CAV in Finchley, which made fuel pumps for diesel engines. The factory was quite near where I had once lived with Wassim. I remember one early morning driving through St John's Wood and seeing the Household Cavalry returning from a pre-dawn ride, their cap badges gleaming and their spurs jingling. Hatred of soldiers was pretty standard on the left although I had heard one Trotskyist refer to members of the armed forces as 'workers in uniform', which was a description I liked.

My job was to sweep the shop floor and to try and keep it clean. This wasn't easy because the machinery was ancient and worn-out and the factory itself was old and dirty, with malodorous lavatories reminiscent of a prison camp. Because of my worries over the state of British manufacturing I'd begun studying articles in newspapers and magazines as well as getting books out of the library that covered management practices around the world. From what I read it was generally acknowledged that Japan was the coming industrial power and in all the best Nipponese factories there would only ever be a single canteen. This dining hall would be an attractive space serving excellent food where everybody ate, from assembly-line workers to senior management. The practice of communal eating was said to foster a collective sense of ownership and enabled all levels of the workforce to exchange views and swap ideas in an informal setting.

At Lucas CAV there were five different canteens, with ascending levels of food and hygiene going from factory-floor worker to clerical, senior clerical to management and finally upwards to the wood-panelled splendour of the dining room reserved for the executives where the chef was from the Savoy and the 'Omelette Alec Issigonis' was famed around the world.

By contrast the fare in the lowliest workers' canteen where I ate reminded me of something out of Dostoevsky and there was no provision made for the many vegetarian Hindu workers, so all they could eat was the watery carrots or mushy boiled Brussels sprouts that accompanied our leathery boiled meats. It occurred to me that the poor quality of British automotive components might be down to the fact that a lot of the people who assembled them were suffering from scurvy.

That summer I felt very low and my mood was made worse by our flat suddenly becoming infested with mice. At night you could hear them skittering about, climbing up and down the curtains; their droppings were everywhere and out of the corner of your eye you would see sudden darting shapes as you watched television. Linda said our best bet was to get a cat. At home in Liverpool we had only ever had dogs but until they'd moved to the tower block her family had owned a succession of ferocious tomcats. Wise in the ways of the slums, the next Saturday Linda simply walked up and down Wornington Road asking kids playing in the street if anybody had any kittens. Within half an hour she was back with a tiny little mewling ginger thing wrapped in a blanket. I couldn't believe that this creature, which we christened Archie, was going to rid us of mice since he was hardly bigger than one of the rodents himself but within a few days they were all gone and Archie was my saviour.

I also found out what great companions cats can be as Archie became my little pal. He was fascinated by everything I did. When I was washing the dishes he would climb up my body to perch on my shoulders, determined to see what was going on.

We called him Archie at the suggestion of Harry Jackson the former bus driver who had moved down to London more or less at the same time as Linda. We only learned later after naming our cat that every single one of the pets in the Jackson family had been called Archie. It was weird listening to him and his brother Clive talking about their animals. 'Do you remember the time when Archie 9 tried to get Archie 12 out of his tank?' Clive would say, 'and Archie 25a got out of his cage and was flying around squawking while Archie 17 was squirting water at him out of his trunk?'

Municipal House of Cards

Then a greater deliverance came when in late summer the whole of Wornington Road was compulsorily purchased by Kensington and Chelsea Council and scheduled for demolition. A letter arrived telling us that if we wished we could be rehoused in a twelfth-floor flat in a tower block in Fulham, some three or four miles to the south. We jumped at the chance, a council flat at a reasonable rent was a wonderful gift. The only sadness came when me and Linda realised we wouldn't be able to take Archie with us since it would be cruel to keep him confined in a flat all day. Instead we took him by train to Liverpool and left him with Molly.

The next time I visited my home town my lovely little mate had vanished completely and been replaced by the biggest, dirtiest tomcat I had ever seen – if you stroked him your fingers came away all sticky and black. He and Molly had also begun screaming at each other.

'Eahyoweahyoweahyow,' Archie would yowl.

'Oh Christ! What do you want? Tell me what do you want!' Molly would scream back.

'Eahyoweahyoweahyow,' the cat would reply.

'Shut up, you little bastard. Just shut up, shut up, shut up!'

'Eahyoweahyoweahyow.'

'Shut up, shut up!'

They both seemed perfectly happy in their own way.

Our new apartment building was on Dawes Road, Fulham, and was called Lannoy Point. Its design was identical to that of a council tower block named Ronan Point in the East End where a gas explosion had caused the collapse of one entire corner of the structure. An enquiry revealed that the panels of the supporting walls at Ronan Point had all just rested on each other like a house of cards and gravity had been given the job of holding everything together. After the explosion, emergency measures were taken to ensure the safety of blocks such as ours. When you opened one of the built-in cupboards in the kitchen or living room you would find a steel beam secured with massive nuts and bolts tying the wall to the ceiling and hopefully stopping the building falling down.

Apart from the possibility of the entire block collapsing it was a lovely flat, spacious and flooded with light from the large, almost floor-to-ceiling wood-framed windows. On a Friday evening as the sun set we would see the arrow-head shape of Concorde climbing out of Heathrow bound for New York.

After the din and chaos of North Kensington the flat was also wonderfully quiet. The only source of occasional noise was the woman who lived above us, an old-school prostitute, tall and statuesque with beefy, muscular arms and a standard towering beehive hairdo. Not so much a 'lady of the night' as a 'dinner lady of the night'. Generally her patch was the red light district behind King's Cross Station but occasionally she would work from home in which case you would hear the strangest and most baffling sounds coming through the ceiling.

Lannoy Point had been built at the zenith of the Greater London Council when there had been a worthy, though perhaps condescending, impulse to provide council tenants at great expense with the best of everything. Looking around the flat though, I got the impression that there was a certain type of crap product that manufacturers reserved solely for selling to local councils. In all the rooms there were massive, grey-painted storage heaters, filled with bricks, that would sigh out a tiny amount of heat in exchange for the input of gigantic amounts of electricity, and the lovely wooden windows would regularly rot then fall out, requiring the entire block to be shrouded in scaffolding while they were replaced.

One night I came home drunk from the pub with the gift of a bottle of cider for Linda, who for once had stayed at home. Sadly before giving it to her I had to use the toilet. As I bent down, the bottle of cider fell out of my pocket smashing a big hole in the toilet bowl. The next morning we rang the council and the very same day a couple of workmen came round and quickly changed the toilet.

I said to them, 'You know I broke this with a bottle of cider?'

One of them said, 'Don't matter, mate. If it's broke it gets fixed, don't matter how it got broke.' Yet it bothered me, this idea that if you were a council tenant there were no consequences to your actions, as if you were some kind of big baby.

Unlike the tower blocks such as those that Linda had lived in in Liverpool, Lannoy Point was not part of some huge estate but instead formed one element of a mixed cityscape. Dawes Road on which our block stood was a long winding main road of shops, pubs and large houses; off it ran streets of more compact two-storey dwellings. I could look down and all around me were laid out the terraced houses of Fulham, two- or three-bedroom homes built of London Stock brick with slate roofs. Though you couldn't tell from twelve floors up, the occupants of these houses were beginning to change. The majority of the population had until recently been Londoners from the East End or Irish immigrants arriving between the wars to service London's explosive growth. But there was a metamorphosis going on: stockbrokers from the City, people who worked at the BBC, advertising executives who a few years before would have lived in Chelsea and South Kensington were being forced by rising house prices to move further west. To show that they were a different kind of occupant these new people would often paint the outsides of their dwellings in bright shades of blue or yellow and they always seemed to fix a pair of carriage lamps to the front door. Given my obsession with cars and my worries about British manufacturing I observed something nobody else seemed to have noticed parked outside their houses, rather than the older residents' UK-built Ford Cortinas, was a new type of vehicle, a small, brightly painted, Japanese-made Suzuki SJ410 4x4 Jeep, which gave the impression that they owned another place in the country, though my sense was that they only used these tough little military-style vehicles to go to the nearest supermarket.

I had never had a 'local' but more or less at the foot of our flats there was a pub built in the 1930s called the Bedford Arms. The public bar was strictly rural Irish but the lounge where we drank was more diverse. Admittedly there were none of the new middle classes but there was a mixture of the native Cockneys who lived in Lannoy Point and the nearby estate as well as other working-class people, Northerners, Scots and Irish drawn from flats in the nearby houses.

At the same time as we moved to Fulham, Harry Jackson began renting a room in an apartment in a private mansion block round the corner. Harry was from a Jewish family in Liverpool and his father had owned a tailoring business until he had gone bankrupt. He'd trained as a TV engineer and was now in London working for his cousin. Harry and I looked quite alike and pretty soon I began to think of him as the brother I never wanted. Me, Linda and Harry would meet in the Bedford at least twice a week, sometimes more. Before we went out, Linda would make the two of us a big meal complete with a pudding and custard then, after drinking four or five pints and the pub closed, we would get a Chinese meal from the little takeaway counter a few doors down but as an economy measure Linda would boil our own rice rather than us paying takeaway prices.

Other times we would stay in and watch TV. We were very excited on the day we bought a colour television. The only one we could afford was a little rotary dial Sanyo. The first thing that was on was Crufts Dog Show and we watched it all the way through, astonished by the green of the turf and the extra detail that colour brought. I think right at that moment that we could not have been happier: there was nothing expected of us, everything was in the future.

After we'd finished our three course meal, but before we went to the pub, me and Linda had a conversation concerning the years to come and why neither of us had given any thought to our future financial security.

Linda said, 'Well I've never thought of getting a pension or saving money in a bank account or buying a share portfolio because by the time I'm old enough to need it Britain will inevitably be a socialist nation led by a vanguard party whose ideology is based on the teachings of Marx, Engels, Lenin and Mao Tse-tung and every worker will have all of their needs taken care of by the state.'

I replied, 'Well I never thought of getting a pension or saving any money or buying a share portfolio because I figured that one day I'd be a famous celebrity, known and admired around the world, a person who'd have tons of money in the bank from whatever the very successful thing is that he does.'

Once my feelings about the future were out in the open it seemed ridiculous to remain a member (no matter how ineffectual) of a Maoist revolutionary party and I stopped attending CPB (M–L) meetings. I never officially told them I'd quit the party but then they never rang up to see where I was either.

A lot of my friends remained in revolutionary groups, others were becoming involved in the new single issue politics, the environment, race or gender, while I became the sole member of the CPA – The Communist Party of Alexei. I continued to think of myself as Left-wing and a Marxist, it was just that I never attended any kind of party political meeting ever again.

The Calm Before the Calm

Unfortunately me having a local pub that I visited up to three or four times a week did not mean that I was in any way 'well in' at the Bedford. Indeed if the Irish bar staff noticed me at all it was with a mild sense of irritation at my peculiar manner and odd clothes.

As I became familiar with the lounge bar of the Bedford, the Naugahyde banquettes, the flock wallpaper and the orange fibreglass relief on one wall that looked like something from a space station in a futuristic movie, I became more and more convinced that after closing time at 11 p.m. the regulars were getting a 'lock-in', i.e., the bar staff would seal the doors and illegally carry on serving alcohol. Try as hard as I might I could not get myself invited to these 'stay-behinds', instead I was always rapidly ejected, sometimes physically, right on 11.15, stumbling onto the pavement. Linda and Harry might have been OK but as long as they were with me they too were thrown out. Behind us the doors slammed shut and turning I would see the shadows of happy figures outlined against the frosted glass and hear the sound of raucous singing beginning to drift into the night air.

This was particularly painful because me, Linda and Harry shared an obsession, which was the idea of getting a drink after the pubs closed. Back in Liverpool it had been an easy task at closing time to locate an ethnic drinking club, the Somali or the Niger, which wouldn't shut until the early hours of the morning, but in London we couldn't discover such a place anywhere. This desire to drink after the pubs closed was not really even about the alcohol but rather expressed a wish to challenge the idea of your life being controlled by archaic laws and puritanical bureaucrats who didn't want you to enjoy yourself but instead wanted you to go to bed so you'd be fresh to service the Machine the next morning.

One night, after drinking with Roberta Gordon-Smith, the ex-president to my vice of Chelsea Students' Union, in a place called Finch's on the Fulham Road, me and Linda were walking home when we passed a gay pub with blacked-out windows called the Colherne. It was a place which attracted a leather crowd who signalled their sexual predilections via a complex arrangement of key chains, colour-coded hand-kerchiefs and small plastic gonk figures scattered about their leather jackets and trousers. David Pearce was stand-ing outside and called to us. He said he was going to a gay bar called the Copacabana and did we want to come with him? Later, once we were signed in, seeing only a late-night drinking club close to our home, I asked him to go and see if I could join. David returned to tell me that membership was closed but he'd informed the manager that I was a gay guy from Liverpool who wouldn't be coming too often so if

I went and had a word with him he'd let me be a member. I walked over to the manager's desk reminding myself not to act too camp but then gave a performance of such extreme gayness that everybody in the club thought a drag act had suddenly begun performing in a corner. They did make me a member but joining a gay club wasn't a viable long-term solution to us getting a late-night drink.

On another occasion, me, Harry and Linda managed to get into a postmen's social club in Fulham Broadway that didn't close until the early hours via a postman Harry knew slightly. After a few drinks the postman's wife who was Austrian started railing against 'ze Chews who controlled everything and were mean and had big noses'. We were all shocked at this especially since both me and Harry were Jewish but it still took us a few minutes before we definitely decided we had to leave, so desperate were we to get a late-night drink.

Not being one of the crowd in the Bedford meant at least that I got to scrutinise the Cockneys who drank in there relatively unobserved. I found them extraordinary. In some ways they resembled people from Liverpool in that they had this really thick, distinctive accent but whereas the Scouser went in for a kind of erudite loquaciousness, a love of a clever-sounding phrase, they did not deal in complex ideas, their talk was all about material things, cars and jewellery, and very loud, they swore an awful lot and they were right-wing and patriotic. On the eve of Prince Charles's marriage to Diana Spencer the occupants of the small council estate opposite us painted a mural on their six-foot-high street-facing wall. This fresco featured the badge of the Parachute Regiment, of which Charles was Colonel-in-Chief, and underneath it the legend

'Good luck on yer night jump, Charlie!' which brilliantly combined crude vulgarity with fawning obsequiousness.

Unlike me, Roberta was 'well in' at Finch's on the Fulham Road. She knew everybody in the place and they all knew her and she was sort of the centre of things but it seemed there was a price to pay in that if you wanted to be that sort of person you had to be much more tolerant of bores. One night when we were with her there was a guy who talked about nothing but the drugs he'd taken, culminating in a long story about some amazing dope he'd smoked which had temporarily paralysed all his limbs, which he thought was a brilliant outcome.

Boulevard of Broken Dreams

Tired of being a casual worker, I went down to the jobcentre and said to one of them, 'Do you have any jobs to do with art?'

'No,' they replied after not looking through their files.

'Well what do you have then?' I asked.

'You can come and work here if you like,' they replied.

So I did or rather I became a temporary clerk, grade T6, at the Department of Health and Social Security on the fourth floor of Euston Tower, a thirty-four-storey 1960s office block on the Euston Road. At the foot of Euston Tower there was also the entrance to Capital Radio, London's only commercial music station, which occupied the bottom two floors of the building. On my first day at work I swore that at some point in the future I would enter via its doors but for now I trudged through a separate, dark, gloomy, civil servants' entrance which led me to the lift and the fourth floor.

I worked in an office which was involved in a major project. The DHSS architects' department had never been allowed to design and build a hospital before but with Greenwich

District Hospital they had been given their chance. My office contained four clerks who dealt with the mail to do with this project while there was enough work to employ maybe one trained chicken. Of the three junior clerks, one was learning to play a Russian folk instrument called a balalaika, one was running a knitwear business from her desk and having an affair with one of the architects while I read books and wrote film scripts. The senior clerk, a woman in her forties, did nearly all the work.

On my desk was a push-button phone. I had always found the process of making a call with a conventional dial phone incredibly tedious, you had to wait ages for the numbers to click round and I genuinely felt I'd wasted a large part of my life waiting for this process to be completed. The push-button phone felt like the future – I couldn't imagine that anything could be more futuristic than a push-button phone.

It was much more congenial being a clerk than sweeping a factory floor, but I found that when you worked in an office you got into this weird kind of tribal mindset where you couldn't see that there was anything wrong with the way you behaved. Occasionally in the course of our jobs we would be forced to have dealings with clerks in almost identical positions to ours who worked for local government rather than, as we did, the Civil Service. In our office we really didn't like having anything to do with those who worked for local government because we thought they were all lazy.

At lunchtime I used to go to the nearby Royal Institute of British Architects in Portland Place where they showed free films though this meant that I couldn't be back at my desk in under two hours and one lunchtime I went see a play called

Christie in Love, an early work by Howard Brenton concerning the life of serial killer John Christie, at the Almost Free Theatre in an alley behind Oxford Street, where you paid whatever you felt the play was worth. As I took my place there was an actor dressed as a policeman already digging at a pile of dirt with a shovel. I'd taken a crusty baguette in with me to eat for my lunch and as I bit into it with a loud crunching noise the actor abruptly stopped digging, the houselights snapped off and staring directly at me he began to recite a limerick in a weird mechanical voice. The fright I got at this meant that the play made a great impression on me but I also found it memorable because I had never before seen something in the fringe theatre that was sympathetic to the police. The play emphasised how hard it must be for those involved in law enforcement to constantly be confronting evil and for that it felt fresher and more involving than the usual empty agitprop.

As a teenager, when I was distressed I would take long walks, backwards and forwards across the entire length and breadth of Liverpool. During my first difficult year at Chelsea I would occasionally find myself in some remote suburb of London with only the vaguest recollection of how I had got there. On one occasion I walked from our flat in Finchley Central to the slip road of the M1. During my lunch break, while working for the Civil Service, I would sometimes walk down what I liked to call the Boulevard of Broken Dreams and labelled in the *London A–Z* as 'Piccadilly'. I was drawn to Piccadilly and its environs because they seemed to me to contain the headquarters of a number of institutions operating with extraordinary and epic uselessness.

First at the western end there was the Arts Council. I hated the Arts Council. The remit of this organisation was to give money only to things that were unpopular, which meant books that nobody wanted to read, plays that nobody wanted to go to and art that people found baffling and unsettling, all displayed in buildings of phenomenal ugliness. After that was the headquarters and booking office of Aeroflot, the airline of the Soviet Union, where only the most persistent could buy tickets for their dangerous and smoky jets. Over the road was the booking office of the French Railway Network the SNCF where they were terribly rude to you if you interrupted them chatting to each other. Further along was the Lebanese Tourist Board representing a country beginning the long slide into civil war, and beyond that the Northern Ireland Tourist Board which at the height of the Troubles wasn't selling many self-catering holidays. Next there was my favourite, a shop that formed the sole retail outlet of a government agency named the Egg Information Council, which was tasked with the dissemination of all ovum-related data. In their dusty unwashed window were displayed eggcups and a device popular in the 1960s which consisted of a pin on a spring-loaded plunger rather like the instrument diabetics use to take blood samples. With this contraption you could prick the egg you were boiling so that all its contents leaked out into the pan.

Then finally occupying a big building on the Haymarket looming over them all was the Design Centre. The Design Centre was a sort of Arts Council for teapots. Its chief aim was supposedly to promote 'good design' in British industry but in reality the Design Centre seemed dedicated to bringing

to British design and manufacturing the same levels of intro-
spection, meaninglessness, jargon and elitism as the Arts
Council was bringing to painting, sculpture, the theatre and
literature.

A few years later the Design Centre would award their prestigious 'Design Centre' label to the only motor vehicle ever
thought worthy of this important encomium. The car was the
Austin Montego, an oddly sized, weird-looking, badly built
lump whose only innovative feature was a talking dashboard.
The philosopher Ludwig Wittgenstein said, 'If a lion could
speak we could not understand him,' and unfortunately the
same was true of an Austin Montego dashboard.

I also imagined, though I never found it, that somewhere in
a quiet side street just off Piccadilly the Society for Promoting
the Injury of Children by Encouraging them to Play on Lethal
Structures had its opulent headquarters in a Regency building spread over six floors with a cobbled forecourt where the
eminent bosses of the organisation parked their Rolls-Royces
and Jaguars.

Day of the Two-wheeled Triffids

In the spring of 1975 I finally got around to applying to the two main UK film schools, the National Film School at Beaconsfield and the Royal College of Art Film School in South Kensington. I submitted my work all beautifully mounted on stationery provided by the Civil Service and was very upset when they both turned me down flat. This despite the fact that I was technically incompetent, didn't care that much about movies and had no idea what sort of films I wanted to make.

Although I couldn't really admit it to myself they were right to reject me. I had gone to art school not because of a love of art but because I had a facility for painting and drawing and wanted an education and the same would have been true if by some freakish accident I had got into film school. We had all been encouraged at Chelsea to believe that each of us had a unique vision to share with the world. It was cruel because most of us didn't. I firmly believed I was one of the ones who did, even though there didn't seem to be an art form right now for me to communicate my ideas with.

To try and regain some control I felt, at least, that I had to stop working in the Civil Service: there was a certain kind of cloying security in being a clerk that I didn't want. My feeling was if I didn't act now I could see myself in twenty years' time still doing the same job, sitting in an office of the DHSS working one hour a day and running a business on the side selling ceramic clowns.

My feelings about work had been conditioned by the fact that I had grown up in an era of full employment. If somebody as unreliable and weird as me could walk in and out of jobs then there was no need for me to ever worry about getting paid work.

My new plan was to try and find some kind of job which would enable me to stay at home and at the same time create whatever great artistic thing it was I was going to create.

It was wrong of me to think that I wasn't part of a network of influence a bit like the one that existed between the rich kids at Chelsea because I was a member of the web connecting those in the British Communist Party and their children. Unfortunately since I didn't want to become a shop steward at British Leyland the network hadn't seemed to be of much use to me. Except on my first day of secondary school an older boy whose parents were in the Party had been appointed my protector, this was Cliff Cocker. After a fashion he did look after me and later we became friends. It was Cliff's older brother Glen who got me out of the Civil Service. Glen worked in advertising as a typographical designer and he had a friend called Martin who owned his own graphic design firm. Through Martin I quickly became one of London's bottom-ten freelance illustrators.

Martin was a person who always took others at their own valuation: if you said you were a singer rather than a dustman (which was your actual job) Martin believed you were a singer, if despite the fireman's uniform you told him you were a sculptor then to Martin you were a sculptor. In consequence Martin was always being taken advantage of by people who assured him they were qualified central-heating engineers or state-registered hovercraft pilots. He told me at his graphic design company they were always on the lookout for illustrators to do record-cover artwork, draw pictures for adverts and so on.

I said to Martin, 'I'm an illustrator.'

'Great,' he replied.

And from then on he would regularly push work my way and I would consistently let him down with my very poor illustrations. The one half-decent thing I did for him in several years was my first job, a pencil drawing for a double LP of the recordings of the US folklorist, ethnomusicologist and writer Alan Lomax called *Murderers' Home/Blues in the Mississippi Night*. These recording were of prison and chain-gang songs so I knew I would need some photos of black prisoners for reference. Unfortunately I was always really bad at getting reference material, basically just looking to see what I had in the house and then if I couldn't find it giving up. For this LP I found one still photo of prisoners on a chain gang in a book about Hollywood films, it was from the movie *I Was a Prisoner on a Chain Gang*. Regrettably all the men in the picture were white, while the people on the cover needed to be black, but I'd discovered another book I owned which was a history of Tamla Motown music and so what I did was simply transpose the heads of members of the Four Tops, the Temptations, and I think in one case Diana Ross, onto the shoulders of the white chain gang. Unfortunately the heads didn't really fit onto the bodies so all the prisoners looked like they had severe neck injuries but still this was the best illustration I ever did.

Being a freelance illustrator introduced me to the world of those who aren't strictly unemployed but don't go to work either. It is a realm of people who rise late, have a lunch of sardines and oranges at 3 p.m., who wear what they feel like wearing and linger too long in bicycle shops trying on the hats. Sometimes I would ride around with Harry Jackson in his van watching as he fixed people's TVs. One time a man with a house in Regent's Park tipped us both a pound. I don't think I have ever been more content.

I also developed an interest in commercial vehicles. Every month I would buy *Commercial Vehicle* magazine and I visited the Truck of the Year Show at Earls Court. This even though I couldn't drive.

Another way I found to fill my time was by worrying about the health of my houseplants. The fashion was to fill your apartment with all kinds of greenery, Swiss cheeses, spider plants, ficus trees. Whenever you went to a dinner party at somebody's flat it was like eating in the Burmese jungle.

Because our flat was full of light I too had a lot of house-plants but they seemed so fragile that I began to worry about their health and I became something of a houseplant hypo-chondriac. I'd bought most of them from a garden centre about a mile away and so when, say, my big ficus tree began to lose some of its leaves I would load it onto the back of my bike and ride round to the garden centre to badger the woman who worked there on what might be ailing my houseplant. She would usually tell me that the most likely explanation for my ficus's ill-health was the fact that it had been for a ride on the back of a bicycle.

About Poor A.S.

Throughout my schooldays Cliff Cocker had been a calming presence in my otherwise rather overheated world of friendship. I didn't have a big circle of acquaintances, rather my pattern was that I would become close to one other boy who I would spend all my time with, I'd invest all my emotions in them, I'd visit their house constantly, dropping in at all times of the day and night whether I was invited or not. Eventually there would come a point where my best friend would let me down in some way, they'd lie to me about where they were going or they'd leave me waiting for them at some agreed spot and never turn up; sometimes their parents would come to our house and have a word with Molly. Either way after that I'd never speak to them again.

But I never fell out with Cliff. And he was also the first person who recognised the performer in me, who saw that I had a talent for comedy. We had been in the school play together, Gogol's *The Government Inspector*. Cliff had a lead role and I played a character only referred to as 'a Jewish merchant' with one line which I delivered in a frankly anti-Semitic manner to huge laughs every night. After that he encouraged me to join him in Merseyside Youth Theatre where we spent a year or so rehearsing a production of *West Side Story* that we never put on led by a couple of teachers, one of whom would go on to star in Channel 4's *Brookside.*

At the same time it was always understood that I was junior to Cliff, he was the leader and one day he was going to be the successful actor. He was also considered to be very handsome with something of the look of his namesake Cliff Richard about him.

But Cliff was not allowed to become an actor right away: his parents insisted that he take an English degree at Newcastle University first. During my career as a cut-price drug dealer I would regularly visit him there and was also supplying Newcastle University students with subsidised dope. After Newcastle, Cliff was free to attend Bristol Old Vic Drama School. Following graduation he got parts in rep and with the agitprop 7:84 Theatre Company but somehow there wasn't the rapid transition to stardom we'd both expected, so now he was living in Paris teaching English. Me and Linda would go and visit him often. We did not, however, get to see any of the sights, rather we seemed to spend our whole time in bars and the odd restaurant. I did see the Eiffel Tower once but it was from the floor of a taxi as we careered back to his flat at six in the morning.

The other thing I did in Paris was to buy several packets of sweets that Anne Rees-Mogg had asked me to get for her. They were small white mints available exclusively from vending machines on the platforms of the Métro and called Mental Blanc.

In 1976 at the point when I was beginning to call myself a freelance illustrator and therefore had a great deal of time on my hands, Cliff Cocker returned from Paris to live in London. No longer interested in being an actor Cliff decided he wanted to be a director of radical plays instead so he set about forming a fringe theatre group. His plan was to mount a production of songs and poems of Bertolt Brecht in a cabaret style but focusing on the more political and overtly Communist aspects of the playwright's work. Cliff named the group Threepenny Theatre and asked me if I'd like to join. The production was to be called *About Poor B.B.* and would be staged initially at a community centre called the Factory in a space where formerly taxi meters had been made.

The cast of *About Poor B.B.* met for the first time at the Factory, in the big open space where we would stage our show. Dust hung in the air and the smell of stale beer wafted from the bar. Suddenly I experienced an overwhelming sensation, a vivid impression of actors two thousand years ago meeting under the hot sun in the amphitheatre at Epidaurus for the first production of *Medea*. Of Shakespeare and the King's Men gathering under the leaden skies of Bermondsey for the first read-through of *Hamlet*. Of Kean and Joseph Grimaldi and Sarah Bernhardt slipping through the stage door of the Theatre Royal in Drury Lane nervous and excited about their latest productions or perhaps I was just a bit overexcited.

It is true though that I did feel a greater and more immediate sense of belonging with this troupe than I had ever felt with any of the other organisations and institutions, the Young Communist League, the CPB (M–L), Chelsea School of Art, that I had belonged to over the years.

The actresses seemed brave and luminous and you got the feeling that they'd do anything you asked them to do. There was a girl called Michelle who'd actually been in a movie, she'd played a lizard in *Flash Gordon*, and another whose name was Saffron and lived in a big decaying house next to Paddington Station, while the actors were different to any men I had met before. The oldest was an American called Joe who had only one eye and wore a flamboyant patch-covering where the other should have been, another was Bill Monks, a little working-class guy from Liverpool, who like Cliff was a Communist but also ate brown rice and mackerel in a bowl and led us in this amazing thing called 'warm-up' where you wiggled your neck about to loosen up your body.

My role was not large. Apart from sharing in a couple of musical numbers with the cast I spent the rest of the performance seated on a stool beside the piano, sipping whisky and pretending to be Bertolt Brecht by wearing a pair of glasses just like his and a leather jacket. I performed only one poem which began, 'At the time of the First World War . . .' It was the story of a Marxist soldier held in an Italian prison cell who carved 'Long Live Lenin' on the wall. The authorities try and obliterate the message but through incompetence only succeed in making it larger and larger until the slogan is carved in enormous letters on the wall. My final line was, '"Try knocking down the wall," said the soldier,' which got a big laugh every night.

One thing that really surprised me about the other actors both in rehearsal and in performance was that they had a very odd attitude to the bits of comedy they did. They would get a funny part right one night so that it got a big laugh but then they'd perform it completely wrong the next night, which meant that it died. I had the odd sensation of instinctively knowing something that all these other performers, actors who'd trained at drama school, women who'd played a lizard in a movie or who'd spent years on the stage, couldn't grasp. To me it seemed obvious that once you found how to get a laugh you should stick with that way of performing it but rather than doing that all the actors in the Brecht show would constantly mess with the delivery of their funny line, slowing it up or adding stupid bits of business, which to me both seemed foolish since they were killing the gag and implied a disrespect for comedy. In my opinion comedy was actually harder to do than straight acting. With comedy you had to do all the stuff you had to do with acting but on top of that you had to be funny as well. It did not seem odd to me that I had such strong convictions about a thing I had never done before.

Ahead of rehearsals Cliff talked to us about Brecht's ideas of how a play should be performed. This was something I didn't know anything about, the idea that you could have theories related to the staging of plays, but having been brought up a Communist there was nothing I responded to more than an all-encompassing and inflexible ideology. Cliff said Brecht didn't believe that the audience should get all caught up in the action and find themselves identifying emotionally with the characters or what was going on on stage. Rather, Brecht thought those watching should be encouraged to maintain a critical distance, should always be reminded that they were watching a performance and this was not real life. Also he believed that a play shouldn't provide those watching with catharsis – the release of built-up emotion – instead he wanted his audiences to adopt a critical attitude. To this end, Brecht employed techniques such as the actor talking directly to the audience, harsh and bright stage lighting, the use of songs to interrupt the action and declamatory slogans written on placards.

I bought into all this completely, it seemed to make absolute sense, but at the same time I rather took to Brecht as a person. I read in a biography of the playwright that though he lived and worked in East Germany he insisted his money was paid into a bank account in Switzerland, which gave me the impression that he was a bit of a Marxist rascal.

I also wondered if all the ideology about changing the world through theatre wasn't probably self-justification and Brecht did these things because he'd thought them up and they looked fantastic. The rationale came later.

Cliff had arranged to have the audience sitting at tables, entrance was 40p and a glass of wine from a makeshift bar cost only 20p. It was remarkable what a difference it made if people could have a drink while they watched a show; it created a proper cabaret-style atmosphere that undermined the solemn way in which productions were viewed in the conventional theatres. This idea of people sitting and drinking while watching a political cabaret was also very much in line with Brecht's theories. One night things got so political that we were heckled by a tall, curly-haired hippy anarchist for the overly Stalinist nature of the show. Some of the other actors were shocked at this and froze, horrified at being interrupted, but I thought it was great and I shouted back at him. This was not the stodgy theatre of the West End or the state-sponsored RSC or National Theatre but a living thing where the audience talked back at you.

After the Factory *About Poor B.B.* went on a sporadic sort of tour. We would play where we could, a few nights at a theatre in Essex or a poorly attended evening in a warehouse in Rotherhithe. But inevitably with a show that was mounted only occasionally and paid the cast very little there came a point where tensions began to arise. There were rows, shouting, crying and stormings-out. A few of the actors found this angry atmosphere upsetting but to me it was exactly the same as being in a political group so it just felt normal. Inevitably after about a year Threepenny Theatre split up leaving only me, Cliff and Bill Monks behind but now with nothing to do and a void in our lives where the show had been.

Didn't Work for Mussolini, Did It?

Though I had not played a huge part in the Brecht show, being a part of it had opened a trapdoor for me, given me a signal that I might become some kind of performer. The problem was that from the outside the world of TV, radio or the theatre seemed like an impenetrable citadel while stand-up comedy in the UK, based as it was on the racist and sexist working men's club circuit, was beyond the pale. When I'd been at Chelsea there was only one visiting lecturer who I'd got on with. He was a young documentary film-maker call Roger Graef. An American, he had recently made a highly innovative series for the BBC called *The Space between Words*. Roger had gained access to various institutions such as the US Senate and the United Nations and then he would simply let his camera roll so that after a while the subjects forgot there was a film crew there and began to behave unselfconsciously.

Roger Graef was also one of the few people in Britain who bought one of my paintings, though sadly it was later destroyed in a fire at his holiday home in Wales. One lunchtime when I was at the Civil Service I went to visit him at the nearby offices of Granada Television. I remember we went to a café round the corner and he talked Spanish to the staff, which seemed to me like an amazing thing to do.

All around us were young film-makers, coming and going dressed in their fashionable Fair Isle sleeveless sweaters, flared trousers and complicated anoraks, men not much older than me making this historic television such as *Seven Up* and *World in Action*. I thought I could probably do that but I didn't tell Roger I'd like to work in TV or anything, I just thought he might offer me a job, but he didn't because he wasn't telepathic.

Then maybe I could be a writer. Linda and I entered a playwriting competition for new writers from the North run by BBC Radio 4. Our play was called *The New Member* and featured a Maoist group on Merseyside. It wasn't bad but didn't get past the first round. The piece that won was *The Man that Comes in Autumn* by somebody called Dave Parker and featured two disembodied voices screaming at each other in a desolate audio wasteland for an hour. In later life I would learn that the things that won playwriting competitions were often two disembodied voices screaming at each other in a desolate audio wasteland or similar.

I was in the flat failing badly to do an illustration of a fish for Martin when a man knocked on the door, he said he was from the BBC and they had just made one of their depressing 'Play for Today's set in a tower block and could they film out of our kitchen window to the adjacent block for the opening titles? I said sure and half an hour later a guy in the regulation complicated anorak came with a 16mm film camera to shoot out of our window. I tried to engage him in conversation about my hopes and fears concerning the entertainment business and my future part in it but he wasn't interested. The BBC gave me £20 for using my window but I lost the cheque.

A week later the man was back once more. I thought at first he'd changed his mind about telling me how to get into TV but instead he said that there'd been a fault in the camera and they needed to shoot the titles again. At least this time I held on to the cheque.

It was a different cameraman who arrived thirty minutes later but he was no more interested than the first one had been in hearing about the little 8mm films I'd made at art school and he said he couldn't help me get a career in television.

Drinking one night in the Queen's Elm, round the corner from Chelsea School of Art, there was a guy who was one of the cast of the BBC sitcom *It Ain't Half Hot Mum*. Me and Linda listened fascinated for hours as he told us stories about Lofty, the character played by Don Estelle, plus indiscreet tales of Melvyn Hayes and Windsor Davies. It seemed like an impossibly distant and glamorous world. In the following months I went back several times to the Queen's Elm but he never returned and after that I was pretty much out of ideas about how somebody like me could get into show business.

Communists were not supposed to like Christmas. In East Germany angels, the kind you put on top of your Christmas tree, were grudgingly permitted but the government insisted they had to be referred to as 'flying end-of-year-celebration puppets'. Yet over time my mother had become more and more obsessed with me spending the holiday with her, though she made no effort to make it either pleasant or comfortable.

Once we were married Linda had suggested to her mum that one year maybe we could eat Christmas dinner at their flat then the next year at Molly's house. Presented with this perfectly reasonable suggestion Linda's mother broke down weeping, crying out over how could her daughter betray her like that. If that was Chris Rawsthorn's reaction we both knew there was no point even putting the Christmas question to Molly.

So for the next twenty years me and Linda ate two Christmas dinners. We would dine at Linda's parents' first, the full three courses with pudding and everything. Then in the afternoon we would walk to Molly's in a vain attempt to work off some of the meal. If we were even a few minutes late, as we approached we would be able to see a tiny figure hopping up and down at the top of Valley Road. This would reveal itself to be Molly who as soon as she saw us would begin shouting, 'That's it, your Christmas dinner's fucking ruined! It's fucking ruined, you fucking bastards!' as on the other side of the road little children walked by wide-eyed and frightened clutching their newly unwrapped train sets and toy soldiers closer to them.

That Christmas of 1977 Linda was staying with her parents so I was alone in the narrow bed in my childhood bedroom. On the landing outside there was a familiar racket. Not long after we'd dumped him on her Molly had had a flap fitted for Archie so he could come and go as he pleased but he must have been bragging about it because all the other cats in the neighbourhood got to hear about it too. You'd often come down in the morning to find an unfamiliar tabby or a tortoise-shell happily asleep in the living room. And Molly would feed them; if you told her not to she'd tell you to fuck off. The only problem was if Archie came home and found another feline on his territory there'd be a huge fight with furniture going flying, clumps of fur torn off and crockery smashed. Rather than just not feeding the other cats my mother had taken to waiting up for Archie to come in at night then once he was home she'd lock his cat flap. A few hours later her pet would want to go out again so he'd start yowling and relentlessly bashing his head against the plastic. After a couple of minutes of this you'd hear Molly's bedroom door fly open followed by the sound of her running down the stairs screaming, 'You swine! What do you want, you swine? You're going to kill me, you little bastard, you swine!' Then she'd let him out. Two hours later the whole process would be repeated when Archie wanted to come in again.

Suddenly an idea came into my head. Comedy! During the latter part of the Brecht show's run Cliff had added in a number for me and Bill. We both played drunken soldiers. I had no lines but simply swayed about with a gormless expression on my face while Bill sang to me about how great the army was. Without saying anything I found I was able to get big laughs and I also discovered there was a chemistry between me and Bill that really worked: he short and moustachioed, me large and clean-shaven. As well as that I'd added in a line. At the end of the song Bill threw the empty bottle he'd been drinking from away and one night after being mute for the whole performance I just said in a heavy Scouse accent, ''Ere, there's money on them bottles!' (At that time there was a deposit of a few pence on alcohol bottles and if you collected enough bottles you could buy more alcohol.) This line got a big laugh.

To the sound of Molly accusing Archie of working for the internal security service MI5 I thought to myself: Why shouldn't me and Bill do a comedy show? Right away I knew this was a killer idea. Doing the Brecht cabaret had shown me how desperate audiences were for humour that was intelligent and had some relevance to their lives, even when it was written by a dead German before the war. Imagine what you could do with stuff that had been written since the invention of the transistor radio and the jet engine.

At the same time as the notion that we should do a funny show came into my head a whole tumble of half-formed ideas appeared there too, about what sort of comedy we should be performing. I found some scraps of paper and a pencil and began to scribble. There was no conception of exactly how I should write down the thoughts that were in my head, there was nobody who could tell me how to get humour onto paper, all I was certain of was that the ideas had to be captured before I forgot them so I just made disjointed notes which I hoped I could later bring to life in performance.

Over the holiday I gradually accumulated many scraps of paper with what I hoped were funny ideas scrawled on them.

My first notion was a bit for me and Bill to do. It was a bingo routine. Bingo callers would add silly little phrases to the numbers they called so they'd shout, 'Key of the door – twenty-one,' or, 'Two fat ladies – eighty-eight.' I thought it would be funny to do phrases that came from our political world so, 'Lenin's Party card – number one.' Then I thought you could hand out cards so the audience would be genuinely playing bingo but if all the cards were identical then they'd all shout out 'House!' at the same time and that could be interesting.

Next was an idea I'd had in my mind since I'd been at Southport Art School, a bit which would go on to form the basis of my whole comic persona, and which was based upon my experiences as a teenager and a bit of a Monty Python influence. In Liverpool in the pubs where I spent my evenings, one common type of drinker was the working-class intellectual. Bright, intelligent men who'd been denied the education they would have got if they'd come from a different class, and who'd been forced by poverty to go out to work, often from the age of thirteen or fourteen. Dockers, builders, factory workers, these people did not accept their condition but had chosen to teach themselves, reading voraciously and often indiscriminately. Small men in caps and scarves, even at the height of the summer, they would talk for hours about Plato, Velázquez or the Marshall Plan. But because Liverpool was also a fighting town and these men were sometimes quite bitter about their lives and almost invariably drunk, the discussions would frequently end in violence. So I scrawled out notes for a piece, for me as a character, a working-class tough guy who is always getting into fights over philosophical ideas in pubs and cake shops.

When I got back to London after the holidays I spoke to Cliff and Bill about us doing a comedy show and they were both enthusiastic and we began very slowly to evolve it. Cliff found us rehearsal rooms at a community centre in north-west London called the Carlton Centre, located in one of those bleak areas of council estates north of Notting Hill so disregarded that the neighbourhood doesn't seem to have a name. For several days each week the three of us would go there and try and work out what we were doing. Our progress was sluggish because we really had no idea how to go about putting something like this together.

One thing was accepted, we did not think for a minute that we would not write our own material. It would be one of the ways in which we would distinguish ourselves from the conventional old-style comedians: they had writers (I imagined sleazy men in greasy suits covered in cigarette ash). But by this time it was the norm that musicians wrote their own stuff, and in comedy *Beyond the Fringe* and the Pythons did it too – and that was our model. On LWT, I'd seen a folk musician turned comedian called Jasper Carrott who had his own show, which only went out in the London area. Jasper performed monologues and sang funny songs which I assumed he'd written himself, making much of his thick Birmingham accent, and the fact that he wasn't doing the usual awful mechanical gags but rather stories drawn from his life really inspired me. Plus the material wasn't that strong and I was convinced I could do better.

In an effort to gain some guidance about performing political comedy we went to see a guy called Roland Muldoon. He had his own political theatre group called CAST (Cartoon Archetypical Slogan Theatre). The style of their work was agit-prop and they often put on plays on the folk-club circuit. These plays would feature what they called 'Muggins' characters who were trying to make sense of the capitalist world and had titles such as *John D. Muggins is Dead*, or *Trials of Horatio Muggins*, or *Mr Oligarchy's Circus*, and were performed in Students' Unions and factory occupations. In 1970 the group split, one half left and set up the Kartoon Klowns and later were the drive behind Rock Against Racism.

CAST had exactly the kind of heavy-handed, ponderous left-wing 'humour' that I wanted to avoid. And Roland mostly spoke to us about grants, allocations, gifts we could weasel out of various organisations such as the Arts Council and the GLC. That wasn't what I wanted at all. I didn't plan to take money off any government organisation. Even though I'd never actually performed any comedy I was already evolving strong ideas about how it should be done. To me the best barometer of whether your work was any good was not whether some arts bureaucrat thought you were entitled to a grant but if people were prepared to pay to see it. To my mind institutional sponsorship led to self-indulgence and elitism. What I wanted was smart relevant popular comedy that paid for itself. I was also certain I didn't want to confirm the opinions of the people in the audience like CAST did, rather I wanted to challenge and mock them. After meeting Roland Muldoon I wrote a bit about agitprop theatre that went, 'People think if you've got baggy trousers and a red nose you're automatically funny. Didn't work for Mussolini, did it?'

What's He Doing Now!?

From the moment we met in the Masque, Linda had seen something unique and original in me, something that others didn't necessarily perceive. A lot of people who knew us were baffled when she insisted that one day I would do something really important, especially since there was a lot of evidence to the contrary. For example my originality of thought came with a range of challenging behaviours which Linda tried to gently alter so I could pass in polite society. She taught me that having a conversation is not the same as describing the entire plot of a science fiction novel and she persuaded me not to hoot like an owl on trains. But I too began to have a reverse effect on Linda so that she sometimes lost her sense of what could be considered appropriate.

Me, Linda and Linda's mum were in the centre of Liverpool one afternoon when I heard Linda's mum who was walking behind us suddenly exclaim, 'Oh God! What's he doing now!?' We both looked round with concern but it was me that she was referring to. I had been holding her daughter's hand and walking with the bandy-legged gait of a chimpanzee, gibbering and making grunting noises, but the two of us had got so used to me doing stuff like that that neither of us had noticed.

I had a fantasy of what my life might have been like if I'd stayed in Liverpool and hadn't met Linda. I imagined myself living next door to Molly, in a decaying house full of cats, fat and pale-skinned, Brylcreem slicking down my thinning hair, permanently dressed in a purple tank top tucked into the waistband of my Bri-Nylon trousers. On a Saturday night I would go next door to do Molly's hair, before murdering my mother with an axe on her seventieth birthday.

When I was little it had been Joe who'd decided where we would go on our holidays and when we went out it was usually to trade union functions connected with his work but with his health continuing to fade and with me keeping a good two hundred miles between us, Molly was increasingly forced to try and make a life for herself. Others her age might have joined a bowling club or the League of Hospital Friends but as a Ukrainian Jew my mother instead transferred her allegiance to the struggle for Irish independence and became a member of the Troops Out movement. She had not stayed for very long in the CPB (M–L) as Maoism didn't offer enough of an excuse for hysterical carryings-on but extreme Irishism suited her right down to the ground. From then on when Molly sent you a Christmas card it would read, 'Season's Greetings from H Block'. This legend would be written in blood against a background of barbed wire and would generally feature a photo of dirty-protest hunger striker Bobby Sands' shit-smeared cell. 'Merry Christmas from Mum, Dad and Archie' she would write inside.

Molly threw herself wholeheartedly into this new personality with her usual lack of balance. I would come home from London to find her sitting in the dark weeping and when I asked her what she was upset about it would turn out to be victims of the nineteenth-century potato famine or those executed by the British following the Nationalist uprising in 1916. On the other hand she felt no sympathy at all for anyone killed or injured in the IRA bombing campaign which had been going on in the UK since 1971.

Living in London, the main target for IRA bombs, I felt particularly aggrieved that I should be at risk since I had been involved in the anti-colonialist struggle almost my entire life, which I thought entitled me to a bit of a free pass in terms of terrorist violence. For instance I'd memorised all the names of the Arab revolutionaries I'd met when I'd been with Wassim and all the leaders of their various organisations, just in case my plane was ever hijacked. Then I could say to the AK-47-toting guy in the keffiyeh, 'Hey, you guys are Popular Democratic Front, right? I once ate sliced octopus in Finchley with Abdullah Habajab, your deputy chairman.' And they'd let me go. (Though there was a pretty good chance given the complexity of the Arab liberation struggle that those holding me at gunpoint were sworn enemies of Abdullah Habajab and I'd be the first hostage they'd shoot.) Or if they were Druze I could tell them I'd watched *Rocky* with Walid Jumblatt. But bombs hidden in department-store toilets didn't give you the chance to argue with them.

In October a device exploded below the revolving restaurant of the Post Office Tower in London causing extensive damage though no injuries but preventing people for evermore from eating in the capital while going round and round. In 1972 six civilians were killed in the Aldershot bombing, in 1973 there was a car bomb in the street outside the Old Bailey. Then bombs at King's Cross Station and Euston Station injuring twenty-one people. In 1974 eight soldiers and four civilians were killed in the M62 coach bombing and a bomb exploded at the Houses of Parliament, causing extensive damage and injuring eleven people. Then there were the Guildford pub bombings and the Birmingham pub bombings plus more in Bristol.

If Linda asked Molly, 'What if your beloved son was killed in one of these attacks, how would you feel about it then?' my mother would simply scream, 'Don't say that! Don't say that!' and try and hit her.

My parents' Communist philosophy was based on an authoritarian view of the world in which people's opinions had to be kept in line via the widespread use of terror, propaganda and repression; making up your own mind on stuff from all the available evidence was not an option. I on the other hand vaguely subscribed to the liberal notion that if you just sat a person with disturbed, anti-social ideas, somebody such as Hitler, Pol Pot or my mother, down and talked to them rationally for a long, long time, possibly aided by a chart, some maps and a list of statistics, then eventually they would change their minds. 'Oh man,' Pol Pot would say after I'd been going on at him for a bit, 'I see it now, Alexei, that whole Year Zero, killing-fields thing was some fucked-up bullshit, man!'

But Molly's conversion to the cause of Irish independence and her refusal to admit even the tiniest flaws or inhumanity in the Provisional IRA's campaign of bombing and murder showed me that there are people in the world who, no matter how many facts you show them, no matter what cogent arguments and pertinent metaphors you deploy, will never shift their opinion even the tiniest bit.

In Molly's case she could not and would not change her views, firstly because she was crazy but secondly because through the Irish liberation struggle my mother had found who she wanted to be and who she wanted to be with. Those in Troops Out were nice, young, idealistic people, students or political activists, who had never met anybody like Molly before. The secret of maintaining successful friendships had always been a struggle for me but Molly's method of shouting at these young people, yelling that they were stupid fucking bastards if they disagreed with her, and then trying to hit them if they didn't do what she wanted seemed to make them all adore her.

One new friend was Mandy who at that time lived in a women-only communal house in Princes Park. When Molly was seventy and Mandy was thirty they held a joint hundred-year-old party at a bar called the Flying Picket, which was in the Unemployed Workers' Centre based in a defunct police station on Hardman Street in the centre of Liverpool. It was fascinating to see my few relatives like Auntie Dorothy and Uncle Ron picking at the vegan buffet food and dancing alongside Mandy's guests, women dressed in dungarees, their skin adorned with tattoos and multiple piercings. The first time Mandy encountered my mother was when she went to a film showing at October Books, the headquarters of the CPB (M–L) in Liverpool, when Molly was still a member. My mother was late but the comrades were too frightened to start the film without her. Finally Molly swept in and regally took her place at the front, and the movie could begin. Bizarrely this made Mandy want to know the woman better.

Often the young people did not have the energy to keep up with Molly. One of the places they frequented was called the Irish Centre at the top of a hill near Liverpool University. It was an odd building originally used for balls and dances with a severe neoclassical exterior and no windows giving it the appearance of a large mausoleum, decorated inside with Republican and Everton FC memorabilia. Molly would stay all night at the bar getting other people to buy her drinks and would often take to the dance floor by herself, even if there was no music playing. She told me she could have been a professional dancer.

In 1974 an IRA gang attacked the upmarket Scott's Restaurant in Mayfair raking it with gunfire and tossing hand grenades at the windows. Defiantly Scott's was open again for business the very next day but with the addition of wire grilles fixed over the windows and doors to prevent more hand grenades being thrown at its diners. Pretty soon even quite modest restaurants and cafés were screwing wire grilles over their windows as if they too were the sort of place where the power elite wined and dined and would therefore have Mills bombs thrown at them. Though what members of the establishment would be doing eating liver and bacon at the Copper Kettle, a shabby tea room on Kensal Rise, was anybody's guess.

Another consequence of the bombings was that all litter bins disappeared from the streets. Often I would see a discarded

Mars bar wrapper blowing down the pavement and think to myself: There goes another victory for the Irish liberation struggle.

By and large the population of London, the most likely victims of these attacks, didn't seem to take that much notice of the danger they were in and went about their business in a stoical fashion. There were so many inconveniences and discomforts at the time, fuel crises, three-day weeks, dial phones, your shoes were uncomfortable, only three TV channels and all the pubs were terrible, either old and unfriendly or hideously modernised with orange plastic walls and brown vinyl toadstools to sit on and you couldn't get a drink after eleven o'clock unless you were gay or a Nazi and the nearest place to get a decent cup of coffee was Turin, that the prospect of being blown to bits seemed like just another inconvenience.

One Sprout or Two?

1977: three years after leaving college, a significant stretch of time in which others had got their lives together and embarked on lifetime careers. I was twenty-five years old and getting very little work as a freelance illustrator, which in turn meant that I brought in such a tiny amount of money that during one year Her Majesty's Revenue & Customs ended up sending me a refund. The days drifted by, occasionally you would hear a crump out of the window as a bomb exploded followed by a rising plume of smoke but by and large these were happy times for us. At night we would go to the Bedford with Harry and during the day me, Bill and Cliff endlessly rehearsed and rewrote our comedy show without ever actually getting round to performing it.

It also meant eventually that I had to take a series of menial part-time jobs to help subsidise my part-time job. There were so many posts available that even somebody as useless as me could be in constant work if they wanted to be. And I really was quite a poor employee. The first part-time position I undertook was as a dinner lady in a private girls' school in South Kensington. When I turned up for the interview the Portuguese woman cook under whom I would work said they wanted a woman for the job but I pointed out that the Sex Discrimination Act had just been passed so they had to consider me, plus I don't think anybody else applied.

My task was to serve the pupils their dinner then afterwards wash up the hundreds of dishes in a big vat. A lot of the little girls were doing ballet and seemed to consume very small amounts of food – 'One sprout or two?' I would ask – and having a big hairy man looming over them caused the girls to eat even less than they normally did. I had an incentive in this since I got to take home the unconsumed rissoles and chips that had been cooked for lunch and me and Linda would eat them that night sitting up in bed.

As with all my jobs I was very poor at timekeeping though I managed to get to my dinner-lady position more or less when I was needed. In my last year at Chelsea I had acquired a bicycle, a big old black steel machine with only one gear. At that time if you rode a bicycle you were thought of as being only one level above a homeless person but I cycled every-where, I liked the freedom that a bike gave you and it meant I could time to the second how late I wanted to arrive for my various part-time jobs.

Next I became the assistant caretaker of the primary school which was more or less at the base of our flats. Assistant care-taker just meant I had to clean the tiny little kiddie toilets and sweep the school yard before school began. This was the worst of all my part-time jobs. I had to get up quite early, about 6.30 a.m., and it was very badly paid. So in what I thought was a reasonable act of redress, I would sweep across the yard towards the gate then hide my broom in a corner and sneak home and go back to bed for an hour but one day I was spotted escaping by the lollipop man who ratted on me to the proper caretaker and I got fired. I already distrusted lollipop people but this just cemented my hatred of these traffic-stopping Hitlers.

Following that I got a job as a part-time filing clerk for a small specialist publisher called Graham and Trotman. I think I was OK as a filing clerk but they were a bit puzzled by me.

I told one of the young editors that I was an illustrator and since they were quite a cheapskate outfit he asked me if I wanted to do a book for them. It was called *Enterprise Zones in the European Community* and my task was to draw each country, then shade in the enterprise zones with some very old Letraset that Glen Cocker had given me because it had mostly gone off.

When I was doing the illustrations I got really bored with the Norwegian coastline – all those fjords, bays and inlets – and in the end I just made them up by drawing random wiggly lines all around the seaboard. In subsequent years I did occasionally worry that somebody in a small boat might try to navigate the coastal waters of Scandinavia using Graham and Trotman's *Enterprise Zones in the European Community* because if they did they'd probably drown.

While I was a terrible employee Linda was the opposite. Wherever she worked she was valued for her intelligence, honesty and calmness, whenever she moved on people pleaded with her not to leave. She also didn't smell of dog shit which was an unusual attribute back then. In addition to her many other qualities Linda had a secret skill which was that she had the ability never to step in canine excrement. At that time people's dogs defecated wherever they felt like and the streets were a constant assault course of piles of dog poop. Most people stepped in some at least once a day and that may have been one reason apart from poor construction why their shoes broke so often due to the soles being rotted with dog dirt. But not Linda, she would be walking towards a heap of dog shit not paying any attention to the ground beneath her but at the last second her foot would always swerve away from it, leaving her shoes unsullied.

It had been a mistake for me to try and be a freelance illustrator: you cannot attempt to do something artistic if your heart is not totally committed to it, you can't try to be any kind of an artist while waiting for something better to come along. Not only did my lack of commitment to being an illustrator give me mental pain but it also made my work a lot worse. When I'd started out my drawing skills, while not phenomenal, had at least been competent but as I went on the lines I drew became more and more wobbly and indistinct, my colour grew wishy-washy and the things I was meant to be representing did not look like they were supposed to: it was sometimes hard to tell if what I had drawn or painted was a duck, a vicar or a T34 tank.

Because it was causing me so much anguish I also spent a lot of time avoiding doing the few commissions that I was contracted to produce so I added the worry of being late and letting Martin down to my other anxieties.

Our flat in Fulham was only a bike ride away from Chelsea School of Art and as long as there were people there that I knew I would constantly call in to chat to them and stop them working. I didn't think there was anything the least bit pathetic about this, just a fellow dropping in to pass the time of day with some old mates.

I don't know why I was pedalling down Manresa Road on a Saturday when there wasn't any chance of anybody I knew being there but as I passed the college I noticed on the forecourt there was a chalk board propped up with a piece of wood. Getting off the bike I went to look at what it said. In big untidy letters was scrawled, 'Tonight. College Dance Featuring The Sex Pistols'. I thought to myself: The Sex Pistols, that's an interesting name for a group, maybe I should hang around and see them, I bet they'll be really good and different. But it was a few hours before the dance so I went home and that night me and Linda went for a drink in the Bedford with Harry instead of seeing the second ever gig of The Sex Pistols but at least unlike a million other people I have definite proof that I wasn't there.

My desire to succeed as an illustrator was further undermined by the fact that at last I thought I might have found something I was truly good at. Finally we had managed to mount a performance of our comedy show. The first Threepenny Theatre comedy gig was in somebody's front room at a fund-raiser for the local branch of the Communist Party in Kilburn. It went as well as doing a theatre show in somebody's front room could go.

So encouraged we now set out to find some paying work. Friends who were students or sometimes already staff were asked to find us shows at their Students' Unions where we thought we'd be guaranteed a sympathetic audience. We called our show *What a Load of Balkans*. Glen Cocker designed a poster for us which we had printed at their father's shop in Liverpool alongside the identical bingo cards.

Cliff also got a friend of his who'd been a photorealist painter at Newcastle University to do us a really nice little set. It was three six-foot-high panels hinged together with portraits of me and Bill on it and in the centre of the central one there was a flap that dropped down. When I'd been at Southport we'd found a tin one day of a mystery substance called Neucolac. From this we developed the idea that Neucolac was a miracle Eastern European product and we would invent TV adverts for Neucolac which we would do in a fake Eastern European language. In our show the centre panel would drop down and Bill would perform these adverts as if he was on a TV screen.

The show began with the bingo routine with me as a very aggressive bingo caller and Bill dressed in high heels and a tight top as my lovely female assistant Sandra. When everybody shouted 'House!' at the same time it really tested my powers of improvisation to deal with the chaos that followed. Later on I did a bit inspired by the druggie we'd met that time in the pub on the Fulham Road with Roberta and his tedious story of the great dope he'd smoked that had caused paralysis in his hands and feet. In my routine I was a character talking about some dope he'd smoked, familiar to everybody in the audience since the drug bore was a common phenomenon, but I ramped up the comic power by exaggerating the effects, saying not that the dope had caused paralysis but that it had given me all the symptoms of typhoid which I thought was great.

And there was a sketch set in a Liverpool restaurant in which we treated Scouse as a foreign language with Bill translating what I was saying out of which I did the philosophical thug.

A lot of this stuff was not the greatest comedy but we were protected by the fact that there was nothing to compare it to. Either for us or the audience.

Glen Cocker, who had never seen us perform, came to an early show at a college in Kentish Town. Afterwards he said to me, 'You've got something special.'

I giggled nervously at this. It was what I believed but I'd never heard anybody say it before so I acted quite dismissively but he was impatient with my coquettishness.

'No, don't pretend you don't know,' he said.

There was a guy I knew from Southport called Philip who was now a student at Hornsey College of Art and he arranged for us to appear at an event he was putting on. When he was younger Philip had been one of the best dancers at the famous Wigan Casino and he thought it would be a good idea to mount an evening that began with a male and female avant-garde dance duo, then there'd be me and Bill while the evening would finish with a Northern soul disco. Unfortunately the only ones interested in the event, in their hundreds, were the local skinheads attracted by the disco. On the night Philip managed to lock the mob out for the dance duo though you could hear them beating on the door as the couple formed jagged shapes in an empty room but they forced their way in for our show.

I came out and started my usual aggressive patter, which caused a skinhead to try and get up on the stage to attack me. Linda for some reason was manning the bar halfway down the hall. She is also very short-sighted and quite unco-ordinated in her movements but seeing her husband in danger she managed to catch my assailant forcefully on the head with three full cans of lager thrown from a distance of maybe fifty feet. Bill then came on wearing his boiler suit though he still had his high heels on from the bingo sketch and asked the audience if they wanted us to stay, or go so the disco could start. They voted that we could go so we left with all our friends surrounding us like a phalanx of security guards. The father of one of our friends had recently died and he had been very depressed but the riot really cheered him up.

There was another show at a place called the Tramshed in Woolwich where we needed to employ microphones but never having had any experience of their use we just pointed them in our general direction and then did our show inaudible to the audience. The crowd got so restless that the guy who ran the place had to come on stage and beg them to give us a chance.

With the little bit of extra money that was coming in from the comedy show, I did not buy fancy clothes or start going to smart restaurants but we did carpet the living room, covering up the institutional red-and-black council tiles with a luxurious dark green wool carpet that we bought on hire purchase from the local department store. I laid it myself and considering that carpet laying is a skilled occupation I didn't do a bad job. The carpet remained reasonably taut everywhere apart from one single lump which I couldn't smooth out no matter how hard I tried. This lump gave the impression that a medium-sized rodent, a ferret or a stoat, was hiding under the carpet and though you could move the ferret around the room you could never get rid of it.

I also bought myself a better bicycle, hand-built by a small firm in Putney called Holdsworth's: a racing machine in Reynolds 531 superlight tubing with 10-speed Campagnolo gears. When it came to choosing the colour of the frame I expected the staff in the shop to be dismissive but in fact they spent hours with me poring over paint charts until we all agreed I'd got the right combination of flame orange with the lugs picked out in a kind of Yves Klein international blue.

In fact, me, Cliff and Bill all rode racing bicycles. One of the old Soviet films we used to show at CPB (M–L) meetings was called *October* and was a highly fanciful dramatisation of the Russian Revolution. In one scene a soldier bursts into a clamorous meeting of soldiers and militias and shouts, 'Comrades!' All heads turn towards him. 'Comrades!' he shouts again and once more all heads turn towards him. 'Comrades!' he shouts one final time. 'The bicycle squad is with you!' Then there is a cut to a shot of hundreds of bicycles being ridden by furiously pedalling soldiers, bent low over the handlebars, long rifles slung over their shoulders, hurtling down the road to St Petersburg. Sometimes when the three of us were racing to a gig it felt like we were the bicycle squad.

Occasionally when I rode to our shows my competitive nature got the better of me. I frequently tried to set myself a time to get somewhere and then break it but one night after a performance in south-east London I had five pints of bitter in a pub then managed to ride back to Fulham in twenty-five minutes. In the middle of the night I got up to go to the toilet then coming back from the bathroom I suddenly passed out, waking up with the hall carpet in my mouth and a cut on my head sustained as I'd hit the door handle on my way down.

Linda came to see what was the matter and I said, 'Call an ambulance.'

'Why?' she asked.

'It's obvious, isn't it? I've got multiple sclerosis.'

Your Drama Teacher
Has Been Kidnapped

For a little while Cliff, like me, had been forced to do menial tasks such as office cleaning to get by but eventually he'd managed to find something much better, a job teaching a subject called general studies, part-time at a place called the London College of Printing. So important was the teaching of general studies considered to be to the nation's well-being that there appeared to be an endless demand for teachers of it so once Cliff had been working there for a few months he got me a position too. This meant I was able give up all the scrappy little part-time jobs I'd been doing, as well as the pretence that I was a freelance illustrator.

Because you were not entitled to holiday pay the hourly rate a part-time teacher earned seemed fantastic compared to anything I had been paid for any of my jobs. For me to be a part-time college lecturer was a definite step up from dinner lady and it was more the sort of thing that people I knew were doing for a living. On the other hand this also made me a bit nervous. While I was cleaning toilets or filing invoices there was never any doubt that it was only temporary, that I was still pursuing my dream of being some kind of an artist. But what if being a part-time lecturer proved to be so congenial and easy that, seduced by a quiet, comfortable life, I gradually began to give up on the notion of becoming a performer? Luckily I proved to be terrible at it.

The subject of general studies as part of the curriculum for technical colleges appeared in the early 1960s. The Ministry of Education report 'General Studies in Technical Colleges' identified its purposes as helping young workers 'to find their way successfully about the world both as consumers and citizens, to form standards of moral values by which they can live in the new world in which they find themselves, to continue and develop the pursuits and activities which they have begun at school, to improve their basic education.' The report might also have added, 'A secondary purpose of general studies is to give any directionless idiot with an arts degree a job where they can get paid for showing films from Cuba and failing to get a discussion going about racism.' At the London College of Printing apprentices who were on block release – which meant they were attending college for a week – took an afternoon of general studies, and those on day release were assigned an hour.

The main college building was at the Elephant and Castle which before the war was known as the Piccadilly Circus of the south but was now nothing more than a gruesome traffic roundabout. Across the road from the LCP was a shopping precinct, the first covered mall in Europe, which could only be reached by foot tunnels whose lavatorial tiles seemed to have encouraged many to urinate or worse in these dank, odiferous and badly lit passages. Built at the same time as the shopping centre, the college was a modernist building composed of a large four-storey workshop block full of the latest printing machines and a thirteen-floor administrative and teaching tower complete with the usual 1960s problems of damp, poor ventilation and general falling-apartness.

Before I began I had a short chat with the head of the general studies department who told me that in his view we were preparing the apprentices for leisure. In the near future due to the extensive use of robots they would only work a twenty-five-hour week and therefore needed to be taught how to entertain themselves for all the leisure time they were going to have. Then I was let loose on Box and Carton Making 2, Machine Printing 1 and Bookbinding 3 with no idea what to do with them.

Coincidentally the LCP had a small film school which I'd applied to the year before and been turned down. On my first day of teaching as I was struggling up the stairs with a film projector planning to show my apprentices a movie from Cuba, I passed some of the film-school staff who had rejected me. They must have thought that I'd decided to turn up for their course anyway since they looked very nervous when I appeared.

I even surprised myself with how bad a teacher I was. After all I knew by now that I could dominate a comedy audience in a Students' Union or rowdy arts centre so I was astonished, when confronted with my first class of printing apprentices, by how nervous and unsure of myself I became. Some of this was the same uncertainty which had dogged my career as an illustrator. Deep down I thought teaching general studies was

My mother and very happy father dancing, probably at some trade union event. Molly would have made that skirt herself which is why it is longer at the back than the front. She achieved a similar effect with the trousers she made for me which always had one leg considerably shorter than the other.

At a demonstration in Liverpool in '68. I've got on the same leather jacket that I'd wear on stage eleven years later for the first night of the Comedy Store. In my top pocket there is a pencil and small sketch pad in which I would have drawn nothing except some guns.

In the canteen of Chelsea School of Art with my 'gay friend' David Pearce who is looking suitably Caravaggesque.

Our wedding. Both me and Linda feeling vaguely solemn over the sanctity of marriage.

Two student union cards. The first is stamped 'September 1975', a whole year after I'd left Chelsea, and I've got my date of birth wrong by 20 years. On the second, for some reason, I seem to have deliberately lied about when I was born, making myself younger by a year.

Me and Bill Monks
on stage in front
of our innovative
portable set.

An early publicity
photo I got my
mate George to
take. The jacket's
getting a workout.

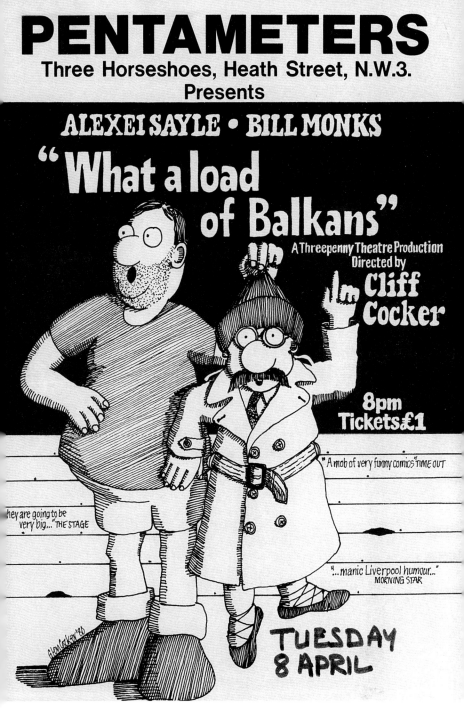

The poster Glen Cocker designed for our show complete with some fairly unenthusiastic reviews.

History in the making. The opening night of the Comedy Store.

On stage at the Elgin, waving the unlucky gun around in the week before 'Black Pistol Saturday'.

© Adrian Boot

Me and Sting backstage at The Secret Policeman's Other Ball. He looks like my care worker.

Sound checking on the Comic Strip tour with Dawn and Peter. What was joyous was that we spent a lot of time making each other laugh.

Me and Linda on the couch in our tower block flat.

The Comic Strip crew. Me and my children plus Arnold Brown.

With the former 'Britain's Most wanted Man', John McVicar, while making the Arena Cortina documentary. We used the same picture for the cover of 'Ullo John! Gotta New Motor?'

Rehearsing the first series of *The Young Ones* at the BBC rehearsal rooms in North Acton.

On location in Bristol. Mad energy crackled out of Rik all the time.

BBC tv
colour

The main set of *The Young Ones* during a camera rehearsal. Adrian looks like he's just noticed the photographer and is planning to hit him.

Doing the Cockney mod poet during a benefit at the Palladium for, I think, mental health. When the benefit was shown on TV my whole performance was removed.

Backstage VIP bar of the Dominion Theatre. This is one of my favourite photos, perfectly illustrating a 'keeping the flies off Coco' moment. In the foreground are Rik, Lise Mayer and Rowland Rivron, tanned, happy and relaxed. In the background is me who has just stormed a show in front of 3,000 people, pasty, overweight and exhausted.

Me and Michael Elphick on our bender in Helsinki. This is me after about an hour.

Doing my revolutionary duty, entertaining the striking miners of South Yorkshire.

a waste of time and if it hadn't been better paid I would much rather have been cleaning toilets.

Also that nihilistic spirit I had which really sparked on stage didn't work so well when you were trying to be a teacher.

The boys would say to me, 'Sir, why are we here?'

And I'd reply, 'Fucked if I know. Do you want to go home?'

This in turn meant that I used to wander around my classes begging, 'Aww, can you please stop playing cards, your head of department's looking through the window.'

Sometimes I would try and take them on visits to museums or art galleries but the apprentices would just sneak off when I wasn't looking and go to the pub.

At least there was no chance that I would give up my dreams of being a great artist for this – it was horrible. The only group I really got on with were the bookbinding apprentices. Bookbinding had been an area where working-class kids could express themselves artistically but mine were the last group to be taught as apprentices. After them bookbinding would move to being an art-college rather than a technical-college pursuit.

There was one bookbinder called Jim and we just used to go out drinking together: I recall us being thrown out of a pub in Covent Garden and me shouting, 'I'm his moral guardian!' It seemed to me I was a bit like Anne Rees-Mogg, socialising with my students, except unlike Anne I wasn't teaching them anything.

A lot of the apprentices saw us general studies teachers as wet liberals with a sentimental and patronising notion of the nobility of the working class. So they would try to wind us up.

One class I had were training to be typesetters on Fleet Street newspapers. It was a family affair, their fathers and grandfathers were often already in 'the Print'.

One afternoon my class gleefully told me all about the extraordinary working conditions for printers in Fleet Street. A daily newspaper is by definition extremely time-sensitive and a tiny amount of industrial action could wreck a whole day's output so weak and lazy managements had over the years made all kinds of concessions to 'the chapels', as branches of the print unions were called. As a result the presses were incredibly over-manned. In fact in a lot of cases the unnecessary extra workforce did not actually exist, rather the men who were printing the papers would sign on twice for the same job using false names to get a second wage packet, except sometimes they were so drunk by the end of the shift they couldn't remember the false name they were using.

And the chapels had been given total control over who could be recruited so there was no chance that anybody black or Asian or female would ever be printing a national paper since these men who were there already were extremely conservative.

I did not react in the way my students would have liked me to react, either horrified and shaken at having my romantic view of the working class challenged or by trying to defend the indefensible actions of the print workers. Instead this turned into what was perhaps my one good lesson as we had a really interesting discussion about how a trade union should behave in the modern world, whether they should fight every innovation or try and find some accommodation with technology. The apprentices told me there were already machines in the workshop block of the LCP that could produce newspapers much more efficiently that the ancient and monstrous presses of Fleet Street and there were computers beside them that could set the type in a fraction of the time requiring much less skill than it took to align rows and rows of lead print as was the current practice. These boys knew that one day there would be a huge confrontation over the introduction of these machines to 'the Print' and they would inevitably line up with the union and the older generation but they wished there was another way to manage things. The next week I tried to repeat my triumph to get another discussion going but the mood was gone and we were back to zero.

Perhaps the main effect of that discussion was on me. Years later when Rupert Murdoch brought modern printing presses to his newspapers and the unions struck I didn't feel able to take part in what was known as the Battle of Wapping. Certainly Murdoch was a reactionary tyrant, there was no doubt about that, but I just couldn't support those printers.

Something like twelve months went by with me teaching at LCP and over that time, while my performing skills were getting better and better due to all the shows I was doing, if anything my pedagogical skills got worse and worse. I began to feel that I was short-changing my students. They might not have particularly wanted to be taught general studies by a failed art school graduate but if they were then they deserved somebody who was better at it than me. (Though as far as I could tell the college would have let me go on teaching there indefinitely.)

This time, unlike being an illustrator, I wasn't going to give up, so in September 1978 I embarked on a one-year degree course in how to be a proper further education lecturer at a place called Garnett College in Roehampton, west London, part of the University of London.

Every morning I would cycle from our flat down Fulham Palace Road to cross the river at Putney, passing at either end of the bridge the bleak slab-sided office block of the British computer company ICL that blighted the view of the Thames both upriver and down. One of the first computers produced by the group that eventually became ICL was called LEO (short for Lyons Electronic Office) and had been developed by the J. Lyons café chain, who were innovators in the application of computers to their accounting and logistics practices. The idea of the company being innovators in improving their horrible cakes, dull sandwiches and watery coffee never seemed to have occurred to them. Then turning right I rode parallel with the river before heading south where the road ran through woodland past the tree that Marc Bolan had driven into and died and up the hill to Roehampton.

The main building of Garnett College, yet another 1960s modernist structure, was set on the main road while behind it in undulating parkland were several eighteenth-century villas such as Manresa House built for Lady Caroline Lamb and later a Jesuit seminary where the poet Gerard Manley Hopkins had lived and which the college used for some of its classes.

There was something leisurely and vaguely eighteenth century about our course of study too. In an undemanding and relaxed fashion we learnt how to do a lesson plan and were instructed in various bogus, outdated and contradictory theories of educational philosophy. I quickly got the feeling that the staff were not exactly at the forefront of teaching practice or were going to allow themselves to be overburdened with work. The tone was set on day one during the induction talk to the whole year. The student counsellor, a large busty woman with a string of pearls around her neck, made a speech in which she said, 'My door is always open to all of you but I would just point out that if anyone tells me anything that is illegal I will go straight to the police . . .' So fucking leave me alone.

It was a nice life, I got a reasonable grant and all my fees were paid and once I left the college at the end of each day I never gave it another thought until I arrived back there the next morning, and in the evenings I carried on doing comedy shows with Threepenny Theatre. I even managed to get us a well-paid gig at Garnett.

The second term then came as a shock as we were dispatched beyond the walls of our Georgian seminar rooms (where light from ancient woodland dappled the rococo plasterwork) to do teaching practice with real students in a real college under the tutelage of a regular front-line teacher. I had chosen more or less at random to become a drama lecturer so I was to be posted to a place in Holloway called North London College to help on their drama course.

There was a great difference between the verdant deer parks of old Roehampton and Holloway, north London. To get to my placement I had to cycle to King's Cross, which took over half an hour, then turning north the ride got harder going uphill along the Caledonian Road for another couple of miles past Pentonville Prison to the college, the usual low 1960s construction on Camden Road. Just before the college there was a semi-circular row of large Victorian houses, facing a pleasant garden planted with cherry trees. This was Hilldrop Crescent where the notorious murderer Dr Crippen had poisoned his wife and then buried random bits of her in the cellar.

The students I was to teach were a lot more diverse than I'd encountered at the LCP: a mixture of Irish, Cockney, Black African and Caribbean, Turkish and Greek. This League of Nations feel was heightened by the security guard. In those days most colleges didn't think they needed protection but North London certainly required a permanent guard in a booth by the door. He was a Jamaican who'd been allowed to design his own outfit, which resembled that of an NCO in a Hungarian cavalry regiment, peaked cap, silver buttons down the front of his jacket and gold epaulettes on the shoulders, in addition to which he showed me he had a secret inner pocket sewn into the jacket that contained a short but lethal-looking black cosh.

The staff at North London College were welcoming enough but it soon became clear that having a student from Garnett provided an opportunity to hand over some of the more difficult classes. One of these was a group of nursery nurses who had become very disillusioned with their course to such an extent that there was even some talk amongst the staff that all of them were going to be thrown out and the course cancelled.

I had a couple of days to prepare for my first lesson. Teaching drama, unlike general studies, was something I believed was useful and I found myself excited by the possibility of bringing them back from the brink of disillusionment through the power of my teaching and so for once I prepared for what I was doing. When the nearly thirty-strong class, mostly young women but a few young men and a couple of older women in their thirties or early forties, came into the drama studio I was not present but instead there was a notice pinned to the board made out of letters cut from newspapers and magazines in the classic kidnapper's style. It said, 'Your new drama teacher has been kidnapped. If you want to see him again you should line up in alphabetical order and walk to the tree outside the college where you will find another note. If you see any staff on the way you must not speak to them or your new drama teacher will die.' So twenty-nine nursery nurses lined up in alphabetical order and walked out of the college. In the corridor they passed their head of department who asked them what was going on but they refused to speak to her.

After that I sent the group all over Holloway picking up various notes I'd hidden in plant pots, tucked under piles of rubbish and stuffed in cracks in walls while I followed watching from behind a newspaper with two big eye holes cut in it.

The final note directed all twenty-nine of them to buy as a ransom one single burger from the local McDonald's. When they tried to do this they were ejected by a security guard at which point I introduced myself and after that we all got on very well and their course wasn't cancelled. It also showed me that I wasn't necessarily a crappy teacher: if I believed in what I was doing then I could be good at it.

Though it was easy to get on with the students my relationship with the staff was more complicated. Many of the lecturers were about the same age as me, some a little older, some a little younger, but they had not messed around as I had. Instead they had gone straight from university or teacher training college into lecturing and had been making a good living for the past four or five years. They were part of the first generation of college-educated, working-class young people who wanted to differentiate themselves from their parents by the things they bought. This meant that consumer items were much more important to them than they had been to earlier generations. Information about the products they should buy was to be found in the Sunday newspaper supplements. Furniture from Habitat, Sabatier knives, Le Creuset pans, jam-making equipment and Italian pasta machines of fearsome complexity were all featured in their pages.

This pioneering consumerism though was not without its martyrs. There was a particular incident in the late 1970s arising from an article in the *Sunday Times Colour Supplement* which promoted a French kit for bottling meat. This was a method of food preservation that had not been truly necessary since the invention of refrigeration and when employed by those who had been not doing it for centuries resulted in the death by food poisoning of several social workers in Sheffield, an educational psychologist in Oxfordshire and schoolteachers all over the country.

There was one lecturer at North London called Gilpin who was the epitome of this new type of person. Gilpin was short and bearded and always wore bright yellow dungarees which he covered in badges. On his feet were French-made shoes called Kicker Boots usually in red, blue or yellow. Gilpin lived in a part of London called Stoke Newington where a lot of college lecturers, social workers or people in the arts were buying up the formerly neglected Victorian houses and converting them back to family homes.

As a result of the influx of these people Stoke Newington High Street was beginning to be lined with entirely new categories of businesses catering to their needs. They worried about their health but didn't entirely trust Western medicine (even though a lot of them worked for the NHS) so there were health-food stores selling herbal remedies for their imaginary illnesses. They liked to give dinner parties so there were kitchen-appliance shops and the off-licence started to stock better wine. When they went out they didn't want to drink in the bleak Irish pubs of north London but somewhere more congenial so there appeared places called wine bars, lit by candles and furnished with tables and chairs from churches or J. Lyons cafés that had closed down.

Realising that these people were often in the audiences at Threepenny Theatre shows, I started adding in mocking references to this lifestyle and predictably they loved it.

Before my teaching practice was over I was offered a job at North London College beginning at the start of the next academic year. The permanent drama teacher was going off on maternity leave and they needed somebody to take over from her for three days a week.

This meant that when I went back to Garnett I already had a job which in turn meant I couldn't really see the point in doing any more studying so I pretty much stopped going to lectures.

Not travelling to Garnett more than once or twice a week allowed me more time to work on the comedy show, which in its own small way was doing well. We were even getting noticed in the press, sort of. The *Morning Star*, the newspaper of the Communist Party, wrote, 'If you are having a social evening Threepenny Theatre can be highly recommended. It puts on a seventy-minute satirical show which was enjoyed by everybody who came along to the York Library social organised by Battersea Communist Party.'

There was only one problem that blighted our lives. None of us in Threepenny Theatre was able to drive so it was a constant struggle to get our stage set and props to the gigs. Sometimes we could use Harry Jackson's van but this was only a temporary solution and we were forced to try for something more permanent. (Curiously none of us thought about taking driving lessons.)

In the classifieds section of the London listings magazine *Time Out* there was a regular advert from a collective of hippies with vans called Gentle Ghost. These drivers and vans weren't expensive but there was still only one amongst them who came into our price range and when he turned up for the first gig it soon became obvious why – he only had one hand, his right arm ending in a stump. To get around this problem he drove a left-hand-drive VW Kombi on German plates. This meant that because the steering wheel was located on the left our driver was able to steer with his good hand while changing gear with the stump of his right. Though the hippy wasn't much use at helping us carry the set at least he got us and our stuff to and from the venue.

Until we did a show in a room above a riverside pub in Twickenham and Julie Christie was in the audience. It seemed absurd that such a huge film star should be watching us and we got so overexcited that none of us behaved well. The presence of *Doctor Zhivago's* Lara along with the wheelchair-bound musician Robert Wyatt who was in the Communist Party caused such hysteria in all of us that after the show the one-handed hippy got drunk and smashed down a beer glass onto the bar. The glass shattered and a shard flew upwards gashing his stump badly. With blood seeping from his arm our driver insisted he was fine but though we were drunk too we all refused to get in the VW so he drove off in a fury, along with our gear. To make things worse Cliff then also got plastered and he too cut his hand open so me and Linda were forced to take him in a taxi to the A&E at Uxbridge Hospital.

While we waited for Cliff to be treated I got chatting to a soldier with a broken arm who was sitting in the waiting area before going for an X-ray. He told me he'd broken his arm while drunk.

I asked, 'Will the sergeant be nice to you when you get back to barracks?'

'No,' he replied. 'I'll get six months in military prison for this. See, I've made myself unavailable to fight. This is what they call in the Army a self-inflicted wound.'

This idea of the self-inflicted wound stayed in my mind because it seemed to me that that was what me, Cliff and Bill were doing to ourselves with our lack of focus and ambition. The decisions we took appeared to sabotage any chance we might have had of success beyond the narrow world of the left. There was a phenomenon I had noticed amongst left-wing people which was not a fear of failure but rather a morbid fear of success. If you never achieved anything then you wouldn't ever have your ideological purity tested by all the blandishments of fame. Breaking out into the real big world would always require making uncomfortable compromises.

Bill and Cliff seemed happy to pootle along doing Students' Unions and CP benefits with the odd mention in the *Morning Star* but I wanted more. I just couldn't see how I was going to get it.

Gong!

Every week Linda would buy the satirical magazine *Private Eye* from a kiosk at Fulham Broadway station to read on the tube going in to work. One day in April 1979 she showed me a tiny advert almost lost amidst the junk in the back pages. It said, 'Comedians wanted for new comedy and improvisation club opening in W1.' I felt a rush of excitement: this was what I'd been looking for, a comedy club such as they had in the United States. Admittedly my knowledge of what a comedy club in the United States was like was patchy as it was based solely on the Dustin Hoffman film *Lenny*, a biography of troubled comic Lenny Bruce (from which I mostly remembered him having sex with a nurse). From this scant information I'd gained the impression that across the Atlantic there was a string of clubs in all the major cities where there existed a hip, politically engaged, radical, anecdotal stand-up comedy that dealt in subject matter such as drugs, lifestyle, sex and social hypocrisy, the comics dressed in sharp suits and narrow ties. With great excitement I phoned the number and was told to come at five the next day to a strip club in Soho.

I had never felt any particular affection for Soho. The self-conscious bohemianism its denizens went in for always just seemed annoying. My friend George Foster took me to Muriel Belcher's Colony Room club only once. Francis Bacon might have been lying face down in a corner with Lucian Freud on top of him but the strongest emotion I felt was indignation at how much the barman was trying to charge me for a tiny can of lager and I made us leave immediately. Clearly some of these people were talented; I just wondered how much better their work might have been if they hadn't been twatting about on Dean Street.

In all fairness it was not a district I knew well. There was an Italian deli on Old Compton Street where I'd sometimes buy complicated pasta and then fail to cook it but the web of sleazy stripteases, tailor's shops and foreign cafés did not particularly attract me. During the day Soho felt more or less all right, seemingly just a slightly ramshackle tangle of narrow streets and ancient buildings, but at night a transformation took place. Occasionally in the evening I might be passing the edge of the neighbourhood, maybe I'd been to see a new David Edgar play at the Almost Free Theatre. From Oxford Street I would glance into Soho. The illumination spilling from the department-store windows was bright and electric but that brilliance did not seem to penetrate more than a few feet into those dark and narrow alleys. Within that skein of streets the few lights atop old-fashioned lamp posts cast a softer glow and there was even one ancient restaurant lit by the guttering glow of flaming torches that jutted out of its walls.

On Oxford Street people hurried with determined purpose heading for a destination but in the shadowy byways of

Soho you would observe indistinct figures, men and women aimlessly leaning against walls or moving about in small repetitive patterns. If you stood still for a while and watched you would see one of these characters slip down an alley only for them to reappear a few seconds later several hundred yards away sidling out of the side door of a Greek restaurant carrying an oddly shaped parcel that seemed to be moving and two minutes later you'd spot that same person getting out of a taxi wearing a completely different pair of trousers.

This louche side of Soho gave Linda one particular worry. She had recently read an article in the *Evening Standard* about tourists being lured into strip clubs in Soho then charged £100 for fake champagne and threatened with violence if they refused to pay. She told me if anybody offered me a drink I was to turn them down flat.

The building where I was to meet the people from the proposed comedy club was at 69 Dean Street, a large, former Georgian townhouse accessed via a side door in a paved alley called Meard Street.

I caught a tiny, creaking lift up to the fourth floor. The door opened with a clatter onto the foyer of the Gargoyle Club, a topless bar, empty at that time of day and smelling like an old pub. Then following the sound of voices I descended a steel-and-brass art deco staircase that I didn't know was designed by Matisse which took me down a floor to the Nell Gwynne Theatre.

If I was going to imagine a slightly faded Soho strip club it would have looked exactly like this. In the auditorium were a hundred or so rickety gilt chairs grouped around tightly packed tables laid with white tablecloths, all facing a tiny stage backed by a glittery slash curtain and a single spotlight illuminating a microphone on a stand.

On the stage a middle-aged woman with a number of kitchen utensils, pans, knives and spoons, plus an old flat iron tied to her body with pieces of string, was singing the Victorian music-hall song 'Any Old Iron?' in a stagey Cockney accent. I had never done an audition before, performing my work to a few people rather than a paying audience, and was justifiably nervous but as I watched the other performers my confidence soared because they were all terrible – the woman with the ironmongery attached to her was actually one of the better ones. On the other hand I could see the two men holding the auditions, Don Ward the owner of the club and his partner Peter Rosengard, visibly fading as each appalling lunatic took to the stage.

For my piece I'd decided to do my standout bit from the Threepenny Theatre show – the thug who got into violent philosophical disputes in cake shops. It was strange performing such an aggressive bit to only two people but it really worked. Soon the pair were laughing and I could see Don and Peter visibly relax. What I didn't know was exactly how much trouble they had been in before my arrival: up to that point they hadn't auditioned one single performer who wasn't hopeless. High on relief they offered me a celebratory drink and were shocked at how vehemently I refused.

As I sipped a glass of tap water they told me how they had both separately been to the Comedy Store in Los Angeles and realised that London could do with something similar, a hip modern comedy club. This sounded like paradise to me, except that there were no other acts.

A few days later I went to meet Don and Peter in Peter's office at a large insurance company in the West End. There was some confusion at the reception desk about who he was because until a short while ago Peter Rosengard had been known as Peter Rose and had only recently re-discovered his Jewishness and re-Semitised himself. For a few seconds I experienced again the unpleasant feeling that it was all some complicated con but once the misunderstanding was sorted out I found them waiting for me at a desk in the middle of a large open-plan floor. The pair were again very complimentary about how funny I was, then they told me they wanted to offer me the position of MC for the opening night and me to sign a contract entitling me to the only wage any of the performers would be getting which was £5 a show.

When I was a child in the summer holidays me and Joe and Molly rode the train right across Europe, my father leading what were termed 'delegations' to the Communist states of the Soviet empire. There came a point in the long three-day journey when suddenly everything changed. At the border between the West and the East in a space between the minefields and the rows of barbed wire officials would examine your passport while soldiers in green uniforms stared down from watchtowers. Then once you were cleared to enter you would climb back aboard the train and with a hiss of steam and a squealing of metal you'd pass into an entirely different world.

Now I felt as if I was once more at a frontier. A border between the small-time ordinary existence that I'd had up until now and the world I'd always dreamed of entering – proper show business. To me Don and Peter didn't seem small-time.

Don already had his own club and Peter Rosengard owned a Rolls-Royce, a powder-blue Corniche convertible. Admittedly he'd got it from selling life insurance rather than from the world of entertainment but still.

The last song ABBA recorded together is called 'The Day Before You Came'. It is a piece of work suffused with the pain of Björn and Agnetha's divorce, both mournful and sad, yet it brilliantly captures the all-consuming sense of being in love. The number achieves this not by describing those emotions directly but by having Agnetha recount in the first person the banal life of a woman on the day before she meets her lover: she goes for lunch with the usual crowd, she reads the paper, she thinks it might have rained but she is not sure because up until then she has been in a kind of trance.

That song expresses what it felt like for me to live the six days before the Comedy Store opened on Saturday 26 May 1979.

> I must have gone to the pub with Harry and drunk five pints
> or so,
> I must have driven with Peter Rosengard to do some stupid
> late-night radio show,
> I must have done a CP benefit that I travelled to in a van,
> I must have eaten some sausages in the week before the
> Comedy Store began.

Because truthfully nothing during that week is real until with a rushing sound I am standing on the tiny stage and there are a hundred and fifty baying, drunken punters in front of me and I am yelling and swearing and sweating and some idiot has put a huge gong at the side of the stage and then I'm bringing on the first act and the audience hates them and shouts out 'Gong!' so within about three seconds I'm back on stage yelling and swearing and sweating again and this goes on till about 2 a.m. when I hand over mic duties to a guy called Bob Payton who owns a couple of Chicago-style deep-pan-pizza restaurants.

He'd told me before the show started, 'I was funny in high school and I wanted to find out if I could be funny now.' He couldn't.

With Bob Payton on stage as compère the evening degenerated into drunken chaos. I didn't care, firstly because I was so relieved to have got through the night but also because after I came off stage a stocky man in a suit with a gold chain around his neck approached the table where I was slumped with a couple of friends. He told me he was a producer from London Weekend Television, gave me his card and said that he'd very much like me to come in for a meeting next week. After that I went round the club showing everybody this card and telling them, 'This is my ticket to stardom . . .'

A few days later, full of excitement, I went to see the producer in his office on the South Bank of the Thames near Waterloo Station. The LWT complex comprised twelve floors of offices in a white tower with studios and workshops below. It was an island of light and activity in a landscape of dilapidation. The riverside, which would in any Continental city have been a tree-lined promenade, was here a row of abandoned warehouses, while out the front facing the main entrance was a very large patch of derelict land being fought over by local people who wished for housing and developers who wanted to build office blocks. There were no restaurants or bars close by, only the occasional old-fashioned tea room or grey pub that closed in the early evening, and beyond that miles of blank-windowed offices. There was a 1960s block near by that had a skein of scaffolding and wood around it at first-floor level forming a sort of basket designed to catch the bits of the building that fell off from higher up.

Along the walls of the corridor leading from the LWT reception area to the producer's office there were large black-and-white photographs, portraits of all the big stars of the channel mounted on shiny board; the one of David Frost had both its eyes poked out.

The producer's assistant asked me if I'd like a coffee and when she brought it there was also an accompanying plate of biscuits. I had never before been to a meeting with anyone where there had been biscuits.

After complimenting me on my performance the preceding Saturday the producer told me he was in charge of a new talent show that LWT were making for the ITV network called *Search for a Star*. The one innovation from the tired formula of the talent show was that the acts each week would be voted for by viewers' panels from around the Independent Television regions. The winner would go on to get their own TV show. He said he'd like me to take part. I felt a crushing sense of disappointment. I wasn't entirely sure what I'd been expecting but it wasn't an invitation to be on some crappy TV talent show. Yet at the same time to be on the television seemed like such a huge opportunity and I had been given biscuits so I felt compelled to say yes. Luckily that same week the unions called a big ITV strike which put the channel off the air for three months and when the talent show appeared it was without me. This was fortunate because I would have absolutely died amongst the line-up of old-style comedians, sentimental singers and terrible speciality acts who appeared on the programme. Thanks to industrial action I avoided TV humiliation (that pleasure came later).

The eventual winner of that season's *Search for a Star* was a comedian who went by the name of Fogwell Flax.

Up until my meeting with the LWT producer I'd been hoping that following the wild success of the first night of the Comedy Store and him giving me his card, my life would be instantly changed and by the end of that week I'd somehow have already become a famous comedian on the television. It didn't really work out like that.

In fact reality began to reassert itself by Monday morning. A few hours after the Sunday show closed I had to return to Roehampton for the first time in weeks to sit the exam for my Dip Ed from Garnett College. I knew that if you'd completed the course they'd award you the diploma, which meant the exam was a formality, and since the night before I'd been in a Soho strip club until 4 a.m. after answering a couple of questions badly I simply wrote, 'However . . .' then I got up and left, two hours early.

It had been a strange week. I was left with the feeling that my life had been completely transformed while at the same time it seemed to go on exactly as before.

The next Saturday I cycled back to the Store. All the way as I rode the streets were deserted, the only people still up were those being served free soup from a van. But outside the Gargoyle Club there was already a queue of eager people forming, though most did not seem like fans of challenging comedy. Some of them were there just for late-night alcohol – the Comedy Store was only £4 to get into and that compared very well with what many seedy drinking clubs charged. If I hadn't been the compère I might have paid £4 for after-hours booze. Many of the rest of them had come to see a freak show and the reason for that was the gong.

In the US clubs they used a spotlight that the stage manager flashed to tell the comics that their time was up; this light of course could only be seen by those on stage. Before opening night Peter Rosengard, realising that he didn't have such a thing, dispatched his friend Ashley, who he knew from the Society discothèques they frequented such as Annabel's in Mayfair, to get one. Ashley, also known as Billy the Kid, was a figure out of Terence Rattigan: tall, blond, muscular and not very bright, he was the lover of a newspaper heiress called 'Bubbles' Rothermere. Unable to find a spotlight Ashley came back from the hire shop with an enormous gong, similar in size to the one used to summon the giant ape in the original King Kong movie, an object so large that rather than being a private warning to the comic it gave a clear signal to everyone. Within seconds the crowd got the idea that they were in charge of this thing and very soon they began to shout 'Gong!' when they didn't approve of an act. The gong did at least provide an illustration of one truism of comedy which is that some performers are liked immediately by an audience while others possess a quality that incites the crowd to hate them on sight.

Putting such a powerful tool in the hands of the audience took away a lot of the authority that performers depended on to survive, so I needed to give myself as much power as possible to stop the night from turning into a riot (it was my proud boast that in all the time I was in charge at the club the police were never called, whereas on the weekend after I left a whole vanload of officers was required to subdue the audience). I would not plead with them though. Instead I chose to be honest. If we were short of acts I'd tell the crowd, 'We don't have many acts tonight so if you gong them off you're going home early, it's your choice.' I would not say, 'What a great audience you are,' because they weren't and I would not say, 'You're going to love these acts,' because they wouldn't.

Then there was intimidation. My mother possessed the ability to fly into a rage, to go from normal to completely crazy in an instant, and I'd inherited that talent. But rather than attacking motorists or screaming at shop assistants I used my anger to control the punters at the Comedy Store.

Nevertheless we couldn't go on like this. After a while the audience would tire of the novelty of shouting down pathetic deluded comedians and the Comedy Store needed more than just me doing innovative material if we were going to survive. The house was packed on the Saturday nights but neither freak-show aficionados nor late-night alcoholics came into town on a Sunday so that was soon abandoned. The next few weeks at the club were like one of those black-and-white films about the Russian Revolution that we used to put on at the Maoist bookshop. A time of suspended animation resembling the months of stasis between the abdication of the Tsar and the October Bolshevik Revolution. Then like a curly-haired Lenin arriving at the Finland station the first of the revolutionaries appeared, a tall man with the look of a dapper gypsy at a racecourse.

His name was Tony Allen and he was the anarchist who had heckled the cast of *About Poor B.B.* over the excessively Stalinist nature of our show. He told me before he went on that every Sunday morning he appeared at Speakers' Corner, which I thought was a weird thing to do, but watching Tony's routine I knew this was who I'd been waiting for: another comic like me but not like me. The subject matter was different – sexual politics, squatting, drugs – and the delivery was slow and thoughtful rather than my manic and aggressive tirades but he was clearly someone who was trying to do a similar thing with comedy. A week or two after Tony came a couple of left-wing actors, Andy de la Tour and Jim Barclay, and suddenly there were lot of comics doing stuff about Northern Ireland, street theatre, and vegan food and no matter how much the audience complained I refused to gong them off.

Then Keith Allen turned up and phase one of the revolution was complete. I met Keith when somebody asked me if I wanted to earn £20 as an extra on an Italian film being shot in a porn club in Soho. He was playing a barman and we got chatting. When the time came for my sequence to be filmed I had managed to somehow get myself locked in the back of a van with a huge stack of pizzas that were steaming up the windows.

Keith said he'd heard about the Store from Tony whom he knew from the squatting scene around Notting Hill, and I said sure, come down. With Tony you could see what the influences were, US comedians like Lenny Bruce and George Carlin combined with an anarchist-hippy-squatter-street-theatre worldview. But with Keith you couldn't tell what his inspiration was. He seemed deranged and dangerous in a way that had the audience transfixed and a little frightened.

Keith could be pretty deranged in real life too. After one early show at the old Albany Empire in Deptford, me and Keith both travelled back to central London on the train but he was on the outside, between the carriages balanced somehow on the buffers. Keith did not adhere to Flaubert's dictum, 'If you want to be wild in your art, be bourgeois in your habits.'

The Society drunks from Annabel's and Barbarella's, the crowd looking for a cheap thrill and the late-night drinkers were not interested in seeing challenging, experimental, Lenny Bruce-style stand-up comedy and slowly they drifted away to be replaced by a different bunch who were closer in attitude to the leading performers. Whatever else was wrong with the left in Britain, nobody else seemed to have noticed that sexism and racism were rife in the entertainment business and needed to be challenged. So from the start, along with the best of the other comics, I set out to exclude it from the Comedy Store. Sometimes even if the audience were going along with it I would impose my own view and gong off a comic I thought was stepping over the line. Pretty soon the idea of being 'non-sexist' and 'non-racist' was universally accepted by anybody who wanted to do well at the Comedy Store.

Though I never consciously thought about it in these terms, what we were attempting at the Comedy Store was to create a whole new art form. Britain had never had a tradition of smart, anecdotal stand-up comedy so we were trying to build that tradition from scratch while at the same time overlaying it with a left-wing political consciousness. It's hard to overstate how unqualified I was to lead this revolution. All my comrades in Alternative Comedy were experienced performers: Andy and Jim had worked for years in the straight and fringe theatre; Tony too, though his arena was often the street or Speakers' Corner; and Keith had been to drama school, whereas I was an ex-art student and part-time college lecturer who, up until the Comedy Store, had maybe done twenty-five comedy gigs.

So I was forced to invent how I behaved both on and off stage from scratch. While the other acts would sit in the club I tried not to mix with the crowd. I figured that since my authority on stage depended on me acting crazy I didn't want them seeing me being normal. I was also happier maintaining my illusions about them rather than knowing the truth. I had this idea there was maybe one boy or girl in each night, a timid lonely kid perhaps who'd saved up their dole money to get the £4 entrance fee and had travelled into London on the last bus from the grey and distant suburb where they lived. Frightened and nervous, they'd then been forced to share a table with horrible people – the bad-tempered celebrity harmonica player Larry Adler perhaps or National Theatre dramaturge Kenneth Tynan – but once the show began all the noise dropped away and for them my performance, or Tony's or Keith's, was like a door opening to a world of bright possibilities they hadn't dreamt existed. Full of hope, they would walk the ten miles back home resolving that they too would become a comedian or at the very least a DJ on independent local radio.

For this new audience we were attracting it was both a thrill and a challenge to come into town late at night to see our show. Soho after dark did not feel like a safe place; there was an air of danger and seediness that hung over the area. Meard Street, the narrow alley where the entrance to the club was located, was lined with eighteenth-century townhouses that were now used as brothels, so there'd be women wandering up and down outside looking for business.

The lugubrious, dinner-jacketed doorman Joe would show audiences into the tiny lift and they would creak past the empty and silent floors of 69 Dean Street, never entirely sure that the groaning cable wasn't going to snap, sending them plummeting to the ground to die at the feet of some Filipino call girl. Then if they arrived early enough, the topless bar would be almost deserted, with only a couple of girls pulling Comedy Store T-shirts over their naked breasts. In a time when pubs closed at eleven it was well after that before the show began and they knew they would not be leaving before 2 a.m., which was an exciting thought, though it did leave them with a problem getting home. The tubes stopped pretty much as soon as midnight fell and there were only about two night buses running, one that went to somewhere like Walthamstow dog track and the other that terminated in an industrial estate in Walthamstow, so you would either have to take a taxi or walk. A few drove into the West End, four or five of them packed inside their brightly coloured little Fiats, Citroëns and Renaults, motoring in from Hackney, Acton and Clapham. One advantage of driving into town was that you could still park more or less anywhere you wanted after nightfall in central London, though there was a fair chance when you got back to your car it would be on fire.

THIS COMEDY LIFE

With the closure of the Sunday show, the Comedy Store was only open for the one night, so it was Tony who came up with an idea for us to be able to work during the rest of the week. He suggested that those of us with more political acts should start our own collective to tour venues where we could perform longer sets to a more sympathetic audience. The first meeting to discuss this was with me, Andy and Jim and a performer called Pauline Melville at Tony's flat, a pleasant housing association apartment just off Portobello Road where he suggested the name Alternative Cabaret. Keith was there too but only to tell us that he didn't want to have any part in our collective. As I'd come to know him a little I realised it was typical of Keith Allen that he would come to a meeting of something just to tell everybody he didn't want to be part of that thing. Especially since he then performed at most of our gigs – though you were never quite sure if it was a good idea having him there or not: at a show in a Students' Union in south London Keith dealt with some hecklers by throwing darts at them. The rest of us couldn't decide if that was going too far or if it exactly embodied the anarchic spirit of Alternative Cabaret, so for a while all of the acts were throwing things at the punters, chairs, fire extinguishers, seafood . . .

This was only a few years after punk, and rather than the crowd passively watching the performer, the interaction between act and audience could often be rather more of a two-way street. I had first met Pauline Melville at the Half Moon, a fringe theatre in Whitechapel on the edge of the City. I had been appearing at a cabaret there, while Pauline was in a band with Andy de la Tour's then girlfriend Maggie Steed. In the audience were a party of obnoxious lesbians in leather jackets and big boots who talked throughout the show. Afterwards these same women barged into the one dressing room to remonstrate with the female performers for wearing make-up. I was standing outside because the women were getting changed.

At the end of the dressing room was the fly tower for the scenery, essentially a big lift shaft that was only guarded by a rail. The first time I saw Pauline, who had been in the band but who I hadn't noticed before, was when I heard a guttural howl and saw her, through the open door of the dressing room, wearing only her knickers, grab one of the lesbians and propel her towards the fly tower. Over the next few years she became one of my and Linda's closest friends. It was Pauline who best summed up the mindset of those of us who were in Alternative Cabaret when she said we were the sort of people who fantasised about refusing to appear in the Royal Variety Performance.

Surprisingly competent as an administrator, Tony took care of nearly all the organisational work, booking venues, arranging fees and so on. My contribution was to design the poster based on something I'd done at Southport Art School ten years before.

I signed my initials 'A.S.' in the bottom corner and me and Tony silkscreen-printed them at a community centre on the Harrow Road where he knew the people who ran the place.

The first Alternative Cabaret gig was at a pub on the Gray's Inn Road called the Pindar of Wakefield. The second was a day later at another pub – the Elgin at the top end of Ladbroke Grove just before the J. G. Ballard Westway flyover.

The Elgin was a big run-down old place of bevelled glass and scarred and varnished wood with a large back room where bands used to play and it became our regular base. The crowd were very much Tony's people – squatters, druggies and activists. Just across Ladbroke Grove was Freston Road, a tangle of boarded-up Victorian houses where squatters in a *Passport to Pimlicoesque* move had attempted to secede from the United Kingdom, renaming the area Frestonia. Threepenny Theatre had once done a show at the National Theatre of Frestonia performed entirely by candlelight.

With a regular audience at the Elgin you needed to come up with a constant supply of new material, although at first I was unsure about this crowd because of some of the language I used in my act. The big split in radical audiences at that time was between the Cuntists and the Anti-Cuntists as to whether it was permissible to use the word 'cunt'. Surprisingly the crowd at the Elgin turned out to be firmly pro-'cunt'.

It must have been around about this time, though I can't say there was a single moment, when I crossed over from being somebody who did comedy to somebody who was, heart and soul, *a comedian*. Years ago we had got chatting to a guy at a party.

Linda asked him, 'What do you do?'

And he replied, 'I'm a poet.'

'No, what do you really do?' Linda said.

'I'm a poet,' he insisted.

'No, what are you really?' she asked again.

'I'm a spinner of words, a rhymer of rhymes.'

'No, what do you really do?'

'I'm a postman.'

Up until Alternative Cabaret I had been a postman, not committing fully to the comedy life, but now being a stand-up comedian was not just what I did, it was what I was. It took up most of my time and comedy was what I thought about in the moments when I wasn't doing it. I would see a terrible car crash and think not about calling an ambulance or assisting the dying but instead would wonder: Can I get five minutes of material out of this? It was not just me, it was all of us. Linda noticed it first. She observed that amongst the Alternative Cabaret acts, if she said anything funny in conversation, where once they would have laughed as ordinary people laughed, now they'd just nod sagely and mutter, 'Hmmm . . . nice line, nice line.'

I say I was fully committed to stand-up, except that during the day I was still a teacher. When I'd got the part-time drama post at North London College it had felt like a tremendous honour: to be offered a job during my teaching practice seemed like a real testament to my teaching ability but now it just felt like an imposition. Through the autumn, as well as hosting the Comedy Store at the weekend, I was performing with Alternative Cabaret several night a week, doing Threepenny Theatre gigs with a very resentful Cliff and during the day lecturing in Holloway. I was covering more miles on my bicycle than a professional cyclist. One class I was in charge of was an after-hours drama group which I allowed to get taken over by a young black teenager who wasn't even a student at North London College. His name was Ricky Beadle. Ricky just turned up one day and seemed to enthuse the students much more than I did so I just let him get on with it. Together they devised a play called *A–Z* which won the *Evening News* Student Drama Competition against many drama groups with older and more privileged members drawn from colleges and universities including Oxford. I tried to take as much credit for this as possible and my students' success made me look superhuman. Not just a great comedian but a brilliant teacher as well.

(Holding a student drama competition wasn't enough to save the *Evening News* though and it closed that same year.)

On one of my days off from North London College I bumped into a fellow staff member on the tube. She was an older woman who wasn't aware of my night-time activities.

'Where are you off to?' she enquired.

'I'm just going into town to be photographed for the Christmas cover of *Time Out* magazine,' I replied. The woman was confused by this. At that time, *Time Out* was the most powerful magazine in London: for all those new consumers it told them where to go, what to wear, what to eat, what to see.

This woman couldn't understand why their substitute drama teacher was being featured on the most significant cover of the year of London's most important magazine.

Anyway, in January the proper drama teacher was due to return so I was able to stop teaching that Christmas. After that I really was a full-time comedian.

Bit Windy . . . Went for a Swim

Alternative Cabaret began to get the odd show outside London. One such early gig was in Exeter where Linda booked us into a boarding house on the edge of the city centre. There were some civil servants on a course staying there who had come in drunk the night before and signed themselves in as 'Mickey Mouse' and other stupid names. Over breakfast the next morning, in front of all the other guests, the owner of the boarding house upbraided them like a schoolteacher speaking to kids of primary school age and these grown men took it, looking down shamefaced into their greasy fried eggs. That was how it was in a small hotel in the late 1970s: like a minor public school but without the Latin.

Like in many boarding houses there were little handmade notices everywhere listing things that were forbidden – making a noise, keeping a squirrel in your room – so many indeed that it seemed as if they'd had a special wallpaper made out of proscriptive announcements. One of the notices said, 'We try and keep notices to a minimum.'

The most common instruction was the one informing guests that they weren't allowed to stay in their room during the day after 9.30 a.m. So me and Linda were forced to wander around the city. This was the first time I had performed in another town and to be in Exeter with nothing to do all day while others shopped or went about their jobs felt slightly unreal and disconnected, a bit like when as a child travelling across Europe with my parents we would change trains in some foreign city, completely unknown and anonymous amongst a crowd of hurrying people.

This magical feeling increased when in a narrow, cobbled back street we came upon a guy I knew from the sculpture department at Chelsea School of Art sitting on a wooden folding chair in the window of what seemed like an abandoned shop. Inside it was a complete mess, floorboards smashed and torn up; in several places there were piles of rubble and brick while in the corner a rusty tap dripped into a bucket.

'Hi, Charlie,' I said. 'What are you doing here?'

'I'm having an exhibition,' Charlie replied.

'In this shop?'

'Yes.'

'When does it open?' Linda asked.

'It opens this evening.'

'Oh my God!' Linda said. 'We'll help you get it ready, you've got a few hours yet. I'll go out and buy a mop.'

'It is ready,' Charlie replied.

Having been to art school I'd kept my mouth shut since I knew it best not to commit myself on a matter such as this. In things to do with modern art I was a great fan of something Francisco Franco, dictator of Spain, had once said, which was,

'You are the slave of what you say and the master of what you do not.'

On my return to London, the offers of gigs increased, not just with Alternative Cabaret but as a solo comedian. I had so much work in fact that I was obliged to buy myself a large diary from Ryman's called a Langham Diary, to record all my bookings in. From time to time before then I had sometimes kept a journal but I had only ever written in it what I'd had for my tea. On 11 January 1977 Linda had cooked sausages and onions with gravy and mashed potatoes while on June the 4th of the next year we'd dined on her famous five-bean salad. As a diarist I'd always admired the style of Tsar Nicholas of Russia who on the day of the Russian Revolution had written, 'Bit windy . . . went for a swim.'

Men who ran pubs with upstairs rooms, the administrators of arts centres, college entertainment officers all approached me to do solo comedy gigs for them, but oddly I also got offers to perform from the managers of old people's homes, guys who thought it would be a good idea if they stopped the music at their local disco to have me shout at the dancers, and primary school teachers seeing if I'd like to do ten minutes of foul-mouthed lifestyle comedy for their under-sevens.

The offers of legitimate work were a sign that I was beginning to be noticed, while the stupid ones were a sign that a lot of people didn't understand what made a good comedy performance. They would see you in a club with a proper sound system, stage lighting and an attentive audience and assume you could do the same thing in the butcher's shop where they worked. The truth was that stand-up comedy was entirely dependent on context and, despite seeming robust, was actually quite a fragile thing. I did not come upon this knowledge intuitively but because I did a fair number of the wrong kind of gigs including one at a children's theatre in Richmond at the instigation of Lee Cornes, a performer from the opening night at the Comedy Store, which ended with me rolling on the floor being attacked by a gang of children who were lashing me with strings of wooden sausages.

Thatcher Stole My Trousers

Margaret Thatcher was elected Prime Minister on the 3rd of May 1979 and the Comedy Store opened a few days later, which must have meant something. At first, her grip on power seemed quite weak. Nobody knew that we wouldn't soon be returning to an era of community-theatre clowns having beer and sandwiches at Number 10 Downing Street, so she didn't at first figure that much in the routines of even the left-wing Alternative Cabaret comics. It was only as it slowly dawned on us that the old consensus was never coming back and we were now living in a more polarised world that she crept more and more into our routines. I chose never to ask myself precisely why I did political stuff. I certainly never thought you could change anything politically by performing stand-up comedy (I didn't even think you could change anything politically through politics). When Peter Cook opened his Establishment Club in 1961, around the corner from the site of the Comedy Store, in Greek Street, Soho, he said he wanted it to be a venue 'like those cabarets in Weimar Republic Germany that had done so much to stop the rise of Hitler'.

And in some ways Alternative Cabaret could be quite Thatcherite. As a reaction to the self-indulgence and irrelevance of a lot of the subsidised theatre, me and Tony agreed that we were not interested in getting an Arts Council grant or any other form of state handout. We both felt that the only thing that made sense was if people paid to see us – that them buying tickets was what would ensure that we remained relevant.

On the other hand, because we inhabited the world of counter-culture radical activism, me and Tony also wrestled with ethical dilemmas that would have seemed absurd to any other entertainers. One evening the pair of us had an interminable debate over the dilemma of if a TV company sent a limousine to collect you and take you to a studio, would it be OK to accept the ride or should you refuse to get in the car and instead travel to the recording on a bicycle or public transport? Finally Tony handed down his judgement, which was that it would be acceptable to travel in the limousine as long as you sat in the front beside the driver.

The first really good comedians who weren't left-wing Alternative Cabaret types to turn up at the Comedy Store were Peter Richardson and Nigel Planer. When they came down the stairs and asked to go on Peter kept saying of Nigel, 'He's David Essex's understudy in *Evita*,' as if a career in musical theatre would mean he'd do all right. I asked them how they wanted to be introduced. Peter said they wanted to be known as 'Severed Head and the Neckfuckers' but after a few nights settled on 'the Outer Limits'. Their act was more physical than the Alternative Cabaret gang which is perhaps why we never asked them to join us, but they would consistently go down well with the audience and they added variety to the show at the Comedy Store, because apart from not being at all political they were also the only double act.

One weekend after the Store had been going for a few months I decided to take a break, have a rest, kick back. At least that was my intention but after a couple of whiskies in the flat my Saturday night began to feel suddenly empty. It seemed, in my drunken state, like it would be a good notion if I went along to the Store anyway. My plan was to perform a brand-new piece of material, a bit that had gone down really well at the Elgin earlier in the week. My reasoning was that the crowd would be absolutely delighted to see their beloved regular MC coming on just to do a new routine. Linda asked me whether this was such a great idea but I ignored her, and around about midnight I cycled into Soho, parked my bike, went up in the lift and told Andy de la Tour, who was taking my place that night, that I wanted to be put on as soon as possible.

What I hadn't figured on was that the crowd at the Comedy Store wouldn't have a clue who I was since there weren't any regulars, they were different every week. Also as soon as I stepped on stage I realised firstly that I was really drunk and secondly how much authority my role as compère gave me: without it I was just another weird act. It also became apparent pretty quickly that there was a problem with the bit that had gone down so well at the Elgin. What I'd forgotten about the crowd in Ladbroke Grove was that they were regulars who knew me and tolerated my experimenting with material, and a lot of them were on drugs. The new piece of comedy was a quiz where if the audience didn't get the questions right I pointed a gun at the punters and threatened to shoot them. I'd bought the gun from Linda's Littlewoods catalogue. It was actually an air pistol that fired little lead pellets but in appearance it was a pretty convincing imitation of a Colt .45 military side arm.

At first the crowd at the Comedy Store were just indifferent to my opener but when I started screaming and pointing a very real-looking gun at them they became extremely agitated and understandably started yelling for the gong, hoping to have me removed before they got shot. Andy wasn't going to gong me off even though the audience were screaming at him to do so but despite that I died a terrible death. After I came off stage I also learned that there was a journalist in from the *Observer Magazine* who was doing the first ever big feature on the Comedy Store in a national newspaper.

And if that wasn't enough this was the first night that Twentieth Century Coyote – Rik Mayall and Adrian Edmondson – appeared. They burst on stage exuding a crazed energy that made them the undoubted hit of the night, especially compared to the drunk, crazy guy with the gun who'd been on just before.

Their success made my failure all the more painful. I wobbled back to Fulham on my bike and when I got home I cried for hours thinking everything was ruined.

But just as the moments when you imagine you've had a huge success don't amount to much, the same is true of the disasters. In the end the journalist from the *Observer* never mentioned me and the article didn't make much of an impression anyway because the writer didn't really understand what he was seeing. The main result was that I made sure I was always the MC from then on, and I never got drunk before going on stage almost ever again.

It turned out in any case that it wasn't my fault, it was the gun's. It had developed a small fault and I'd refused to pay Littlewoods the balance of what was owed on it so the pistol may have collected some bad karma.

Once I got to know them better I lent the gun to Rik and Ade for a sketch they wanted to do which involved them being terrorists who held the entire audience hostage, and like my quiz bit that sketch went down very, very badly. Then, later on, the pistol was stolen from the horrible council flat in Kennington they shared and was used to hold up a post office. During the robbery the guy with the fake pistol was shot and wounded by police armed with real weapons. So it was a very unlucky gun.

Been Great Working with You, Les

Gradually, with Tony, Keith, Jim, Andy, the Outer Limits and Twentieth Century Coyote, the Comedy Store became the place to visit for a small number of people who wanted to be at the cutting edge of what was going on in London. And our friends. With its success, the Comedy Store turned into a bit of a clubhouse, both for the comics and the place's owners. Don Ward felt safe enough to invite down his old mates from when he too was a comedian, people such as all-round entertainer Des O'Connor – who seemed very nice though his skin was tanned to the same colour as a roast chicken.

Peter Rosengard appeared to always be surrounded by models, skinny girls who possessed a surprisingly comprehensive knowledge of the makes and capacities of German sports cars. He was also somebody to whom weird stuff kept happening, so one of the models would tell you a story that went, 'Me and Peter were in Paris and Peter was driving like a convertible Mercedes 280 SL, the one with the fuel-injected 2.8 litre straight 6, and suddenly this guy on the street pulls out a rifle and there's this elephant charging down the . . .'

Tony's companions by contrast were often fierce mad women who always seemed to have just got off a train with all their belongings while Keith's mates, wild boys with hungry eyes, travelled in a pack like wildebeests and Peter Richardson's friends were often slightly seedy hippies who owned things like roller-disco rinks in west London.

My friends had to be invited in small numbers because they all hated each other. I had always envied those whose mates hung around in a big pack, a large interconnected social group, since everyone I knew seemed to dislike every- one else I knew. Me and Linda had a very busy social life but that was because we would have to travel all the way to Clapham to have a drink in a pub with just one other person.

To put together the running order of acts I would hang about at the foot of the stairs in the small foyer between the club itself and the door to the kitchen, a space which also served as the dressing room. Holding a clipboard, pen in hand, I'd see who was coming down to perform that night and would start to build the show, placing energetic acts in the middle when audience energy might be flagging, alternat- ing no-hopers with people I thought had the ability to do well, and placing anybody who'd annoyed me right at the end of the show in the early hours of the morning. I was staring down at my clipboard when I heard a softly spoken voice with an American accent address me. 'Surr . . . do you mind if I go on tonight?'

'Sure,' I replied without looking up. 'What's your name?'

'Robin Williams.'

'Gak!' I said, looking at him for the first time.

To most people in Britain at that time Robin Williams would have still been unknown. The only reason I was aware of who he was was because on Saturday mornings ITV would broadcast his sitcom *Mork & Mindy* in the mistaken belief that it was a kids' show.

Robin had been in Malta working on the movie *Popeye* directed by Robert Altman, his first starring role. As soon as the production had wrapped he'd flown to London and asked a taxi driver at Heathrow to take him to a comedy club. The taxi driver must have been a particularly cool one since the Comedy Store was the only club in the country of the type Robin was looking for and most people still didn't know it existed. If he'd chosen another cabbie he could have found himself at the Circus Tavern, Purfleet, Essex, sharing the bill with Jim Davidson, Jiminy Cricket and Fogwell Flax.

I put Robin on as soon as I could and he did forty-five minutes. The effect he had on me was like I had been pushed down some stairs laughing. Only after seeing him perform several times over the next two years could I work out how he did it. A lot of the audience thought he was making it all up on the spot but I knew that couldn't be true yet at first it did seem like there was just this torrent of brilliant unconnected stuff. However if you watched long enough the same bits came round again so you saw that he had maybe four hours of brilliant material in his head that he would access in a different order every night. This made me respect him more – if he'd been just making it up there would have been no artistry.

Afterwards Peter Richardson and Nigel Planer took Robin to a party in south London thrown by a friend of Nigel's in a squat where a lot of people were taking heroin. Then they dropped him back at the Dorchester.

Not every professional stand-up did as well as Robin. There was a Lancashire comedian called Lennie Bennett who inexplicably was quite big on TV: he had his own series with his partner Jerry Stevens and he hosted a couple of panel shows, *Punchlines* and *Lucky Ladders*. Lennie came down one night and since he was a well-known turn assumed he could just get up on the stage and get laughs with his ancient, hackneyed material. That didn't work at all with the audience at the Comedy Store and he left the stage to howls of derision, his final words to the audience being, 'Well I'm going home in a Rolls-Royce tonight and you're going home on the bus!' And I thought: Yeah, but you're still going home feeling really bad about yourself and with the niggling sense that your career and the entire world as you know it is about to vanish.

But then I thought: Yeah, but he is still going home in a Rolls-Royce, which must be pretty sweet, and I'm going home on a bike.

Then I started thinking about something else.

There was a lesson to be learned there about what makes a good comic. Don Ward had his old friend Les Dawson come down. Les saw right away that it was way too much of a risk for him to get up on the stage and politely refused when I asked him if he fancied performing. There was an old-school guy who came down most weekends dressed in a tuxedo and bow tie, a silver-haired museum attendant who died every week. After he was howled off as usual he went up to Dawson, shook his hand and said, 'Been great working with you, Les.'

Looking the Part

When I'd begun at the Store I'd worn a leather jacket and chinos but one day I saw hanging on the rack of an Oxfam shop in Putney High Street a suit made in the USA that seemed to me to be a most remarkable item of clothing. It was fashioned from a dark grey, almost black mohair-and-silk mix that appeared to shimmer and change with the light. The trousers were narrow and tapered and there were three buttons on the jacket. At that time I still bought my clothes mostly from Army-surplus stores. For our honeymoon me and Linda had taken a cheap four-day holiday on the island of Guernsey – £9 for four nights in a B&B, a coach trip and a bottle of duty-free spirits thrown in. I bought a new jacket for the holiday from a surplus store in Euston called Laurence Corner, where I shopped for my clothes amongst the gas masks, tin water bottles and ammunition boxes. My new jacket was light grey cotton with large black cuffs which I thought looked really smart. It was only when we were on Guernsey and people kept asking me what time the next bus to Saint Peter Port left that I realised that I was wearing the top half of a bus driver's uniform.

So the idea of buying a suit, and particularly a suit like this, was a big step for me. I don't know how such a thing came to be in south-west London. I imagined that sometime in the 1970s a member of Tamla Motown group The Four Tops had left the suit in a rather unpleasant bed and breakfast in Richmond where they'd been staying during a low point in their career when they'd been playing Blaze's Club in Windsor and the landlady had kept it. Recently the landlady had died and her stuff been taken to a charity shop. I tried to barter the women in the shop down from £10 to £8 but they wouldn't budge.

I wore it every time I went out and felt like a million roubles. Then I went on stage in it. Unfortunately as soon as I hit the stage something seemed to happen to my beloved outfit. Even when we'd been poor me and Linda had eaten and drunk a lot, but somehow, being young and also cycling everywhere meant I had not put on weight. But now that I was making a little money we were consuming even more food and alcohol, and so perhaps I was putting on fat that was being held back like water behind a dam, or maybe the material shrank under the hot lights, but the suit suddenly seemed to stretch tightly over my stomach and the trousers appeared to abruptly hike themselves up by about two inches. From the point of view of me wearing my suit out and about socially this was a disaster but as a stage outfit there was something about this ill-fitting mod outfit that really worked.

To perform in a suit at that time was a revolutionary act. The only musicians who wore suits when they performed were avant-garde groups such as Kraftwerk. Once it happened it seemed absolutely right that I should wear a costume while performing and that by being a suit it represented a kind of deranged subversion of what the conventional club comedian would wear. I added a dark blue shirt and a narrow striped tie. On my feet I wore a pair of Doc Martens paratrooper-style boots called Para Docs. Even my shoes were a play on words and a philosophical concept.

After a little while with the constant rubbing together of my thighs the fragile crotch of my suit wore out but rather than getting it professionally patched I fixed the hole myself with silver gaffer tape which would work loose as I performed leaving strips of fabric dangling from my groin.

My hair had also not been that short when I'd started at the Comedy Store but one day I suddenly noticed two strips of baldness like a fire break in a forest travelling parallel along my skull. I was going bald! It was a horrible moment from which in some ways no man ever quite recovers and it presents you with a dilemma: what to do with the hair that remains? The late 1970s and early 1980s was when the era of the baroque comb-over peaked; Arthur Scargill, Bobby Charlton and Liberal leader Jeremy Thorpe were all devotees of the pathetic and vain attempt to hide the shame of baldness by shaping what hair remained into a kind of threadbare thatched roof for the skull. Without ever thinking it was going to happen to me I had resolved that if I started to lose my hair I'd have my head shaved. So I went to the barber's at the corner of Dawes Road and that's what I did.

Fuck, Cunt, Shit, Piss, Wank

Sitting in the living room we heard a muted crump that rattled the big ill-fitting windows of our tower block. Looking towards the West End I saw beyond the grey slate roofs of Fulham a line of dirty smoke curling slowly into the sky from beside the distant pink towers of the Victoria & Albert Museum. For once it wasn't an IRA bomb, this explosion was all the work of our own government. 'They've gone in,' I said to Linda. It was Bank Holiday Monday 5 May 1980 and the sixth day of the Iranian Embassy siege, the first news event to be covered live on TV. Two miles away on a clear early summer evening the SAS were storming the embassy and shooting dead the hostage takers, members of the Democratic Revolutionary Front for the Liberation of Arabistan (DRFLA).

Over the next few days there was an unprecedented surge of national pride due to the successful outcome of the SAS raid and a definite increase in support for Margaret Thatcher. The left had hoped that an afternoon of general studies once a week and fifteen years of Wednesday Plays on the BBC, with their messages of anti-colonialism and liberality, had been enough to cure the working class of this mindless jingoism but it seemed all along to have been lurking just beneath the surface.

One of the most enduring results of the siege, apart from helping Thatcher increase her grip on power, was that it introduced the world to the Heckler and Koch MP5 9mm. submachine gun. Since I was a child I had been fascinated by guns. Although Molly and Joe were Communists dedicated to the dictatorship of the industrial proletariat, there were ways in which my parents, particularly my mother, held opinions on daily life that were closer to those of the more avant-garde elements of the upper classes than the rest of the people in Valley Road.

There was a theory, prevalent in liberal circles, that giving children warlike toys could awaken in them aggressive, anti-social and overtly male tendencies which were unsuited to the modern world.

At first this wasn't too much of a problem – all the boys in the street just ran around pointing their fingers at each other shouting 'Ack, ack, ack' or 'Krplow!' – but soon their parents began buying them plastic or metal toy guns which usually fired a paper roll of percussion caps and this left me pretty badly outgunned with just my fingers. Yet no matter how much I pleaded with her, Molly refused to buy me a toy gun. In the end out of desperation, tired of spending every evening lying dead on the pavement, I started making my own imitation weapons out of bread. What I would do was I would chew an L-shape into a slice of Hovis, then smuggle it out of the house so I could run around the streets shooting other kids with my wholemeal pistol. I brought such conviction to my play-acting that the other children accepted the fact that my bread gun possessed a degree of firepower and as long as it didn't rain I was fine.

After a while though my parents could see that I was being made to look a little bit too eccentric shooting children with my edible pistol so in an echo of the UN Disarmament Commission, which was formed under the Security Council and which met intermittently from 1954 to 1957, we held our own arms-limitation talks. After furious bargaining the final outcome agreed by all parties was this: I would be allowed toy firearms but they would be limited to non-automatic weapons, a restriction which basically meant I could only own revolvers with a Wild West flavour. No automatic pistols, rifles or submachine guns would be allowed. Like all prohibitions my parents' partial weapons ban had the opposite effect and left me nursing a lifelong obsession with firearms. Which was also why I'd bought the unlucky air pistol from Linda's Littlewoods catalogue.

My time at Chelsea might have put me off painting but I still drew, not landscapes done in charcoal or portrayals of the naked human form, but almost exclusively sketches of guns executed in biro. Drawing had always been a way for me to give my internal life a degree of reality. When I was nine or ten I'd invented the state of Saylovia whose buildings, armies and cultural life I'd reproduced in a series of drawings reminiscent of an Uccello with a muscle-wasting disease. Now what I drew was guns. And not just in a sketchbook either but almost anywhere, in the margins of newspapers, down the sides of legal documents and at the top of electricity bills. It was a barometer of the more relaxed attitude to security which existed at that time that you could send in your tax returns decorated with illustrations of Kalashnikovs, 5.56mm M16s and .303 Lee-Enfields all around the edges and nobody would think to inform the police or the intelligence services.

Roland Barthes the French literary theorist, philosopher and critic wrote in a 1957 essay about the then new Citroën DS, 'Cars today are the exact equivalent of the great Gothic cathedrals.' By this I took him to mean that just as those great medieval places of worship were objects of wonder and awe which embodied all that their era was capable of both technically and philosophically so the motor car now fulfilled that function. Barthes was saying that cars represented exactly where we are as a society, both in terms of design and in terms of technology. In my opinion you could say the same about guns. Plus guns had this tremendous lethality that cars didn't possess, unless they were being driven by somebody who was drunk, that is.

Each decade seemed to get its own gun, a weapon that seized the public imagination and was reproduced everywhere, a firearm that appeared somehow to embody its era. In the 1960s that gun was undeniably the Kalashnikov assault rifle, the weapon of liberation movements all around the world, seen on news stories, printed on banners at demonstrations and featured on the flag of at least one African country.

The iconic firearm of the 1970s, by contrast, was a weapon of the United States, of capitalist decadence and the libertarian right, the Smith & Wesson .44 Magnum revolver. Big, heavy, chromed, with an enormous phallic barrel producing an awful loud noise, terrible recoil and an enormous muzzle flash, the Smith & Wesson .44 Magnum was the disco boom, but in a handgun.

When I saw the footage of the SAS men storming the Iranian Embassy with their MP5s I was intrigued. Up until then the British Army had been equipped with a full-sized battle rifle, the 7.62mm FN-FAL (sometimes called the elephant gun by soldiers) and for close-quarter combat the eccentric-looking Sterling submachine gun, a close relative of the WW2 Sten.

By contrast this new gun was sleek, elegant and undeniably European with synthetic materials widely used in its construction. The MP5 really seemed like a gun for the 1980s, a Porsche 911 of a weapon. A machine pistol not in the hands of liberation fighters or maverick detectives but of the death squad of a right-wing monetarist government.

I found out later that one of those held hostage by the Democratic Revolutionary Front for the Liberation of Arabistan was a friend of mine and Wassim's, a Syrian journalist by the name of Mustapha Karkuti who had been trapped at the embassy while waiting to interview the cultural attaché. Mustapha became ill and was released by the DRFLA on day four of the siege, forty-eight hours before the SAS stormed the place.

That Saturday at the Comedy Store Keith Allen, full of fury, performed his whole act wearing a black balaclava pretending he was one of the SAS soldiers who'd stormed the building. It was thrilling that an event could happen in the news then that same day or week you could do a bit about it at the Comedy Store. I loved that about the club. Then one night I quit.

During the summer of 1980 Keith Allen and I took part in a show called *The Last Benefit* at the Albany Empire in south-east London. Located in a former balloon factory or possibly a bow-tie warehouse on Creek Road in Deptford it was the site for community health projects, children's theatre, holiday play-schemes, housing-estate-centred outreach theatre and all manner of community-based awfulness. In the evening there was music and comedy with a bar at the back and tables and chairs for the audience with a gallery running round the first floor. It was the venue after the Comedy Store where we performed most often.

The place had been gutted by a major fire the previous year which, though the culprits were never found, everybody who worked there ascribed to the National Front, since the Albany had hosted so many Rock Against Racism gigs. In my view the arsonist could just as well have been somebody with a grudge against jugglers and clowns.

The Last Benefit was a semi-improvised play about a group of people performing a benefit to save their community centre which ended with me and Keith both doing long stand-up bits for no particular reason, bits that got longer and longer as we competed against each other for more and more laughs.

The audiences at the Albany were always good, receptive and intelligent, so there was not too much stress in doing the show, my main problem being that every night Keith wanted to perform naked. 'That's it, Lex,' he'd say. 'I'm going to take my clothes off tonight.' And every time I'd try and stop him. I was like Scheherazade in *The Thousand and One Nights* who has to tell the king a different tale every evening in order not to be beheaded. For each show I needed to think up a new reason for Keith to keep his clothes on, like my mother was in the audience or there was a party of nuns in the front row. 'Fair enough, Lex,' he'd say. 'Not tonight.' But we both knew it was coming.

On the Saturday when I quit the Comedy Store I'd first of all cycled to Finsbury Town Hall from our flat in Fulham, a trip of five miles or so, to perform an early evening benefit with Threepenny Theatre, doing our entire ninety-minute show. I was riding Linda's bike, a very cheap ladies' machine with no gears, because mine was off the road. Afterwards Cliff told me the benefit had been a great success because it had only made a small loss. Then I pedalled a couple of miles to Charing Cross Station where after carrying the bike up and down several flights of stairs I put it on the train to Deptford. From Deptford Station I rode to the Albany Empire where I performed *The Last Benefit* until about 10.30. It wasn't my best night because unlike Scheherazade I finally ran out of stories and the people of south-east London were treated to their first but not their last sight of Keith Allen's penis.

Then I rode back to the train station, pushing through the beer-smelling crowds returning from a night in the West End as I was going the other way. Once back in London I pedalled my girl's bike to the Comedy Store in time for the show to start at midnight.

The Store could be a volatile environment. One week the audience would be attentive and cultured, the next the whole place could feel on the verge of collapse. This was one of the febrile nights. There was a hysterical feeling in the air and Peter Rosengard, frenetic and twitchy, seemed to have got high on the aura. Keith Allen, having put his clothes back on, had followed me into town and was sitting in the audience but he had told me already that he just wanted to watch the show.

Rosengard however was desperate for him to perform. I dutifully asked Keith again if he wanted to go on but he said once more that no he didn't. I told Peter this but he was insistent and got some of his friends to start chanting 'Keith, Keith, Keith' while I was on stage introducing the next act. As I came off stage getting into the frenzied mood myself I grabbed Peter by the throat and dragged him into the kitchen where I tried to strangle him while banging his head repeatedly against the tiled wall, then I told him I was quitting at the end of the night.

I knew that without me the place would close, which made me sad. All those comedians with nowhere to go, but at least we'd all had the most amazing year. Linda summed it up best: she said when you were young you always had the feeling on a Saturday night that wherever you were there was always a more exciting party going on somewhere else. When you were at the Comedy Store you never had that feeling: there was no better place to be in the whole world.

In the following weeks I would check the papers to see if the ad for the club was gone or casually saunter past on a Saturday night, every time expecting the Comedy Store to be closed, but it is still going strong thirty-five years later.

There is a kind of fiction called counter-factual which imagines different outcomes for world events, such as what if the Nazis rather than the Allies had won the Second World War. But when I hear of a novel that conjectures on what life would be like if Martin Luther had been killed by a wasp so the Protestant Reformation would never have occurred I always think: But he wasn't . . . it did. So what actually happened was that modern comedy as we know it began at the Comedy Store and for the first few months I kept that place going more or less by myself. That is until Tony Allen then Keith Allen, followed by Pete and Nigel, then Rik and Ade came along, though even then I set the tone. Maybe if Linda hadn't seen that ad in *Private Eye* or if I had chosen to stay on in Guernsey and become a bus driver because I already had the jacket the whole comedy revolution and the gigantic arena-filling business that is modern stand-up would have occurred anyway. But it would not have been in that place and not at that time and it would not have looked like it did. You're welcome.

A few months before I left the Comedy Store a very smooth young man called Simon Oakes approached me and Tony and asked if we would consider coming up to the Edinburgh Fringe Festival as part of a number of shows run by a group called Bristol Express based at that city's university. We were to go on at midnight in a lecture hall at the Heriot-Watt University building.

Just after my twenty-eighth birthday Linda and I caught the train up to Scotland. Though we were still in the United Kingdom it was surprising how foreign Edinburgh felt. All the craggy grey-stone buildings set about with towers and tiny windows appeared designed to repel some nameless invading horde; even the libraries, schools and the family-planning clinics looked like they could be defended against a determined enemy. The streets around Edinburgh Waverley Station were swarming with mime artists so maybe it was them the buildings were designed to hold off.

Outside the station we caught a red-and-cream corporation bus heading for the Pentland Hills. Because accommodation in Edinburgh during the festival was so expensive Linda had booked us into a tiny caravan in a woman's garden just beyond the edge of the city where the suburbs gave way to small farmhouses and fields full of rust-coloured Highland cattle who all looked angry as if they were nursing a bad hangover.

From the bus everything appeared very old-fashioned. There didn't seem to be even the small Asian-run supermarkets that you got in London, only tiny and dark general stores often down a small set of stone steps.

On a main shopping street we did see one very distinctive and colourful clothing store. Sigmund Freud had said, 'The great question that has never been answered, and which I have not yet been able to answer, despite my thirty years of research into the feminine soul, is what does a woman want?' This chain was called What Every Woman Wants and the answer to Freud's question seemed to be a pink nylon cardigan with a sequined butterfly stuck on its back.

We got off at the last stop. Behind us the bus turned in a small lay-by and headed back into the city as we dragged our cases over the road to our caravan half hidden amongst hollyhocks and sweet peas in the garden of a pebble-dashed bungalow. The dining table became the bed at night and the toilet was a plastic chemical affair in a sort of walk-in cupboard, little more than a bucket with corrosive blue liquid swilling about in it. At first we felt unable to use this primitive arrangement and instead walked over the road to a nearby petrol station but within days we were happily taking books into the cupboard with us.

The plan was that me and Tony would alternate who went on first for each show. On our opening night I appeared second and I still don't know what went wrong. I think perhaps it was inexperience. I saw myself as a veteran but in the States a comic like Robin Williams would have done over a thousand short, ten-minute spots in front of a diverse range of audiences in basement rooms, bars and clubs before he graduated to a longer set. I had maybe performed comedy just over a hundred times to audiences that were by and large of a similar mindset so in this alien place with a crowd I was unsure of I tried to be ingratiating, to make them like me, but with aggressive and unusual material like mine that didn't work at all. After I came off stage Simon Oakes said to me, 'I think Tony should close the show from now on.' The pitying looks everybody gave me were hard to take.

I went back to the caravan in the same sort of state as I'd been in on Black Pistol Saturday and so my performance on the second night came after me not getting any sleep and spending the entire long day in a frazzled semi-coma. Such was my state of rage and resentment that without conscious thought I completely exploded my act. What had before been in neat packages was now a jagged demented rant, punchlines came before set-ups, stuff started and then stopped dead and into this mix I added something which had been evolving since the start of Threepenny Theatre. This was my Cockney mod poet, not exactly a 'character', more a demonic possession. Inspired to a certain extent by Ian Dury and dub poet Linton Kwesi Johnson and partly by the Cockney drinkers in the Bedford, at some point he had acquired a pork-pie hat which I wore tipped down over my eyes. Originally he'd only performed an early version of my song 'Ullo John! Gotta New Motor?' but that night, fired up as I was, I suddenly just started swearing, a huge torrent of obscenities in a Cockney accent. 'Fuck, cunt, shit, piss, wank!' I began shouting. 'How's your old fuck, cunt, shit, piss, wank? How's the old motor? You cunt, wank, bollocks, shit, wank. You old fuck, cunt, shit, piss, wank.'

A man called Mike Scott who was head of Granada TV tried to get out during my act and left under a torrent of abuse. When I came off after thirty minutes I was greeted with applause not just from the audience but from a crowd that had gathered backstage, people who had drifted in attracted by the sound of me shouting and the accompanying waves of laughter.

After that, every night I would take the last bus into town to do the show. To get back I caught one that stopped about a mile away and then walked through the dark streets past the sleeping cattle up the hill to our caravan. In the afternoons me and Linda would often go to the nearby artificial ski slope, have a hot chocolate and watch people injuring themselves. The only thing we never did was see any shows.

One afternoon Tony came to our caravan and we went for a walk across the fields and lanes, surprisingly for an urban hippy he was able to name all the wild flowers and hedgerow plants. When Tsarist Russia wanted to deal with its radical opponents it would often exile them to Siberia, which from the accounts I'd read seemed like quite a pleasant experience. The conditions were spartan but the revolutionaries were often allowed to bring their wives, and female radicals were also present in the colonies. In the brief Siberian summer there'd be walks and picnics and during the long winter the exiles would organise plays, concerts and discussion groups. This felt pretty much like my Edinburgh Festival.

The Fringe then was entirely university review shows or plays; there was not a single piece of stand-up comedy until me and Tony arrived. The student newspaper's reviewer while liking the show also said something like, 'I don't understand what these guys are doing. It's not a review by medical students and it's not a play. They just stand at a microphone and talk. What's all that about?'

This idyll was nearly ruined when one day towards the end of the first week Molly turned up unannounced at the caravan and tried to stay for a week. She'd chosen her time well because the night before Linda had caught the sleeper train back to London. By then she had given up working full-time so that she could come to as many of my shows as possible but had a part-time job finding accommodation for accountancy students. My mother said she'd been planning 'to stay with this woman I know in Edinburgh'. She hadn't bothered to get an exact address or anything but had gone to a street which more or less sounded like the right one then had knocked on a door at random. The people who answered the door predictably knew nothing of her friend so after telling them to fuck off she had come to our caravan. I put up with this for two nights, sharing a tiny mobile home and the bucket in the cupboard with my mother, but as soon as Linda returned she dragged Molly to the centre of town and forced her onto a coach embarking on a week-long tour of the Highlands. I pitied those poor people on the bus with my mother.

Occasionally when I'd been MC-ing the Comedy Store me and Peter Richardson would cycle home together, westward through the early mornings, he towards Battersea and me on my way to Fulham. As we pedalled past the Ritz, Green Park and a dark and silent Harrods we would talk about how the Comedy Store wasn't really working out but the Alternative Cabaret collective didn't do the job either. What we agreed was perfect about the Comedy Store was its location; being in a strip club gave the show an edgy, authentic, demi-monde feel that the Alternative Cabaret gigs in rooms above pubs, arts centres and Students' Unions lacked. Those shows just felt like a continuation of the old fringe theatre circuit. What Peter and I imagined was finding another strip club in Soho but one where we could choose the acts, control the atmosphere and perform our best material every night without having to cope with an out-of-control audience.

I had forgotten all about these conversations but sometime in my second week in Edinburgh I got a message at the theatre to phone Peter. When we spoke he told me that while I'd been rampaging around strangling people he'd been quietly going about finding us our own place. Peter had secured finance from theatrical impresario Michael White for a new comedy club located in a theatre within the Raymond Revuebar just around the corner from the Comedy Store and he wanted me to be the MC.

MERRY CHRISTMAS, MR SAKAMOTO

Despite me not liking Soho much, for the second time in eighteen months I was a major part of the opening of a new club right in its heart.

A few weeks before opening night there was a meeting at his house in Battersea of the comedians Peter had invited to be the founding acts at what was now called the Comic Strip Club. They were: me, Peter Richardson, Nigel Planer, Rik Mayall, Adrian Edmondson, Arnold Brown and Pamela Stephenson. I think Pamela had sort of invited herself. Unlike the rest of us she was already a big star from appearing in the TV show *Not the Nine O'Clock News*. She had decided she wanted to do stand-up comedy but had made the rather odd decision to have an act written for her by several leading British playwrights. Harold Pinter might have been adept at claustrophobic comedies of menace or elegiac evocations of the shifting nature of memory but he couldn't write a killer gag to save his life so she was there on the opening night but not for many nights after.

Sitting with the others in Pete's little house I experienced a sudden surge of affection for this new group I was joining, then I remembered I'd felt exactly the same thing during the first meeting of Alternative Cabaret. Now those comics in my old gang were starting to get on my nerves. The fondness I had once felt for them was fading because when you were on a bill and there were two or three comedians all covering the same topics – the riots, Thatcher – followed by Keith Allen throwing things at the audience and/or taking his clothes off it was hard to stand out. But now at the Comic Strip I would be the only one doing the political stuff.

My affection for the Comic Strip gang (including Dawn French and Jennifer Saunders when they turned up a couple of months later) might not have been entirely authentic at first, but these were the people whom I would spend the next four years with: we would embark together on a rollercoaster ride that would take us all ultimately to success, wealth and fame. Over that time my affection for every one of them would deepen into a profound and sentimental love which as Linda always pointed out was almost certainly not reciprocated.

Our new club, the Raymond Revuebar, home of the Festival of Erotica, was in a flagstoned alley named Walker's Court, a pedestrian passageway which linked Berwick Street Market, even at night still slick with discarded cabbage leaves, to Beak Street, a narrow and sunless road of hardware stores, pubs and old-fashioned tailors. After dark the alley was brightly lit by the light spilling from the windows of the little shops that lined both sides, tiny outlets selling either falafels or sex toys. The Raymond Revuebar was all gilt mirrors, flock wallpaper and red carpet, resembling a fancy Piccadilly tea room where all the female staff were inexplicably naked.

The Boulevard Theatre, one of two auditoria within the Revuebar, now renamed the Comic Strip Club, was a more theatrical venue than the Comedy Store. The seats were arranged in rows rather than tables and chairs, though you could bring drinks in from the adjacent bar. There was a proper stage with wings and a corridor giving access to two backstage dressing rooms and Peter had hired a house band, Rowland Rivron, Simon Brint and Rod Melvin, which brought a proper cabaret atmosphere to the proceedings and encouraged us all to use music in our acts.

Almost as important in the early days as the acts was Michael White who was providing the money. Just before we began I had been whining about some performance problem to Michael. He simply stared at me and said in his languid voice, 'You haven't chosen an easy profession, Alexei.' I don't know why this remark has stayed with me. I certainly found it bracing to have my self-pity challenged in this way but also I'd never before thought that I'd actually chosen comedy or that standing on a stage yelling was a profession.

Nobody I've spoken to remembers a single thing about the opening night of the Comic Strip and neither do I, which is odd. It certainly happened and there are many vivid recollections of the next nine months but of that night there remains not a scintilla of memory in the minds of all those that were there. Perhaps this lack of recall is because it did not have the magical, riotous feel of the first night of the Comedy Store a year before.

All the core performers had instinctively begun wearing suits though throughout the following year none of us had thought to get these suits cleaned ever, so pretty soon they were all stiff and stinking with sweat. Rik and Ade had bought their outfits at a discount place called the Houndsditch Warehouse. They had been made in Communist Romania out of what looked like cheap purple carpet and cost £10 each which wasn't a lot of money even back then.

And on stage there was not much mucking about. Everybody made sure they did their best material, even the oddest member of the troupe, Arnold Brown. Arnold was still working as an accountant and much older than the rest of us. At the Comedy Store he had been a bit of a joke, dying most nights, but both me and Pete had been there to witness this one show when somehow he had suddenly caught fire and performed for over half an hour, sophisticated ideas pouring out of him, an expression on his face which suggested that even he didn't know how he was doing it.

Given that the Comic Strip was part of a long-term plan to establish our own place and build our careers the second weekend of a club could be almost as important, indeed sometimes more important than the first, but the following Friday and Saturday I wasn't there because of a long-standing booking with Alternative Cabaret to play a series of gigs in Dublin. Peter Richardson pleaded with me not to go but I mulishly insisted that the engagement had to be honoured. This was one of the things I did, be stupidly and stubbornly loyal when there was absolutely no reason to be, while on the other hand I would often let down those who'd been good to me. The gigs in Dublin were by way of a farewell because, as my future was now firmly tied to the Comic Strip, they were the last that I would play with Alternative Cabaret.

The last time I had been on an aeroplane was when me and Linda had taken a holiday to Greece in 1977. We had come into land at Athens Airport during a lightning storm in a rickety old Boeing 707 which had confirmed in me a nascent terror of flying. Over the next few years, Linda became increasingly adept at finding innovative and original ways to get us to distant places in not much more time, and at not much more cost, than it took to get there by plane. In this case to travel to Dublin we first took a train from Euston to Liverpool. At Lime Street a bus was waiting that transferred us from the station to the Pier Head. At the Pier Head a long gangway led to a pontoon that gently bobbed up and down on the brown river and from where there operated an experimental, water-jet-powered hydrofoil service that on a good day got you to Ireland in just over three hours.

To be in transit in your home town felt odd. On the bus we passed Central Station where I used to sell our Maoist newspaper to nobody and the pub where the man looking for a fight called me a 'greebo', while from the river we could clearly see Linda's parents' block of flats. We had not told any of our parents that we were there. Linda's would have probably been all right about it but I still half expected Molly to leap out and stop the bus with her lollipop.

After we cast off the craft turned in a wide arc and headed slowly towards the mouth of the Mersey. Once out in open water the engine note grew deeper as the craft rose up on its underwater wings and charged towards America. This service did not survive one harsh winter on the Irish Sea but it was still a spectacular way to arrive in Dublin swooshing across the water until we splashed down right in the centre of town where from the dock we were able to walk to our hotel. On the way I was surprised to see beggars posted every few yards on the bridges over the River Liffey; it made Ireland seem very backward and inhumane. I could not imagine such a thing ever happening back home but almost by the time we returned they were a common sight on the streets of what I liked to think of as 'Thatcher's so-called Britain'.

The working lives of the old-time British comics and their US counterparts would have been ones of endless travel, nights or weeks spent in unfamiliar and unfriendly towns where in the evening you were supposed to make the inhabitants laugh. The lives of the Comic Strip/Alternative Cabaret comics were unusual in that we had largely worked in our home towns, where we understood the lives of our audience and slept in our own beds at night. By travelling to Ireland I felt like I was embarking on another step towards the true life of the comedian, a world of bizarre hotels and strange encounters that flavoured, poisoned and distorted your view of the world.

Linda had paid 50p to the Irish Tourist Board for a booking at one of their recommended small hotels. This turned out to be a gloomy building in central Dublin named the Adelphi. It was much shabbier than we expected, dingy with peeling paintwork. I think I might have imagined the chalk outline of a body on the floor in reception but there was certainly an empty fish tank. As the taciturn receptionist showed us to our room on the top floor we noticed that the landing light wasn't working and the stair carpet ran out after the first floor. When we finally reached our room he had to give the door a substantial shove to get it open and inside it was dark and dirty. We put our bags down but hanging up my coat I noticed that carved with a sharp object into the broken door of the wardrobe were the words, 'If you think the room's bad wait until you have the breakfast.'

We checked out immediately though this left us in a bit of a fix because we didn't have any Irish currency. However as we wandered the rain-slicked streets a man in a top hat suddenly stepped out of a doorway and said to us, 'If you're looking to change money this is the place,' pointing to the only illuminated shop in a darkened row which turned out to be a bureau de change experimentally staying open late for that one night. After that we walked a little further until we came upon a grand old hotel called the Clarence where we took a room.

As we were sitting in the bar late that night a drunken priest came up to us clutching a fresh-faced young man by the arm and said, 'I'm going to take up a post in Rome tomorrow and this is one of my pupils, Declan. He's the one who's organised this lovely party for me.' Then he reeled away.

The young man watched him stagger off then turned to me and asked, 'Are you Declan?' Molly's adoption of all things Irish, the blarney and the bollocking rebel nonsense, had given me an aversion to the idea of the country as some sort of magical place but you had to admit that some mad stuff did go on there.

After we got back home I wrote a letter of complaint to the Irish Tourist Board which said, 'If the Adelphi is one of your recommended hotels I would hate to see one that failed to meet your stringent standards.' In return they refunded our 50p.

This was the first time I had performed in a foreign country. In a shabby arts centre the way the Dublin audiences responded was explosive. Our acts were shocking enough in Britain, still a country with a relatively liberal climate, but here in repressive, corrupt and priest-ridden Ireland nearly anything you said caused a jolt of horrified and scandalised delight. This is turn spurred me on particularly to say more and more outrageous things until I made some unpleasant remarks about the Pope that would in later years come back to haunt me.

The rest of Alternative Cabaret set off for a tour of other towns in Ireland but having fulfilled my commitment I returned to the Comic Strip for the third weekend. My missing the previous Friday and Saturday did not seem to have affected the health of the club.

Slowly we began to gain press attention, though the first intelligent piece the place got was not in the *Sunday Times* or the *Observer* but from that erudite publication the *London Review of Books* – a long article written by the critic and author Ian Hamilton. He wrote:

> The Comic Strip's compère and guiding star is a Comedy Store veteran called Alexei Sayle, a portly, spring-heeled Liverpudlian with a convict haircut, a Desperate Dan chin and an Oliver Hardy silkette suit well buttoned at his bulging gut . . . Sayle hurtles onto the stage, spraying the audience with saliva. A big man who can move like lightning; a pathologically aggrieved pub lout who's read some books. Sayle's posture is manically contemptuous, his rhythm a hysterical crescendo of obscenity with spat-out satirical asides. Both the stance and the timing are near-perfect, and within seconds he

has the audience agape. Most of them, it seemed, had never been called cunts before.

The bouncers at the Raymond Revuebar had a simple rule of thumb for who was directed where. If they reeked of after-shave they were sent to the strip show, if they smelt of beer they came to us. These men also had very fixed ideas about what anybody Japanese wished to see, which meant that Ryuichi Sakamoto – musician, activist, producer, writer, actor and member of the pioneering electronic music group Yellow Magic Orchestra – got shoved into the Festival of Erotica no matter how much he protested that he'd come to see the comedy. He was one of the celebrities who began to visit the Comic Strip. Dustin Hoffman sat unsmiling through the show while Bianca Jagger's visit was celebrated with a *News of the World* front-page headline splash as 'Bianca's Four-Letter Night Out'. I was quoted as saying, 'I won't tone down my act for Bianca nor none of the nobs.' Which though the paper had never actually spoken to me was sort of about right.

When we'd had our initial meeting at Peter's house there had been some talk about the Comic Strip becoming a co-operative with each member having a single non-transferable vote, yearly elections and an upper and lower house based on the Norwegian parliamentary system, all of which horrified me. Having spent years in left-wing politics I never wanted to attend that kind of meeting ever again. No good ever came from meetings: the Russian Revolution was just a meeting that got out of hand. As it turned out I needn't have worried because Peter Richardson ran everything apart from the show itself, which suited me. Peter had always had a vision of the club as a springboard to bigger things and in the middle of our run there he raised finance for a film, part documentary, part fiction, based around the Comic Strip.

On the night when we had a large crew in – lighting, sound, two cameras filming the show on stage – Robin Williams turned up and said he wanted to go on. I told him he could but he'd only be able to do fifteen minutes rather than his usual hour because if we went past midnight we'd go into terrible overtime with the film crew. 'I have to do an hour,' he said. 'David Bowie's with me, I've told him I do an hour.'

'I don't care,' I replied.

'I'll buy the club,' he said.

'You can't, we don't own it. It belongs to a bouffant-haired pornographer.'

So Robin, accepting the ruling of the MC, only did fifteen minutes in front of the crowd. Then he came off stage and performed the other forty-five minutes of his act to me alone, pressed up against a wall in the corridor outside the dressing rooms. Occasionally out of the corner of my eye I would see people appear round the corner, realise what was going on and slowly back away. This was the first time I'd encountered what I came to think of over time as 'comedian's disease': a compulsion to perform, whether you were on the stage or not, to constantly be 'on', to relentlessly make people laugh. Anybody who knew me could attest to the fact that I didn't suffer from that particular addiction.

TV and record producers as well as celebrities began to show up at the Comic Strip, which meant that my days started to fill up with meetings. Not the political type, but ones where you met somebody in a bar or a restaurant or an office and then you discussed a project that was never going to happen. I had lunches with the editors of women's magazines, drinks with dodgy chancers who wanted to put comedy bits into the soft-porn videotapes they sold and I worked for ages with a woman photographer on a comical photo strip that was supposed to run in the *Daily Mirror*. At first I didn't realise that most of these projects were never going to happen; I obsessed about how I was going to fit them all in.

I'd say to Linda, 'If I move the documentary about the Soviet Union those guys who've got backing from the Yemeni Oil Fund want to make to mid-June, that means I'll be able to fit in the comedy special in Carlisle I've been talking about with Border Television in August, but then I'll have to say no to the puppet show at the inner-city farm at least until autumn . . .'

Finally Linda said, 'Look, chances are not a single one of these things is ever going to happen ever so you can just relax and say yes to everything, then if one of them does go ahead you'll be able to sort it out.' Which was reassuring and depressing at the same time.

One of those wanting to work with the whole group of us was a film director called Richard Loncraine, who had made a film with the band Slade called *Slade in Flame*. He invited the whole Comic Strip to dinner at a smart Chinese restaurant called Gallery Rendezvous in Soho which featured on its walls several large photographs of the chat-show host Michael Parkinson accompanied by his fulsome encomium to the restaurant. The only Chinese restaurants I had been in before had been the takeaway at the bottom of our flats or late-night places in Chinatown that served white wine in teapots after the pubs closed. Unfortunately Keith Allen found out about the dinner and came along in his role as our own personal Lord of Misrule and started a massive row so we all ended up shouting and screaming at each other; even the normally placid Dawn and Jennifer joined in. The following day Richard Loncraine sent us an angry and hurt letter saying he had never before come across a group of performers who behaved so badly.

Our relationship might have ended there, but as well as being a film director Richard Loncraine was an inventor of novelty items. A company he owned manufactured a room light called Jonathan Livingroom Seagull, which was a pendant light set inside a plastic seagull. When we'd first met, he'd offered to give me one for free. Most days in the following weeks I would ring him or his assistant, send telegrams or write letters asking them when my seagull light would be arriving, until finally, months later, a badly wrapped parcel with the minimum amount of postage stuck on it appeared at our flat. By then I'd gone off the idea of having an illuminated seagull in my living room.

The television company that showed the greatest interest in the early days of the Comic Strip was Granada TV, based in Manchester – the company Roger Graef had been working for. Unfortunately, while they had a sure touch for documentaries and dramas, they were less competent with comedy. Granada would get various members of the Comic Strip up to their home town to make all kinds of different programmes, then they would panic and not transmit them. This experience of going up to Manchester became so regular that I developed a routine. Having a bit of money to spend, I had recently bought myself from Harrods a big old-fashioned Raleigh bike in traditional green with an enclosed chain case, which you could ride while wearing a suit. I would pedal to Euston then load it onto the Manchester train and at the other end cycle through the centre of the city to the Granada studios in Salford. I liked the idea of riding a bike through a town I didn't live in.

While most provincial British cities appeared run-down and bombed-out, Manchester, Italianate where Liverpool was neoclassical, had an almost European air – a city like Turin or Munich that was energetic and in some parts even prosperous. There were a couple of Italian restaurants that I was taken to by TV producers that weren't entirely terrible and a thriving, garishly neon-lit Chinatown where the cooking was often as good as or better than in London.

Granada had plans for a late-night show starring the Cockney newspaper editor Derek Jameson called *It's All News to Me!* and they kept paying for me, Rik, Ade, Dawn and Jennifer to come up to Manchester to make endless non-transmission pilots. They would tell us how great and talented we were and how they were going to be the ones to make us famous but then they would get us to perform terrible old-fashioned material. At one point they wanted me to do some racist sketch. I should have just come out and said that the material was rubbish but somehow I didn't know the way to do it, so instead of refusing I just performed it very badly, slurring my words and moving my body in a robotic fashion. I found a pair of headphones lying around and noticed that if you plugged them into a jack socket in the wall you could hear what they were talking about in the gallery. The subject under discussion was me. 'He's completely out of control,' they were saying.

One TV show that did get made was called *Boom Boom Out Go the Lights,* produced and directed by a young BBC producer/director Paul Jackson and featuring the best acts from the Comedy Store, the Comic Strip and Alternative Cabaret.

When the first *Boom Boom* . . . went out in October 1980 I rang Molly to ask her what she'd thought.

'Well . . .' she said. 'Keith Allen wasn't very good either.'

I'd thought that my being on the TV would make a huge difference but it didn't seem to have any effect at all.

At the end of the summer we closed down the Comic Strip Club. Peter had booked us into the national tour which began on the 18th of September. We travelled in a proper large coach striped in contemporary colours of brown, beige and yellow with a toilet, seats and tables at the front and a lounge area in brown velour at the back, just like a rock band.

The tour manager too was from the rock business: a tall muscular man with thick glasses by the name of Nigel who had previously worked for The Damned and was inclined to treat us as if we were the same sort of dissolute outfit as they had been. 'I don't want to find no fucking slags in your room, you cunts!' he would bellow, and, 'I want you down in the lobby at nine firty or the coach is fucking leaving without you, no matter how fucking wasted on scag you are!'

Sometimes he'd threaten to hit us. None of us had the nerve to point out to him that several of us were married and our wives were accompanying us on tour, or that we had been college lecturers, accountants or schoolteachers in our previous lives.

Peter's plan was that we would try and re-create the dangerous atmosphere of the Soho venue by playing places that carried a similar sense of loucheness. Our opening night was in a porn cinema on Sauchiehall Street in Glasgow followed by a nightclub in Edinburgh then an old cinema in the Jesmond district of Newcastle and after that a German-style subterranean *Bierkeller* in Leeds. This didn't really work out, the venues often being poorly equipped in term of sound, lights and basic hygiene.

Peter also seemed to have tried to find hotels with a similar demi-monde feel to the venues. In each town we appeared to have been booked into places that were Sheffield's or Leeds's closest equivalent to New York's Chelsea Hotel, the place where Sid Vicious stabbed and murdered his girlfriend, except that Ipswich's version of the Chelsea lacked any of the charm of its rat-infested New York cousin. For years afterwards when me and Linda were in some town and we'd see a hotel that was mouldy and decaying with drug addicts stumbling out of the doors or police tape around the entrance we'd say, 'There's the Comic Strip hotel.'

But struggling every night against inadequate auditoriums and awful hotels – in Glasgow, Dawn and Jennifer shared a room with a terrible smell that they finally tracked down to a soiled nappy stuffed inside the television, which warmed up every time they turned it on; Peter's wife Marta found a boiled egg in the desk drawer of their room; in Sheffield the room was so cold I had to sleep with my hat on; in Leeds, Adrian and

Rowland tumbled over and over down the sweeping central staircase of the faded station hotel wrestling each other for the ownership of the insides of a wine box which resembled a bladder full of urine – meant that we all grew much closer to each other. Because we were a little bit older, Linda and I sort of evolved into the rest of the group's parents, though my parenting style would probably have got me flagged up by social services even in those more relaxed times.

The Secret Policeman's
Career Opportunity

In the early 1980s a staple guest of TV chat shows was a drawling, affected, upper-class, corpse-like fop called Malcolm Muggeridge. Muggeridge had in his youth been extremely left-wing, to the extent that when he was a newspaper correspondent in Moscow in the 1920s he had suppressed stories of the famine created by the Soviet government's forced collectivisations. In later life he changed completely and became an extremely reactionary, religious 'moral' campaigner. Muggeridge was partly credited with turning super-Albanian nun Mother Teresa into a media superstar and was a leading figure in something called the Festival of Light, a hysterical Christian group that protested against sex on TV and more or less everywhere else. This was rank hypocrisy since in his youth Muggeridge had been a sexual libertine and only embraced abstinence once his own ravening libido began to diminish. To me there was something sad and tortured about this man, his sweaty self-loathing and religious mania part of an attempt to try and locate the certainties of his youth. I didn't believe that his earlier left-wing conviction was any different to his later right-wing Christianity. He had simply gone from being one kind of bastard to being another kind of bastard.

One of the unexpected ways in which my upbringing as the son of Communists had helped prepare me for the challenges of celebrity, an advantage that my fellow comedians didn't have, was in the matter of staying true to yourself. The idea of the traitor, the sell-out, the apostate was central to Joe and Molly's state of mind. Even when I was quite small we would be out shopping in town and my mother or father would gesticulate towards some harmless-looking individual and say in a whisper, 'See him over there trying on gloves, he left the Party over Hungary in 1956 and now he's . . .' Here they'd pause before revealing the full horror. 'A Labour councillor!' Or, 'Don't look, but that woman by the bacon counter, she used to be in CND but now she's . . . joined the Air Force!' At first I couldn't see anything different about the people my parents pointed out but over time it did seem to me that they possessed a certain haunted quality, an air of sadness, and though their mood probably wasn't helped by being whispered about in shops by a red-haired woman and a man in a trilby hat accompanied by a silent watchful boy I sensed that the main critical voice was within their heads, that they themselves were aware on some level of the abandonment of their younger more idealistic self and it corroded them from the inside.

I did not want to end up like that. The trick it seemed to me was to not be blind to the many faults of the left while at the same time to try and stay true to those core values of workers' rights, social justice and equality.

Me doing fund-raising benefits for left-wing organisations was an attempt to stay connected with those ideals.

As a left-wing entertainer it was accepted that you would inevitably perform unpaid at concerts in aid of various radical causes – doing benefits had become a sort of national service for alternative comedians. There was very little pleasure in appearing at them though. I did a bit about benefit concerts in my act: how you told a joke, then there was a pause while the audience vetted the joke for its political content, possible sexism, any hints of neo-colonialism, adherence to the theory of dialectical and historical materialism, and only once it was cleared would they laugh – it was like doing your material over a faulty phone line.

I went up to Sheffield to appear in a show at the Crucible Theatre in support of Nicaragua's revolutionary, anti-American, pro-moustache Sandinista government. Following the show the cast and their friends were introduced to the guest of honour – David Blunkett the radical left-wing leader of Sheffield City Council. After the line-up Linda said, 'I don't like that man, there's something funny about his eyes.'

That same summer I agreed to appear at an open-air show in Hyde Park: speeches, music and comedians protesting at the Thatcher government's assault on the GLC's enlightened policy of subsidising bus and tube fares. On the same day, as part of a coordinated twenty-four hours of action, the transport unions mounted a well-supported strike, the efficiency of which meant that there were no buses or tubes running and therefore there was not one single person at the benefit.

But then in the time between the Comic Strip Club closing and the nationwide tour beginning I received a phone call offering me a spot on a fund-raising show which promised to be both an experience to perform at and potentially a massive boost to my career. The person on the other end of the phone said, 'Cleese has given you the call.' What they meant was that the man from Monty Python and *Fawlty Towers* was inviting me to take part in *The Secret Policeman's Other Ball*, the latest in a number of benefits in aid of Amnesty International he'd organised over the years. The show would take place at the Theatre Royal, Drury Lane, on four nights starting on Wednesday 9 September 1981.

On the afternoon before the show there was a sort of press-conference-come-rehearsal at the Theatre Royal with most of the cast present. Apart from me, who was unknown outside Soho, everybody on the bill was a famous name. There was Sting, Bob Geldof, Eric Clapton, Phil Collins, Rowan Atkinson, Jeff Beck, Alan Bennett, John Bird, Donovan, Jasper Carrott, Graham Chapman, John Cleese, Billy Connolly, Barry Humphries, Griff Rhys Jones, Pamela Stephenson, Pete Townshend and Victoria Wood. In my arrogance I felt sorry for all of them because they were the past and I was the future coming to wreck their cosy world. The previous *Secret Policeman's Ball* had made a gigantic star out of Rowan Atkinson and I believed this one would do the same for me.

Stephen Pile the *Sunday Times* columnist who was there that afternoon described me as 'eschewing the bourgeois comforts of a chair to squat on the floor'.

The only impediment to me smashing it on opening night was that I first had to have a row with Jasper Carrott over ownership of the word 'Guildford'. Each of us knew that the other had a gag in his act which ended with the name of the town as the punchline and neither of us wanted to change it because we knew no other town would work as well, but we also knew that two comedians couldn't both say 'Guildford' on one night.

After protracted negotiations I said to him, 'Who's on first?'

'You are,' he replied.

'Well fuck you then,' I said. 'I'm using it.'

So I did. I said, 'And people come from Guildford to see it!' and it got a huge laugh while Jasper was forced to change his punchline to 'Basingstoke' which died a terrible, terrible death.

Danny Baker wrote in the *New Musical Express* that he found the first half of the show dull:

> Except for Alexei Sayle who thundered through his slot like a train. Whereas what surrounded his spot came measured and perfunctory his punchy script boomed all over wherever it wanted. His rock-hard distaste for just about anything 'went a little too far' for more than one half-time bar dweller. He was great. For the first time that night, well, in years, I felt I was at a live concert.

This was my favourite kind of review: not only saying I was brilliant but that everybody else was shit.

But although I was the hit of the live show it was perplexing to discover that that achievement did not turn me into Rowan Atkinson.

Danny Baker also wrote that the music got in the way. It was certainly true of Bob Geldof. I quite liked The Boomtown

Rats but my memory is that he turned up uninvited and insisted on performing 'I Don't Like Mondays', and when he sang the line 'I'm going to shoo-oo-oo-hoo-hoo-hoot . . .' Geldof paused portentously, eyes jammed shut as if amazed at the depths of his own emotion, for such a long time that the audience began laughing at him.

Jasper Carrott didn't hold a grudge. After we'd both been on we fancied a drink, so me and Linda took him during the show to a very seedy after-hours actors' club called Macready's that I was more or less a member of. It was only a short walk away but Jasper suggested we drive there in his Jaguar. 'Don't worry,' his manager said. 'Bob [which was Jasper's real name] always finds a parking space. It's his secret talent.' (Just like Linda's ability not to step in dog shit.)

And it was true. In the heart of busy Covent Garden magically a Jaguar-sized space appeared right outside the club and then, when we returned to the theatre, there was a space there too. To this day whenever a brilliant parking spot appears me and Linda say to each other 'Jasper's space'.

Apart from performing duties at *The Secret Policeman's Other Ball*, there was a life backstage, people I had been watching on the TV for a decade, musicians whose records I had bought, actors I'd seen in the theatre came and went. I could see what a powerful drug it was, the warm, narcotic embrace of celebrity, the cloud nine of limousine, manager, agent, entourage and being mates with big stars. I chatted to a few, John Bird and Graham Chapman, but the only one I was really interested in was Alan Bennett, so one night during the run I went over and sat down next to him and began talking but after I'd said a few sentences he just got up and ran away.

Pamela Stephenson's interest in doing stand-up comedy had morphed into an interest in doing one particular stand-up comedian – Billy Connolly. They had recently begun an affair and when I left through the stage door with them one night it was the first time that I walked into that waterfall of clacking, blinding flashbulbs exploding in your face. I felt guilty because I'd got to know Pamela's husband, the actor Nicholas Ball, who was then starring in the detective show *Hazell*. Sometimes he'd come down to the Comic Strip Club looking for his wife because she'd told him she'd been performing with us, but she was never there.

At the end of the show all the cast were supposed to troop on stage and sort of stand there looking soulful while the musicians played Bob Dylan's 'I Shall Be Released'. It felt awkward and self-congratulatory and I refused to take part, so instead I just sort of lurked in the wings, gawkily jigging about.

I could see the attraction of it all but I considered I was done for if I didn't face the world clear-eyed and unencumbered by megastar friendships. A lot of my comedy came from pointing out the hypocrisies of other entertainers and if they were my mates I wouldn't be able to do it so I resolved never again to appear in a celebrity benefit show and never to become close to any massive show business stars.

Except for Sting. Backstage he'd said to me, 'You're funny, aren't you?'

And I replied, 'Yes.'

And we became friends for a while before Linda could stop me. After all, I figured his background was quite similar to mine: he was a working-class grammar-school boy and an ex-teacher from the North who had raised himself by his own talent. Plus I thought if you're going to be mates with a super-star it might as well be the biggest of them all.

Boom Boom Out Goes Your Career

The new consumers, the ones shopping at Habitat, were about to get their own commercial TV channel, a channel on which they could watch programmes that appealed exclusively to them, and in turn advertisers could show them things that they really wanted to buy: wines from Bulgaria, small cigars in a tin and different kinds of cheese. Channel 4 was scheduled to begin broadcasting in mid-1982 with a remit to be edgy and modern, but some had concerns. There was a group led by Jonathan Dimbleby called something like the Channel 4 Third World Advocacy Group comprised of those in the media who were worried that the new station wouldn't commission enough depressing programmes about Africa and Asia (their apprehension, at least in the early years, proved unfounded).

Twelve months before the station launched, this group asked me if I would appear in a video arguing their case, which would to go out as part of some advocacy slot in the dead hours of Sunday morning on ITV. With my new policy of saying yes to any old bollocks I agreed and arranged to meet the writer at a big house in Hampstead where we would also shoot the video. The writer's name was David Stafford and the house he lived in belonged to Bill Oddie of the Goodies. When Bill and his wife Jean Hart separated they bought houses next door to each other overlooking the southern ponds on Hampstead Heath so that their children's lives wouldn't be too disrupted. Jean had also become a feminist, and the money from the hit songs Bill had written for the Goodies ('The In-Betweenies', 'Black Pudding Bertha', 'Nappy Love' and 'Funky Gibbon') paid for her house to be filled with angry women while Bill's was occupied by sad single men. There was an opening on the first floor next to a noticeboard announcing pap smears and gestalt therapy workshops where the men's house and the women's house were joined, though the men, like vampires, were not allowed to cross the threshold to the women's side unless invited. David Stafford was in the men's house because he was in the process of getting divorced from his first wife.

Me and David got on immediately. He was from a working-class family in Birmingham and his Third World piece was very funny when it really didn't need to be. The team from Thames TV turned up to shoot the video but the director was obviously not too committed to the piece – his first words were, 'I'm going to the pub,' hinting perhaps at why he'd been relegated to filming solemn crap for early morning access slots. A young boy of about fifteen whose job as far as I could tell had been up until that moment to get coffee and bacon sandwiches for the rest of the crew took up directing duties, actually turning his baseball cap backwards as he did so to denote his new role.

Despite all the shows and programmes that never happened I was still very busy. When we finally got a video recorder ourselves, we didn't own it but rather it was rented from one of the many TV hire companies on North End Road Market. The VCRs you got from the rental companies all bore the name of some established British electronic company such as Pye, Rediffusion or Bush but with my concerns about the health of British manufacturing I would always check the maker's plate on the back, which would inevitably reveal that the machines were in fact made in Japan by a Japanese corporation. The rental shop had merely stuck a plastic badge or a flimsy transfer on the VCR with the logo of the British company on it. I suspected that even the plastic badge wasn't made in the UK.

What I found almost as impressive as watching the recorded programmes (which after all were still just programmes, though a lot more blurry) was the fast-forward facility. To be able to press a button and suddenly see people running around at high speed, cars hectically whizzing about and clouds in the sky scudding by at supersonic velocity was an amazing thing. As my career took off I was reminded of those speeded-up tapes because that's what my life felt like. I met more people, did more things, ate more snacks, went to more places in a week than I had done in a whole year before I had become a comedian. In my fast-forward life I certainly encountered a lot more of those who'd been to public school and Oxford or Cambridge University than I would have ever done in a hundred years outside show business. It seemed to me that those working-class kids such as Bill Oddie who'd gone to Oxford or Cambridge struggled greatly with who they were. In the early days of the Comic Strip Club we'd received a letter from Bill addressed to all of us. He congratulated us on our success but also urged us not to make some of the mistakes he'd made, to stay true to ourselves and not to assume that things would always be easy. The others sneered at the earnestness of this missive but I found it touching.

With David Stafford we had lunch with Bill. The houses backed on to Hampstead Heath's Number 1 pond so out of the large rear windows there was an idyllic vision of reeds and silver water. We all got very drunk and Linda insisted that Bill come to our flat because there were some amazing rare birds that could be seen outside our twelfth-floor window, which, when he questioned her, turned out to be seagulls. In the bathroom there were some fluffy white towels that had printed on them 'Property of the BBC Make-up Department'. I thought how wonderful it was to have towels like these and I vowed one day I too would steal them from the BBC.

The policy of saying yes proved itself when I got the offer to make a series for Capital Radio who wanted something other than music to broadcast. I immediately thought of David Stafford and asked him if he'd like to help me write it.

This became *Alexei Sayle and the Fish People*, which won the Pye Radio Award (forerunner of the Sony Radio Award) for 1982. This was the first time ever that a comedy prize had gone to a station other than the BBC but I didn't use that in any way. In that year I also won an advertising award for a radio voice-over I'd done and in both cases the crusty old moustachioed chairman of the organisation giving the award began his speech by saying, 'It's been a very poor year but . . .' Apart from winning the award I had also achieved my ambition of going through the doors of Capital Radio in Euston

Tower rather than the Civil Service entrance. It didn't feel as big a deal as I'd hoped.

At that time London had three listings magazines of which two were related to each other, *Time Out* and *City Limits*. When it had been founded in 1968, in accordance with the spirit of the age, *Time Out* had been a collective in which everybody from the cleaner to the restaurant critic got paid the same and they all got to vote endlessly on editorial policy. In 1981 the owner decided to end this practice, so some of the more idealistic staffers left to form *City Limits*. You can judge what kind of a person read *City Limits* from the fact that in 1981 I won the magazine's Comedian of the Year award, the only time in my entire career when I got an award decided by popular vote. The trophy was a saucer and I said in my acceptance speech, 'I can't tell you how little this means to me.'

These days I would give anything for any kind of award, no matter what it was I would accept it with gratitude, but back then my arrogance kept me from appreciating what these prizes meant and from utilising them to further my career.

The editor of *Time Out* took me to lunch and offered me a weekly column. I had already done some writing for women's magazines and such but I was particularly excited to get the offer of a regular column, because for somebody who didn't believe almost anything said by anybody about anything I had an inordinate amount of respect for columns and columnists. The journalists who wrote them always seemed to speak with such certainty that I would find myself getting swept up by their conviction. One would thunder, 'Israel is on the brink of making peace with the Palestinians,' and I would think: Oh that's nice, Wassim will be able to go home soon. Then another would declaim, 'Israel is not interested in peace ever,' and I would think: Oh dear, Wassim's never going to get home. (A more likely outcome.) I was also strongly influenced by columnists who wrote such things as, 'This album marks a stonking return to form by David Bowie.' Which was how I came to own so many terrible David Bowie albums.

My column was called 'Great Bus Journeys of the World' and, like the radio series, was written with David Stafford. It was ostensibly the record of a different bus journey I took every week but that was just a hook on which to hang whatever we could come up with. One night David got drunk on mescal and for a week wrote piles of hilarious dreamlike stuff that he could never replicate no matter how much of the Mexican spirit he subsequently drank.

In December 1981 I was appearing on a mixed bill at the Albany Empire in Deptford. By then David Stafford, as well as writing with me, was providing the music for the songs I sang in my live act. I had observed that no performer functioned alone, rather they gathered a group around them of writers, musicians, agents, managers, people who helped them in their work. I had that too, except that they were all David Stafford. Sting came along to the Albany too, we travelled to southeast London together in his Daimler limousine. As we swept in, the door of the Albany was opened for us by a uniformed commissionaire: it was my ex-partner Bill.

My memory is that Sting got out of the car and so that he wouldn't be recognised by the public he put on a motorcycle helmet, which he wore as he walked to his seat before taking it off, at least I think he took it off because I've also got an image of him watching the entire show wearing a full-face crash helmet.

Keith Allen was the MC that night – an authority role he should never have been given. The day before the show the Communist government in Poland had declared martial law in response to growing dissent, and a number of people had been killed by security forces. For his opening bit Keith went out and made some unpleasant comments about the opposition movement in Poland, I don't know why since he was never that political, but they'd obviously got on his nerves. What he didn't know until they began shouting at him was that there was a large group of Polish people sitting at a table near the front, but they soon made their presence known.

Keith came off shaken. 'I don't know, Lex,' he said. 'I can't back down now.'

But when he went back out it initially seemed like he would. 'I realise I made some unfortunate remarks,' he said in a contrite voice. 'So I'd like to apologise in a song.' Then he sat down at the piano and began singing. 'All Poles are cunts, all Poles are cunts. Fuck you, Poles, you're all cunts.'

The whole audience started shouting and as Keith moved to the microphone somebody threw a bottle at him from the balcony. It missed and instead hit a tall bald man in a black sweater and black trousers who was at the same moment getting up on the stage to remonstrate with Keith. This man stepped into the spotlight, blood pouring from the deep wound in his shiny skull, to moan, 'I came here to have a nice Christmas but instead I'm going to spend it in Greenwich District Hospital.' (Which I of course helped to build.)

In response Keith said, 'Ladies and Gentlemen, please welcome Alexei Sayle!'

After I came off stage for the interval I discovered Keith had climbed out of the dressing-room window so I had to MC the rest of the show myself.

Sting thought all this was brilliant, all this chaos was a reminder of his wilder past. Afterwards we went to the Joe Allen Restaurant, which they kept open especially for us. David Stafford was also in the party but he was suffering from a cold and had drunk too much Night Nurse. Then we also drank a lot of champagne.

At one point David tried to discuss guitar technique with Sting. 'Do you use open plangency?' he asked.

'No, I generally play a curved fretboard in D.'

'Fucking hell!' David shouted.

Then his second wife took him home but on leaving the restaurant the night air hit him and he was sick all over the bonnet of Sting's limousine.

A little while later on the night before my late-night, live TV debut –1 January 1982 – feeling restless I popped in, unannounced, to see Sting at the house he'd just bought on a long, secluded, tree-shrouded lane high on a hill in Hampstead. He didn't seem that pleased at my impromptu visit, which caused me to congratulate myself on how far I'd come. A few years ago I'd been dropping in unwanted on art students in Maidstone, now I was dropping in unwanted on the biggest pop star in the world. We chatted uneasily for a while. Sting had just bought himself a clavichord, a predecessor of the piano, which had once belonged to Dr Johnson.

'Did it cost a lot?' I asked.

'Well I had to bid for it against the Smithsonian Museum,' he replied.

This was something I'd begun to notice that rich people did. They bought stuff that was the same as ordinary stuff but cost a lot more. So if you wanted a piano you could either get a nice cheap electric one in a shop or you could be like Sting and buy a piano only if it had first been owned by Dr Johnson. I wondered how far down that road he'd go, if he'd end up only buying things that'd been owned by a famous historical figure so his knives and forks were Shakespeare's and his underpants had once belonged to Einstein.

The next day I travelled to Birmingham. Linda and I had not been familiar with the Saturday morning children's show *Tiswas*, because our local ITV station, London Weekend, had until recently chosen to broadcast a thing called *The Saturday Banana*, made in Southampton and presented by a very bad-tempered and clearly child-hating Bill Oddie.

When I finally watched *Tiswas*, although it didn't really appeal to me I was impressed because they had managed to pull off an interesting trick. On an initial viewing it was a Saturday morning kids' TV show like any other, though perhaps a bit more shouty and chaotic – with 'the Cage', where children and their parents were locked up and peri-odically doused in water, the Phantom Flan Flinger throwing pies around, teen pop groups, comedians and puppets. But anybody grown-up could see that there was something else going on. The female presenter Sally James exuded a kind of naive sexuality while the lead male presenter Chris Tarrant treated the kids with breezy contempt rather than with the patronising chumminess that children's TV usually adopted, and all this was somehow knowingly acknowledged in what was perhaps the first example of an 'ironic' attitude towards presenting a mass market show.

During the summer, Tarrant, who was also the producer of *Tiswas*, had asked to meet me in a pub in Marylebone. He said he was planning to produce an adult late-night version of *Tiswas* and wanted me to be part of it. Over the following months, once I was involved in the project, I would go through an emotional parabola which resembled the Kübler-Ross Model for the Five Stages of Grief: denial, anger, bargaining, depression and acceptance. The particular emotions I would experience were those linked to the Experience of Being Involved in a TV Show that Is Doomed but which You Hope Against Hope Will Somehow Turn out to Be a Success. Those feelings are excitement, confusion, bargaining-with-the-producers-to-try-and-get-out-of-this-mess-but-unfortunately-you've-signed-a-contract-which-is-legally-binding, bollocks! and fuck it.

In December of 1981 I was involved in the making of two non-transmission pilots for the show, now called *OTT*, which was to go out live on January the 2nd of the following year. Recording these programmes meant I had to travel to the Central TV Studios in Birmingham. If Manchester seemed like a cosmopolitan European city, Birmingham felt like a town that nobody visited and nobody left, as if the population stayed exactly the same from one day to the next, which was probably why everybody was so ridiculously nice and friendly.

The cast would often rehearse at a hotel in the suburbs that the core team – Chris and his mates – used for overnight stays. We would sit in a function room for hours on end waiting for somebody to come up with an idea. My friend Philip from Chelsea School of Art would sometimes drive me up there for the day and he'd sit in and often come up with better concepts that any of the show's writers. What was clear to me was that the chaotic, throw-it-together approach of Saturday morning TV could not be applied to a late-night show, but while I could see this nobody else apparently could.

At first I said I'd take part in some of the filmed sketches but the quality of the writing was so low that I changed my mind and refused to appear in any more, insisting that I'd only do my own separate stand-up bits.

It did not make me happy to be uncooperative. The rest of the cast were basically decent, friendly fellow performers who found my attitude perplexing. As far as they were concerned all they wanted to do was entertain people in an unconfrontational way and make money. As the cast of *Tiswas*, John Gorman, Bob Carolgees, Sally James, Chris Tarrant and Lenny Henry were in such demand for personal appearances and supermarket openings they frequently hired a helicopter to get from one lucrative PA to the next and they were surprised that I didn't wish to do the same, that I didn't long to travel around the Midlands by air opening branches of Kwiksave. Bob Carolgees was formerly a DJ in the North West whose big break had come with the creation of his partner, a hand puppet called Spit the Dog. About five years out of date, Spit was a punk dog with spiky fur and a tartan collar whose only attribute was that he would spit all the time with a fruity hawking noise.

My brother-in-law Jimmy came to one of the pilots and later when we were having dinner together with the cast he said to Bob Carolgees and his wife, 'Don't you ever get sick of that dog? I mean he doesn't do anything except spit. Don't you find that somehow unsatisfying?'

At this Mr and Mrs Carolgees' faces contorted with rage and hurt as they shouted at my brother-in-law, 'We owe everything to that dog! Don't you dare criticise that dog! Don't you dare! We love that dog!' I too thought Jimmy's question tactless and offensive, especially since Spit was sitting with us in the restaurant propped up on his own chair.

Though he had recruited me onto his show, Chris Tarrant had no great liking for modern comedy or its practitioners. He preferred instead the company of old-style comics, the sort of comedians who were very slowly being forced out of business by the new wave of alternative stand-ups but were still making a good living on TV, hosting panel shows, game shows and working the club circuit. At Central TV I got to observe these men for the first time as there always seemed to be a few hanging around. What struck me was that despite their family-friendly image, a lot of these comics were deeply unpleasant, miserable people.

One odd trope was that these mainstream comedians didn't appear to be able to have a normal conversation with each other: everything turned into a gag. They might begin by saying they were ill or the wife was away but this would just turn out to be the set-up for the punchline of some lame joke. Perhaps it was no wonder then, given how repressed their feelings were, that their behaviour was appalling. No woman was safe from their attentions, they all drank heavily and a lot took cocaine as well. In contrast all the comedians I worked with, despite our acts often being aggressive and

248

challenging, were in stable relationships, were non-racist and non-sexist, didn't drink or take drugs to excess very often and were able to have a normal conversation that didn't end in a punchline. I came to the conclusion that mainstream comedians were nasty men pretending to be nice whereas alternative comedians were nice men pretending to be nasty. (Apart from Keith Allen.)

The majority of these old-timers also seemed to act in a very miserly, penny-pinching way, scrimping and saving as if they were vaudeville acts travelling around the US during the Depression rather than well-paid TV and club comics. Chris told me that if he'd been working in Birmingham the night before, the Northern Irish comic Frank Carson would always call into Central TV for his breakfast because the canteen was subsidised and therefore a lot cheaper than even the grottiest café in town. On his most recent visit when Tarrant joined him, Frank was in high spirits because not only was he delighted with his cheap meal but the previous night he'd also been able to stay at the Holiday Inn next door due to a reduced rate, also courtesy of Central TV.

'It's not like you to stay in a posh hotel,' Chris said, 'even if you got a deal.'

'Oh no,' replied Frank Carson, 'I was sharing the room with The Bachelors.' The Bachelors were an Irish singing group composed of three brothers and the four of them had shared the bed as if they were navvies in a cheap boarding house.

Once in the endless days of rehearsals I was sharing a taxi back to New Street Station with a comedian, one of Tarrant's mates, who though young was one of the old-fashioned sort working the Northern working men's club circuit. This guy was aware that I too was a comic but didn't know anything about alternative comedy or what my material was like.

'So what do you do in your act?' he asked.

'Well,' I replied, 'basically I talk, I talk about politics, social hypocrisy of course, consumerism, the legacy of post-colonialism, the fissiparous nature of ultra-hard-left political groupings. But you have to be aware if you can imagine it that this is all done with a great deal of physicality, allied to a kind of surrealistic overview, evocative perhaps of the French situationists.'

The comic thought for a few seconds then he said, 'Oh . . . you're a patter merchant.'

To be making television so late at night and trying to do your best work in a few concentrated minutes, when you'd normally be in bed, was extremely nerve-wracking so by the time the red light above the camera came on I was in a state of hysterical mania. I'd also chosen to perform some of my strangest and most esoteric material, a lot of it about the remote Communist Balkan country of Albania.

My hope was that TV reviewers would acknowledge that while the show as a whole wasn't great I was the sole beacon of originality and modernity. As it turned out, the only act that the press really paid attention to was a group I knew from the Albany Empire in Deptford led by Malcolm Hardee called the Greatest Show on Legs, who performed the naked 'Balloon Dance'. This was also the bit of the show that Molly said she liked the best.

I refused to stay in Birmingham and go drinking with the rest of the cast but insisted on going home to London after the show. That night, after what was as far as we knew a success-ful transmission, I was driven back to London in a Jaguar

XJ6. Then later in the week the hundreds of outraged letters arrived from disgusted viewers and the producers got to see the log of the thousand angry telephone calls so the vehicle waiting for me outside Central TV after the second week's show was a Ford Transit van.

Over the following programmes there was little improvement. Each week's show appeared to start from zero because there was no stockpiling of material. I would turn up on a Friday to rehearse my bit for the next day and there would be no script for the rest of the show, it was as if the writers didn't start work on bits for the Saturday show until maybe the Thursday evening. Then early on the Saturday morning, the day of transmission, Chris went fishing, so it wasn't until about 11 a.m. that scripts started to be passed around for that night's programme.

When I got to my dressing room for the second week's show there was what I thought was a lot of fan mail waiting for me. The week before I'd said something slighting about Milton Keynes and most of the letters were from the inhabitants of that town threatening to kill me. Except there was one other letter criticising me and including the line 'it's no wonder your dad's in a loony bin'. It was clearly from somebody in Valley Road since how else could they have known that Joe had recently been confined permanently to a hospital because his mental condition had deteriorated so badly?

From then on Linda read all my mail before showing me the few positive and friendly letters and throwing the majority in the bin.

Receiving this poison-pen letter touched a raw nerve because I did feel unhappy that Joe was now in hospital but there was a degree of relief as well. If my mother could have such a complex relationship with her cat then her feelings towards the man who had once been everything to her but was now more helpless than a baby became complicated beyond measure. In her way she had tried her best to look after Joe but Molly was not suited to such a task though she also refused all offers of help from us so in the end though it marked the beginning of my father's final months I considered that he was better off where he was.

But to be the recipient of such toxic, anonymous abuse showed me that national fame was definitely not what I had expected.

There was too a professional version of the poison-pen letter and that was the negative newspaper review. Clive James writing in the *Sunday Times* was the only TV critic of a broadsheet paper who liked and supported the show, and once it had finished he wrote a very perceptive piece. He said that the reasons so many in the media establishment – critics, TV executives and so on – disliked the show were twofold. One reason, he said, was that it was the first television show to have completely abandoned the Reithian idea of morally elevating TV – rather *OTT* revelled in its dumbness, which he found invigorating. The second reason the establishment hated it, he wrote, was because it was determinedly non-metropolitan. All the elite were based in London or desperately wished they were, whereas *OTT* celebrated the fact that it was provincial, that it came from unfashionable Birmingham, it possessed no desire to come from the capital. The only bit he didn't like about the show was me.

COMEDIANS AT HANGING ROCK

Whether or not it had been a good idea, me appearing on *OTT*, the show did bring me something which I had always wanted which was not exactly fame but national notoriety. Barmen had never liked me. I was terrible at small talk. In the lift at Lannoy Point, because of my shaved skull and my weird attempts at small talk, some of the neighbours thought I was Linda's mentally challenged brother. Now after *OTT* everywhere I went people were pleased to see me. They chatted away like I was an old friend and sometimes I got preferential treatment in chip shops. Of course there was a price to pay, and it required subtle adjustments to my behaviour. When we were out walking, Linda would weave over the pavement, sometimes getting in the way of people coming up behind her. I didn't do that. Almost without noticing, I began taking a quick glance over my shoulder, checking every few seconds to see if someone was at my back, like an overweight Jewish deer. When we were visiting Liverpool I stopped going into pubs in the city centre, places I'd been drinking in since I was fifteen. My reckoning was that if you could get into a fight in town for having the wrong opinion about the *Art of War* by Sun Tzu then being on the telly in a controversial show would virtually guarantee your involvement in a scrap.

But sometimes you were trapped. Once Linda and I were on a train coming out of Lime Street, and opposite us at another table were four tough-looking men drinking cans of beer they'd brought with them. One of them, recognising me, got up and came across to our table. Of the four he was the toughest-looking, muscled with thick glasses and a shaven head.

'Fucking hell! Alexei Sayle!' he said in a thick Scouse accent.

'Hi,' I replied.

'Oh God, he said. 'I wish my grandma was here, I really wish my grandma was here because she fucking loves you.'

I tried to act modest at this compliment and said, 'Well thank you and her very much.'

'Oh yeah,' he said. 'Every time you come on telly she says, "I love that boy, he's getting paid for shite!"'

Then there was the press. By that point I was used to being interviewed by publications such as *Time Out* and the *London Review of Books* but now being on national TV made me a fit subject for the tabloids. One lunchtime I was taken out by a couple of journalists from the *Sunday People* newspaper. The journalists appeared to be very nice, not at all what you imagined but really interested in my opinion on a wide variety of topics. There was quite a lot of wine drunk during the meal which was at an old-fashioned Italian trattoria in the West End where the pair seemed to be well known.

When I returned home and Linda saw me weaving around the living room bumping into the furniture she asked, 'What did you say to them?'

Annoyed at being questioned in this way I replied testily, 'Well actually I told them mostly all about my theories of post-industrialisation, that Britain, being the first manufacturing nation, is now the first to come out of the era of industrialisation and this could represent possibilities in terms of new political and social alliances and new forms of production. I also talked quite a lot about situationism.'

'Did they ask you any questions about other comedians?'

'Oh they might have, I don't know, why are you bothering me?'

When the article was printed the headline read, 'You Boring Lot!' and underneath it said, 'Newcomer Alexei's verdict on Britain's top TV funny men'. Below the headline there were small photos of various beloved British entertainers and next to them my view on their talents. Beside Bruce Forsyth it said 'Zombie of the trade', next to Eric Morecambe there was printed 'Good days are over', and beside Tommy Ball it said 'Flogs a joke to death'. About my views on post-industrialisation and situationism there was not a word.

From that point on Linda became more vigilant. Before I went out to meet any journalists she would give me a talk, saying, 'Remember, you're trying to get good coverage, don't say anything mad or act weird.' Most of the time I didn't take her advice but by and large the coverage remained kind.

I always made certain I showed Molly all my press coverage. I would point to some article in the paper about me and say to my mother, 'Look, Mum, look at this two-page feature all about your son, I'm famous.'

Molly would reply, 'I'm famous too.'

I was so famous that it was actually front-page news in the tabloid press when in March I left *OTT* after nine shows. In fact it had always been planned that I would leave then because the Comic Strip, minus Arnold Brown, had been booked to appear at the Adelaide Festival in Australia for a fortnight, then to go on and play at a comedy club in Melbourne for two weeks and finally a theatre in Sydney. Instead the newspapers implied that I was fleeing the country in shame because of my disastrous performance on *OTT.*

Tarrant replaced me with unpleasant old-school comedian Bernard Manning, but if he thought it would, that did not lessen his troubles. In rehearsal on his first day Manning finished going through his bit then they were supposed to cut to a piece featuring Lenny Henry. 'Cue the Nignog,' Manning said. This too got into the papers.

After taking off from Heathrow our 747 landed for its one refuelling stop in Jakarta, Indonesia. I had never encountered the tropics before and as the cabin door swung back the humid jungle seemed to seep into the plane. In a line we walked across the baking tarmac to a transit lounge whose walls were lined with bamboo like a cocktail bar from an episode of *The Saint* and inside we found the comedy pop group The Barron Knights, who were also on their way to Australia. I was to learn it was an elephant's graveyard for British entertainers, music-hall acts, the casts of long-vanished sitcoms – comedians you thought were dead were in fact working the RSL (Returned

Servicemen's League) clubs of Australia. To save money, The Barron Knights were flying to Sydney on the Indonesian airline Garuda. Their plane had taken off from Heathrow long before ours but then its first stop had been Gatwick, then its second touchdown was at Frankfurt and so on, slowly travelling east and landing every few hours. They had now been in transit for fifty-eight hours and they were still only at Jakarta. Apparently, they said, it always seemed to be morning wherever they were on the plane so they had up to that point eaten seven Indonesian breakfasts of congealed-rice porridge. Nobody ever saw them again.

It had always been a core belief in our family that the Sayles were really good at foreign languages. Molly apparently spoke fluent German because she'd grown up in a Yiddish-speaking home and Joe supposedly had an excellent command of both French and Esperanto. So confident was I in my natural linguistic ability that for five years I paid hardly any attention in French classes, refused to hand in any homework and as the exam grew nearer did no revision, instead relying on my genetic inheritance to see me through. It was only when I was met with complete incomprehension during the oral part of the exam that I began to suspect that things were not going to go well. '*Quoi?*' the examiners kept asking me with puzzled expressions on their faces, and saying, '*Je ne comprends pas,*' while I thought I was eloquently and fluently conveying complex ideas of political philosophy in perfect, slightly Marseilles-accented French.

When the O level results came through the door they confirmed that this idea of our polyglottism had been a collective delusion. After that shock, when I thought back to our overseas holidays, there arose several uncomfortable and long-suppressed memories of foreigners staring in stunned bafflement at one or both of my parents as they talked at them. Now those incidents began to make sense. The more I reflected on it the more memories surfaced of perplexing incidents abroad which were now understandable: why for example we were served boiled cod in Stuttgart when we thought we were getting an ice cream.

This was when I first began to suspect that Joe, rather than being fluent in any foreign language, got others to understand him and do what he wanted simply out of sheer niceness, while people did what my mother wished because they were frightened of her. The other illusion I held was that, because of all the Continental journeys I'd taken when I was a child, I was a good traveller. In fact I was a terrible traveller, easily spooked and prone to panic at unfamiliar things, which meant that Australia completely threw me because more or less everything was not as I thought it was going to be.

I'd been expecting, given the climate, that Adelaide where we landed first might resemble some Mediterranean city – perhaps it would be as Wassim had described the Beirut of his childhood: pavement cafés and whitewashed cinemas; glittering colonial architecture curving around an azure bay; narrow back streets and tree-shaded squares. Instead Adelaide recalled a mildly hallucinatory Stoke, plonked down in the middle of a botanical gardens. It combined the worst of British civic architecture from the 1890s and the 1960s and instead of pavement cafés there were tiled pubs where, behind firmly shut doors, men drank lager and they served a roast lamb and gravy dinner on a Sunday.

I was particularly bothered by the cars. The products of the native motor industry resembled Australian flora and fauna in that having no natural predators they had evolved into vehicles unlike any others on the planet. At this point in the early 1980s the products of Australian vehicle plants were changing stylistically. During the 1970s they had looked like mad American cars, now they resembled mad European cars. The latest Australian Ford Falcon recalled a Granada that had grown under the hot sun to an impossible length and width, while the Holden Commodore was like an Opel Senator with fluid retention, and there are no words to describe the various products of the dying Antipodean arm of British Leyland.

Because of my fear of flying, Linda had looked into ways to get me there other than on an aircraft. She had found it could be done if we went by ferry and train including the trans-Siberian railway to Hanoi in Vietnam, then travelling onwards to Singapore using a mixture of shared taxi and local train, followed by a hovercraft to Indonesia with the final leg aboard a passenger-carrying freighter to Perth, but in the end the only practical way to cope with the flight to Australia was to take a combination of Ativan tranquillisers to calm my mind and beta blockers to deal with the physical symptoms. These worked so well on the journey to Adelaide – even though I became convinced that there was a dog on board the plane and spent a lot of time looking for it before passing the rest of the flight with my anorak on backwards and the hood up, my Walkman headphones on top of the hood – that I believed I had somehow cured myself of my terror.

So when we boarded the flight to Melbourne I didn't take any pills at all. But as soon as the plane had accelerated down the runway and the wheels were off the ground, still on climb-out with engines screaming, we hit terrible clear-air turbulence, the whole cabin shook and the craft seemed to plunge repeatedly towards the ground. Behind me a group of terrified Samoans all well over six foot tall and as wide as Land Rovers were fervently muttering prayers to their many gods. The rough ride continued more or less the whole way to Melbourne, and as soon as I could I threw a large number of tablets into my mouth but the drugs didn't really kick in until we were almost on the ground.

That night the Comic Strip got to see a different side of their normally restrained MC. 'Sayley's finally loosed up,' Rik Mayall murmured in admiration as in the beer garden of a Melbourne pub I danced on a table with my T-shirt on my head to a tune only I could hear.

Rik was right though, I did need to relax because I was being a pain. Perhaps due to being unhappy about how *OTT* had turned out I was fretting over the Comic Strip show. It seemed wrong to me that what had been forged in the sleaze and grime of Soho should now be appearing alongside the mix of ballet and avant-garde dance, classical music and art that was the Adelaide Festival. And the decision to leave Arnold Brown behind in the UK meant that the Comic Strip show was now a series of double acts broken up only by me, which I worried meant that it was unbalanced.

One day, exasperated, Linda said to me, 'Look, I know you're serious about wanting the show to be perfect and everything but here in Australia it's as good as it's ever going to be, there's nothing more you can do. It's time for once for you to take it easy. Look at everybody else, they all know with absolute certainty that when they get back home they're going to do great work and they're all going to be famous. Here, right now, the sun's shining, there's parrots in the trees and you should just see this as a holiday, try to enjoy it.' And though I never completely relaxed, I did try from then on to have a reasonably good time.

The Festival had put us up at an elegant hotel, the Oberoi – an Indian-owned 1960s block in north Adelaide with an authentic curry restaurant on the roof that had views over the city of the tropical vegetation, which seemed too alien, and the English architecture, which seemed too familiar.

During the day we hung around beside the swimming pool. One afternoon the moustachioed jazz musician Keith Jarrett, also appearing at the Festival, was sitting at a poolside table eating this most amazing thing. It resembled a sandwich but it resembled a sandwich in the same way that our house in Valley Road resembled the Victoria & Albert Museum. I was later to learn that this marvel was 'a club sandwich'. Chicken breast, salad, bacon and cheese was all coated with mayonnaise and layered between several slices of toasted white bread (it had never occurred to me before that you could use more than two slices of bread in a sandwich) with a large toothpick through the middle to hold it all together because it was so enormous. I think we must have all been staring at his lunch because after a few minutes Keith Jarrett looked up and said, 'Here, you guys can have the rest of this,' and withdrew from the pool leaving most of his club sandwich behind. We all fell on it like savage schoolchildren in a post-apocalyptic novel. I was reminded of Miranda's words in *The Tempest,* 'Oh brave new world that has such sandwiches in it.'

For the Melbourne leg of the tour the promoter of our venue, the Last Laugh, had booked us into a purple velvet-walled place favoured by rock bands called the Diplomat Motor Inn on a street set just back from the beach in the seaside suburb of St Kilda. At night in order to drown out the sound of the screams, groans and gunshots coming from the adjacent rooms I found out that if you turned up the rattly air-conditioning unit to full power it usually did the job.

Julian Cope's The Teardrop Explodes were touring Australia at the same time as us and they too were staying at the Diplomat. Though we never saw Julian, the Comic Strip troupe took under our wing one of the members of his band who, because of the eccentric nature of their tour and its management, hadn't eaten properly for several weeks. All of us but especially Dawn and Jennifer, kind girls that they were, fed him, invited him to the comedy club where we got a free dinner and after the show bought him drinks and slipped him a part of our daily living expenses. The only problem was that we never really knew what this musician was called because he insisted his name was not words but a small drawing of a mythical creature he'd done in pencil on a scrap of paper that he carried around with him. Maybe that's why he didn't get anything to eat because his tour manager didn't know what to say to call him when his dinner was ready.

About two weeks into the tour there was a relief flight of girlfriends and wives – Nigel's partner Roberta, Peter's wife Marta and Rik's girlfriend Lise Mayer – who all arrived in Adelaide on the same plane. They were then not seen for twenty-four hours.

When they emerged the women brought news from home that soon Britain would be at war with Argentina. When the fighting began we were in Melbourne and I went on stage that night and announced bombastically, 'Britain is at war!' expecting cynical laughter, but instead there was a mighty warlike roar, which reminded me that we weren't in Soho.

On that trip a lot of the group were going through great personal changes. Peter's wife Marta was pregnant, the first of our gang to have a child, which seemed like a huge thing. And on the way back to the UK Dawn diverted to Sri Lanka to finish with her long-term boyfriend who was a tea planter, while Adrian had recently separated from his wife prompting him to radically change his formerly 'straight' look by buying a pair of tight, striped 'punk-style' trousers via mail order from the back pages of the *New Musical Express*. One day in Sydney a police car pulled up alongside us and one of the officers said to Adrian, 'You going to bed?'

'What?' Ade asked.

'You going to bed? Because you've got your pyjamas on.'

'No,' Adrian replied. 'I come from Britain where we're allowed to wear what we like.' Which I thought was one of the quickest and bravest things I'd ever seen, given that Australian policemen weren't always the most easy-going and genial of individuals.

'Well you still look like you've got your pyjamas on,' the policeman said in a feeble voice before driving off.

Rik and Lise were less free than the rest of us to behave as if they were on holiday because they had work to do: writing the scripts for the first series of *The Young Ones*. With all the different stupid projects I was involved in, the failed pilots for Granada and the documentaries that would never get made I knew as soon as they told me about *The Young Ones* that this was my chance to be in something truly brilliant. Which did not stop me being difficult when they asked me if I wanted to take part in this TV comedy they were writing. The pair were forced to endure a long speech about how I would agree to be in it but didn't want to play a single character because 'I don't want to be stuck as one person . . .' Rather I wished for a multiplicity of roles, so they had to write a different character for me in every episode.

Rik and Lise had realised that our whole comedy project was still not a done deal, the only one of the Comic Strip who had achieved national fame so far was me and that was only for being an oddity in a controversial show. We all knew the only way to break out to a mass audience was via television but television so far had failed us, it had not in any way been able to capture the originality, the danger, the excitement of what we'd been doing live. During the recording of *Boom Boom . . .* the audience had been seated cabaret-style at tables in an attempt to reproduce the exhilarating atmosphere of the Comedy Store and the Comic Strip but the drinks on those tables were wine- and beer-coloured water produced at great expense by the props department because the BBC didn't allow the consumption of alcohol on set (though several of the audience still got drunk on these freebies).

Finally Rik and Lise settled on the sitcom as a mode of TV that they could twist and explode in the same way as we had collectively twisted and exploded the cabaret format. Then when trying to come up with a setting – the 'sit' – they thought about their student days and a dilapidated house Rik had occupied in Manchester, the types of students in it and the things that went on there. Rik and Lise decided early on that they would try and make all the lead characters so obnoxious that the viewer would find it impossible to feel affection for them, which though ultimately doomed was a very Brechtian notion – which showed all those drama lectures hadn't been wasted. After they had the initial idea Rik brought his friend from Manchester University Ben Elton on board to help with the script and add jokes. Once they had a rough pilot they took it to Paul Jackson who we had all worked with on *Boom Boom Out Go the Lights*.

Rik and his girlfriend were not the only ones working on the scripts for a TV series while we were in Australia. Peter Richardson had flown out his writing partner Pete Richens on the same plane as the girlfriends and installed him in a separate nearby cheaper hotel in each town we visited. Then he would go every day to write the Comic Strip TV series which was to launch on Channel 4 alongside eleven depressing documentaries about the Third World just as Jonathan Dimbleby had wanted. Peter had asked me if I wanted to be in the Comic Strip films but I refused because I had this mad idea that it was wrong for me to appear on the BBC and Channel 4 at the same time. Even the people inside my head whom I was trying to impress thought this was a stupid idea, but I wouldn't be deflected.

Mrs Doonican Gets a Surprise

Linda always told people I was a pagan because my parents raised me with no concept of religion whatsoever. The first ceremony in a church that I ever attended was Peter Richardson's wedding in Devon in the summer of 1981 and I had absolutely no idea what was going on. Pete and Marta were preceded down the aisle by the man who would perform the marriage ceremony, the Bishop of Exeter. I said to Linda, 'Who's that bloke dressed as a chess piece?'

On an intellectual level I could appreciate the architectural beauty of churches and cathedrals but the first time I entered what felt to me like a holy, sacred space was when I stepped into BBC TV studio Television Centre TC8 for the first time. It was when we were making the original *Boom Boom* . . . Accompanied by a young man in a headset clutching a clipboard, we passed through an airlock of double doors that brought me to a vast space suffused with pure white light radiating from a hundred lamps high in the vaulted roof, while a cool breeze resembling some calming zephyr blowing from snow-capped mountains gently ruffled my jacket. Across the wide shining floor the initiates went about their business in a hushed, pious manner, whispering into their headphones as the cameras seemed to float above the ground on their pedestals. On the monitor screens hanging above our heads the images glowed brighter than the paintings of Caravaggio in the church of San Luigi dei Francesi in Rome.

That sense of wonder has never left me. A TV studio remains the one location where I feel completely safe – a place of sanctuary as the medieval cathedrals once were.

The recording of each episode of *The Young Ones* was spread over two days. All of Thursday was spent in the studio with no audience present, taping what were called the 'pre-records'. These were complex sequences that would have taken too long to do in front of an audience: mostly stunts and special effects, and this was usually the day when Rik (and sometimes Ade) went to hospital.

I had not imagined that making TV comedy would be almost as hazardous as working on a building site but it was. Perhaps it was to be expected since the tools of our trade were firearms, explosives and complicated stunts and in those care-free days the guys in charge of the special effects – the many fires and explosions in the script – were extremely relaxed about what was then not known as health and safety. In the pilot episode of *The Young Ones* there is a scene where Adrian bites into a brick which then explodes. This was done by the simple expedient of putting an explosive in a brick and then having it explode, which cut his mouth quite badly. During a later episode there is a scene where Rik falls down the stairs collecting the banisters (later used as firewood) between his legs as he goes. You might expect that given the danger of doing this he would be strapped into some kind of complex safety rig which controlled his descent, but in fact the effect was achieved by Rik simply throwing himself down the stairs, stopping only at the end by the newel post coming into sharp contact with his genitals.

There is also a section where Rik lights a stove which then explodes. The special-effects guys loaded the stove with explosive then went to the pub for lunch. On their return, having forgotten that they'd put the explosive in the stove, they loaded it with the same amount again, then put in a bit more for good luck. In the shot Rik lights the stove then as it detonates the picture goes into slow motion. This was not Paul Jackson the director being artistic, rather it was because there were only a few frames of tape that existed before the massive fireball caused the camera to burst into flame and the blaze spread to Rik's clothes and he had to be taken once more to hospital.

In the episode where I play armed robber Brian Damage I fired a shotgun on the set. The armourer had loaded the gun with a half-charge blank cartridge but the noise and concussion was still thunderous in such a confined space. Later on during the live recording of that same show I had to hit Rik with the butt of the shotgun. Out of shot I switched it for a rubber version of the weapon but when I hit him it still was a tremendous blow that knocked him over and cut his head open, but he couldn't go to hospital then because we had the audience in.

Danger also came from some of the people who appeared in the show. We were compelled to have a band on every week because Paul Jackson's official designation was as a variety rather than a comedy producer, so *The Young Ones* was therefore technically a variety programme, in the same category as *The Black and White Minstrel Show*, which meant that a music act was required. This was turned into a strength by having the bands perform in various bits of the house.

The musicians could be very scary though. While we pretended to be mad and out of control for our acts these people really were like that. In the episode called 'Interesting' where the boys hold a party, the guest band were Rip Rig and Panic and I can remember one of their members grabbing a bottle of beer and saying, 'Wow, this beer is real!' and trying to open it with their teeth and me shouting, 'No! No! No! That's a prop! It might be needed for continuity!' The musician looked at me like I was the most pathetic thing on earth.

Then for the scene in which the party is invaded by gatecrashers in that same episode one of the assistant producers had hired a load of extras from a company called something like the Real Psycho Hire Agency so when they broke in at the end of the show they were really quite convincingly violent. As the closing credits roll I can be seen crawling on my hands and knees trying to get off the set.

After the recordings each week it felt like a big party. BBC Television Centre outdid Lucas CAV in the multiplicity of its staff restaurants with their different clientele and varying rules: from the wood-panelled Grill Restaurant used exclusively by the executives, where service was by uniformed waitresses and a suit and tie was required, to the various canteens where the cameramen, scene shifters and secretaries ate. But there was one space where all crafts and callings came together and that was the BBC Club, a large bar on the fourth floor where we would go after the shows, that is if you could get past the commissionaire on the door who was particularly determined to stop performers and their friends from entering. Often I would go up there then be refused and have to go running around the darkened corridors looking for a scene shifter to sign me in.

When I finally did set foot in the club, Linda would always be sitting there waiting for me. That was another secret skill she had: there was something about her calm, self-contained manner that meant she was invisible to doormen and security guards, so she was able to wander unchecked into restricted areas such as generator rooms, the bridges of cross-Channel ferries and MOD rifle ranges.

Linda was, anyway, a semi-official member of *The Young Ones* team and after the final show of the first series in a simple ceremony she was awarded a certificate attesting that she was one of only a very few people who had attended all six recordings. Her main job, as soon as we met after the recording, was to tell me that my performance was better than anybody else's. After that she was free to pursue her own agenda.

Rather than the bar of the greatest dream factory in all of Europe, the BBC Club resembled the lobby of a 1950s library: austere and harshly lit. In one of the few dark corners there always seemed to be a young woman, a floor assistant or a make-up girl, weeping. Seated beside her would be an older man sometimes wearing a cravat, a director or a producer, who'd be whispering, 'Look, honestly, I promise I will leave Felicity but not until the kids are out of school, you've got to understand . . .'

Yet despite its lugubrious aura, that bar seemed like the most exciting place in the world. We were drunk on alcohol subsidised by the licence payer, high on relief and a sense of achievement. We would jabber away with our friends about how well it had gone and then at the end of the evening they'd send you home in a taxi that you didn't have to pay for.

Then all we could do was wait. In interviews I would say, 'I've just finished this TV series called *The Young Ones*. If people across the country appreciate our style of humour it'll be huge.'

But the question was, would they? The first series of *The Young Ones* was transmitted in November 1982 and its effect was slow to kick in though gradually we began to be noticed. On one review show ex-Guardsman and football manager Lawrie McMenemy described our show's humour in his Gateshead accent as 'hoortful' and, though he referred to me as 'funny as a funeral', the *Evening Standard*'s critic Ray Connolly wrote a perceptive piece about how he had noticed his children watching this strange noisy show that he couldn't figure out, but which seemed to exert a massive attraction. For me it was just a relief to be in something that I was one hundred per cent proud of.

The BBC with its profound generational wisdom going back half a century knew *The Young Ones* was going to be good and that year, even though it still hadn't really taken off, they invited the cast to the Light Entertainment Christmas Party – a real vote of confidence. No younger comedians had been invited to the Light Entertainment Christmas Party, the high point of the year for all comedians and comic actors, since a dark day in the 1970s when the Pythons had been asked to this black-tie event and had turned up dressed in jeans!

I felt it was a sign that the BBC believed that acts like mine, despite all the references to Marxism and Brecht and the left-wing propaganda, were still in many ways conventional show business turns. I didn't wear a tuxedo but did dress up in a smart suit and tie and tried very hard to behave myself. I nearly succeeded until the moment when Jim Moir the head of Light Entertainment came over to me leading the Liverpool-born comic performer and radio DJ Kenny Everett. I bridled immediately. A few months previously, during a Young Conservatives rally held at Wembley Arena Kenny had inflamed the reactionary, right-wing, tweed-jacketed crowd by coming on stage and shouting, 'Let's kick Michael Foot's stick away!' and, 'Let's bomb Russia!'

Jim said to me, 'You know who this is, don't you?'

'Yes,' I replied, turned and stalked off. My high-minded gesture was undermined by Kenny being way too stoned to notice what had happened and Jim assumed it was probably just some gay thing.

Later on Rowland Rivron showed his penis to Mrs Val Doonican in the lift. It was an indication of the corporation's priorities that all this was still considered better behaviour than the Pythons attending the Light Entertainment Christmas Party wearing jeans.

A Bag of Balloons and a Pencil

For 1983 in anticipation of me starring in a hit TV show I'd booked myself a nationwide solo tour. My plan was to start out with small theatres and arts centres then build up to the bigger venues. In fact the previous year I had already begun doing my show in two- to three-hundred-seaters. Billy Connolly was my model. He was constantly on the road around the UK playing multiple nights in two- or three-thousand-capacity rooms such as the Liverpool Empire, Glasgow Playhouse and Hammersmith Odeon. But there was a difference between my show and what Billy Connolly, or those other ex-folkie comedians Jasper Carrott and Mike Harding, were doing which made things more difficult. Their audience was clearly defined: a variant of those who'd come to see them as folk singers, and their comedy though anecdotal was still mostly warm and cosy, not aggressive, unpleasant and frequently upsetting as mine tried to be.

My audience were an interesting mix. A lot of them, late twenties to early thirties white males in mid-level managerial or industrial jobs who felt that they didn't quite fit in and considered themselves superior to those around them, almost exactly matched the profile of the serial killer which FBI analysts doing pioneering work at their headquarters in Quantico were coming up with during that period. Then there were those like me, working-class kids who'd been to university or teacher training college and now had good jobs in the public sector which they didn't like much, the wine-bar-visiting Habitat shoppers, but there were also always a large number drawn from whatever the local industry was, miners in Nottinghamshire and Yorkshire, car workers in the Midlands, and there was often a large contingent of either soldiers or policemen, sometimes both.

A lot though not all were left-wing but what I thought they all shared was a sense of being marginalised, of not quite fitting in. They felt they saw the world more clearly than the mass and I articulated their worldview. After a gig in Leamington Spa at a thousand-seater which was more or less full, a teenage boy who came backstage told me, 'I thought I'd be the only one here . . .'

By my touring solo me and Linda became joint owners of a family business, except that, rather than being an unfriendly corner shop or a remote hill farm our business was a man who travelled up and down the country in a van shouting at between two hundred and fifty and two thousand people. The enterprise, just like a fishing boat or a hat shop, had employees, which came as a surprise to me. I never thought that I would ever be employing people.

My tour manager, the man who took care of the driving and looked after hotel bookings, transport and payments, was a guy from Liverpool called Kenny Smith. He'd been to the same school as me a couple of years before me and had been old enough to get caught up in the whole Merseybeat scene. Just as in an earlier age the young men of Liverpool had gone away to sea, manning the sea lanes of Empire, so now they became the foot soldiers of the pop business. Kenny had worked his way up until he attained one of the ultimate postings and become part of the Beatles operation as personal assistant to Ringo Starr. I don't know what had gone so wrong in his life that he was now working for me, but Kenny possessed a kind of Samurai dignity and treated me as seriously as any other act.

I had an agent who booked my stand-up tours, but Bob Gold of Wasted Talent was more used to dealing with acts on the scale of REM and U2, and was doing me because he liked my act and it gave him satisfaction to see me live. However, Mr Gold had never bothered to amend the contract he sent out to each venue for what was called 'the get-in'. The point where the bands moved their stuff into the building. This contract was tilted towards the requirements of one of Bob's big rock acts so there were always four 'humpers' – big burly men in black T-shirts waiting ready to haul the amps, speakers, back line and instruments in through the scene dock.

Except I had no gear. All I had was a black cardboard box with a pink hippo in it. This was Pipi, a furry glove puppet I'd bought at a charity auction and to whom I did terrible things on stage. Nevertheless Kenny carried this box, proudly accompanied by cries of derision and catcalls from the burly men. He had a number of expressions: if he saw a pretty girl he'd say, 'That'd look nice on the end of my dick.' Something worthless was 'a bag of balloons and a pencil', and he didn't like Rolls-Royces – he said, 'Rolls-Royce? That's a woman's car.'

Wherever we went he would shield me from non-existent paparazzi. Once in Manchester in a completely empty Chinese restaurant he demanded, 'Alexei Sayle's here, he needs a table and he needs it now!' On the return journey to London after a gig I would ride in the passenger seat next to Kenny and sometimes if Linda was making fun of me from the back I'd say, 'Kenny, the girl with the glasses in the back seat, throw her out.' With a screech of brakes the van would come to a halt, the side door would open and cold night air blow in before I could countermand the order.

Apart from Kenny there was a musician or musicians to accompany my songs, either David Stafford or a duo called Studio Two – Harry Bogdanovs and Jim Bamber – who also played the support slot when needed.

While I took care of the comedy, my wife's area was the more nebulous stuff. Some of the venues, particularly Students' Unions, could be quite lax on security so Linda would put herself in overall charge of that. She would patrol the backstage areas to ensure they were guarded (on at least one occasion during my performance we'd had a theatre employee wander on stage while giving his girlfriend a backstage tour). And she'd cover the auditorium as well. If somebody in the audience was very raucous Linda would get the bouncers to hold off on hauling them out, because she knew that would cause too much disruption and put the crowd on edge, plus I was able to deal with them from the stage for a while. Instead Linda would wait until they had to go to the toilet, which they inevitably did, and then she'd refuse to let them back in.

After eighty minutes I would come off stage soaked in sweat and Linda would be waiting in the wings with a towel. As I paused before going back to do my first encore I would check with her on things that had worked, particularly bits I'd improvised, and she would sometimes remind me of material I had forgotten to do so I could slip it into the encore. Then I'd head back on stage.

On ITV of a Saturday there was football analysis of a very rudimentary kind: clunky graphics and elephantine humour provided by a pair of retired players known as 'Saint and Greavsie' – Ian St John and Jimmy Greaves. Greaves, a recovering alcoholic, always seemed a slightly tragic figure. After he helped get England to the 1966 World Cup final, the manager Alf Ramsey dropped him and there is a shot in the official film of the match of Jimmy, standing in his suit, forlorn on the touchline, watching as he misses out on the greatest moment of English football. But he'd obviously given some thought to what it was to be a player. I saw him being interviewed once and he said something profound about the nature of performing at the highest level. Greaves scored 357 goals in his career and he said he couldn't remember a single one – the reason he gave was that he was so focused on the game, so completely caught up in the moment, that there was no space left for memories to form, though he might have just been pissed. I too recalled very little of my own shows, although, on stage, every second was filled with a thousand thoughts.

Afterwards there was the buzz, which was composed of fifty per cent relief it was over and fifty per cent feelings of infinite powerfulness. This state lasted for maybe half an hour and then I would fade into an exhausted haze. After that it was either back to London passed out in the van, or if we were staying overnight I would sit slumped in some hotel lobby bar unable to form a sentence, watched over by Linda.

Through Martin, the graphic designer, I'd met a comedy writer from Leeds called Dennis Berson. Dennis had provided gags for comedians such as Ken Dodd and Les Dawson but he was open-minded enough to be interested in what I was doing. In an earlier life he'd been an academic working on a history Phd. Dennis Berson described Linda's job as 'keeping the flies off Coco'.

It was also Dennis who summed up my contribution to comedy by saying that I was the first comic he'd ever seen who didn't want the audience to like them. I wanted to make them laugh but I didn't wish to do it by gaining their sympathy or trust, I wanted them to laugh despite my goading them and turning on them and mocking their most profound beliefs.

But the performance, the show, that hour and a half on stage, was the smallest part of the life of the touring stand-up, everything else was the road. We travelled in a Volkswagen LT van with a sliding side door, brown velour swivelling captain's chairs, a fridge, an air-conditioning unit on the roof and a TV, none of which worked. The words 'Space Cruiser' were written down its sides.

Rock and roll myth said that at the Blue Boar Services at Watford Gap on the southbound M1 all the bands who were touring would meet in the early hours of the morning. Rivalries were forgotten and The Smiths, Brotherhood of Man, Alvin Stardust and The Bee Gees would improvise Chicago blues until the sun came up over Northampton. And it wasn't just bands who met there. New wave French film director François Truffaut might be returning from giving a lecture at Nottingham University and he too would sit in on the jam session. But all I ever saw was a cheerless neon-lit canteen where gravy went to die.

There's a motorway sign on the M1 that says, 'London 17 miles'. It always seemed like a strange number to choose. Seventeen miles – did it mark some ancient Druidic boundary? Every time we passed it Kenny would say, 'That's the sign I've been looking for.'

I had a landmark too on Hendon Way which linked the M1 to the Finchley Road. I think I must have first noticed the Garth Hotel when Harry gave me a lift down to London from Liverpool in his van just after I left college. In the early 1970s it occupied one house on a block of 1930s semis between Garth Road and Cloister Road. The next time was when me and Linda took the coach rather than the train to Liverpool because it was cheaper, and I saw, glancing out of the window, that the Garth had taken over a couple more adjacent houses on the block. Now each time we passed it, it seemed to have occupied another building, spreading gradually like a contagion along Hendon Way and down the side streets. The only thing was that as far as I could tell there didn't seem to be anybody ever staying there. No cars were parked on the forecourt and all the little bedroom windows remained permanently dark. I sometimes wondered what it would be like to spend the night at the Garth – it couldn't have been worse than some of the hotels we did use.

In Britain in the 1970s and 1980s these establishments more than any other typified an attitude prevalent at the time, which the author Kingsley Amis referred to as 'sod the public'. Hotels appeared to be run for the benefit of those who owned them and those who worked in them rather than the unfortunates who stayed in them.

In Manchester the closest you came to a place that wasn't a stuffy old relic but had a more rock and roll ethos was the Britannia, a converted Victorian office block where if you drew back the curtains to the 'window' in your room there would only be a brick wall, and once darkness fell the corridors were overrun with prostitutes so it was easier to get a blowjob than a cheese sandwich in your room after 9 p.m. Things were so bad in the North that if we were playing anywhere near Liverpool I would usually stay at Molly's house. Linda would go to her parents' and Kenny would stay with his and David Stafford slept in our front room. The first time we stayed there Molly had bought whisky which David didn't really want to drink, but I told him she'd got it specially so he had some and then had a terrible hangover in the morning when my mother tapped on his door and asked if he'd like breakfast. Thinking she might have got some special stuff in he said yes, then he heard her yelling up the stairs, 'Lexi, get up! Your fucking friend wants his breakfast!'

In Hull, Kenny had booked us into a place in the suburbs called the Adelphi. After the incident at the hotel of the same name in Dublin I should have been apprehensive, but I was still shocked by the cold, dank cell we were shown to. I immediately phoned my tour manager and told him the room was unsatisfactory. 'Don't worry, Lex,' he said. 'You go and sit in the foyer and I'll fix it.'

Me and Linda went and sat in some armchairs beside reception while Kenny spoke forcefully with the manager. Then there was a pause and after a few minutes I saw a woman in full bridal dress crossing the foyer with her unhappy new husband by her side, both of them carrying suitcases and the bride weeping miserably.

They were followed by Kenny. 'Hiya, Lex,' he said. 'I've got you a much better room, there's a lovely four-poster bed and everything.'

Because this kind of comedy had never been done before, nobody had a clue about what was the best way to present it live. When playing the smaller places you were in the hands of local promoters, some of whom were good, some incompetent and some dangerous fantasists. I found myself doing comedy in such locations as Tiffany's – a Newcastle upon Tyne discothèque where the audience had trouble seeing me because their view was obscured by the hanging gilded cages where bikini-clad girls usually danced, or Central London Poly – a crowded and rowdy bar with a stage in the corner, about six foot by six foot and made of some boards balanced on milk crates that could only be accessed by me fighting my way through the crowd. Or Park Lane in the Scottish town of Hamilton, another disco, where when Linda touched a guy on the shoulder to get him to shut up he fell off his stool onto the floor in a drunken stupor. Still I did the full show and two encores.

The best promoter was an ex-college entertainments officer from Preston called Phil McIntyre. If it was a McIntyre gig there would always be fresh towels in the dressing room and photocopied signs pinned to the walls – a large arrow and the words 'Stage this way' above it. Because of this kind of innovative thinking, in 1983 Phil McIntyre was promoting *The Young Ones* live show too. Excited by the thought of seeing my mates performing live, I went with Linda and a couple of friends to see Rik Mayall, Nigel Planer and Adrian Edmondson play the second of two nights at a packed Oxford Apollo. On stage they explained the absence of Chris Ryan's character Mike by saying he was dead, which got a massive cheer from the audience but which I thought was a bit mean. We had planned, my friends and I, to stay at Chris Walker's place near Banbury, but after the show I suddenly experienced the most crippling flu-like symptoms – shaking, sweating and dizziness – so I persuaded my friends to take me back to London in their car.

It turns out the symptoms of flu are almost identical to the symptoms of envy. Every single theatre on *The Young Ones* tour had sold out in minutes and Phil had been quick to put in extra dates. For me it had never been that easy to sell out the venues I would be playing. Some would always go pretty quickly – Reading Hexagon or Nottingham Concert Halls – but there were others that for whatever reason stubbornly refused to sell, so I would have to do endless publicity in provincial papers and radio stations, being interviewed by disc jockeys who did not want to hear about the profound influence of situationism on my work. A local newspaper photographer once told me, 'I've brought a cabbage along so you can do something funny with it.'

Turned out it was something I hated, a venue not being full. It made me feel worthless and insignificant to think that only four hundred and seventy-three people wanted to see me in Hastings. It was also harder to play a room that wasn't packed since it required more energy to lift the audience up and carry them along. Linda would plead with Bob Gold not to tell me how ticket sales were going but I would ring him up about some unrelated matter and then casually ask, 'Oh by the way, Bob, how's sales for Dartford Orchard Theatre doing?'

He'd reply, 'Diabolical!'

I'd just got used to Kenny making the tours run smoothly and terrorising my wife when he asked if he could go off and tour manage for a few weeks for an unknown band who were playing a very small-scale tour of beer *Bierkellers* and small rock clubs – gigs that they were being forced to do in order to pay off the massive debts they'd built up with a record company whom they were no longer with. It was a common experience at the time that musicians would find out that all the limos, publicity and hospitality that the record company had been so generously providing were in fact being paid for, down the line, by the band themselves.

After Kenny returned from that tour he told me that the band had asked him to become their personal manager, looking after their whole career and in return taking a percentage of their earnings rather than just a wage. He said he wanted to take them up on the offer. I told him, 'Well I don't know, Kenny, you're on to a good thing here with me. Fifty pounds a week is not to be sneezed at . . .'

'I know, Lex,' he said, 'but I feel this could be my big chance.'

'Well I suppose so,' I grumbled, 'if that's what you really want.'

'Thanks, it is.'

'By the way,' I asked, 'what's the name of this band?'

'They're called The Eurythmics,' he replied.

A Sunken Fence

Constantly refining her work, never standing still, my mother had developed another response to when I showed her an article all about me in a newspaper or magazine and pointed out how famous and celebrated I'd become. She'd still say, 'I'm famous too,' but now she'd add, 'I'm known for my quiche.' Which wasn't even true!

Before, when I had been working in a series of badly paid, part-time jobs, Molly would go on and on at me over how little I was being paid. Though I begged her not to she would also inform others about my lack of earning power. 'This is our Lexi,' she'd say to people on the bus. 'He's only making £7 a day as a part-time filing clerk.'

After I became a successful entertainer and began appearing on the television and playing big theatres she lost a topic with which to berate me. My mother chose to deal with this by not altering her behaviour at all, and by carrying on acting as if I was still poorly paid. 'When you do one of your programmes for the BBC,' she would ask with genuine concern, 'do they pay you then?'

'Of course they fucking pay me!' I'd yell. 'I'm making loads of money!'

Then Molly would respond, 'Why are you so angry, Lexi? Are you worried about money, is that what it is? Do want a loan?'

But if I tried to turn the tables and said to her, 'Yes, OK, will you lend me £1,000, Molly?' she'd reply, 'But I'm just a poor old pensioner.'

By contrast the rest of the country was not doing at all well. Outside the grey, stone-faced 1930s Town Hall on Upper Street, Islington, the Labour-run council led by an unpleasant woman called Margaret Hodge erected a large electronic scoreboard which each day recorded in glowing lights the ever-increasing number of unemployed people in the borough. It always seemed like they were boasting.

Nationally, the tally of those out of work was at a record high of over three million. The Thatcher government seemed to have decided to concentrate on only two industries: arms manufacture and financial services. If you didn't have a business dedicated to either killing people or robbing them you could expect no help.

The poisonous right-wing newspapers were full of made-up stories about the left and the trade union movement, so the atmosphere in Britain had never been more angry, fractious, and disillusioned. Many felt let down, disenfranchised, excluded, enraged and it was my role to travel ceaselessly up and down the country in my Space Cruiser giving expression to these feelings, and at the same time I couldn't avoid making money. I never felt any middle-class guilt about this; the contortions the rich girl in

Liverpool had gone through were not for me. After all as far as I was concerned I simply sold my services and exploited no one. This attitude was the result of me spending years planning an irrefutable Marxist defence for the time when I began to accumulate wealth.

Rik and Ade, with the income from the TV series and the live show, did start acting like a pair of students who'd found a large stash of used banknotes hidden in a bag behind a wall and needed to get rid of it before the real owners turned up. At the weekend they would drink all evening in one of two or three rough pubs on Upper Street in Islington and then continue after closing time in an Indian restaurant. In the restaurant there would be a fair amount of damage caused: a degree of singeing (especially if Rowland Rivron was there – if you were ever short of fireworks Rowland could help you out as he always had a pocketful of bangers, pinwheels and rockets), a quantity of breakage and inevitably some stainage. The next day they would have to compensate the owner with a large wad of cash, which seemed to give them as much, if not more, pleasure than the drinking and rampaging and blowing up of the night before. In fact it was generally the same Indian restaurant in the Holloway Road that they wrecked week after week so soon the owner stopped making repairs and just collected their money.

For them there also arose the question of how far you would go to make money. The most controversial area of temptation was advertising. People from the music business and music press were some of the first to come down to the Comedy Store, sensing something new was happening; the television industry was next to appear, with newspapers and national magazines following a long way behind. But it was advertising, with its parasitical relationship to art and culture, that was the quickest to sniff out that there was a radical shift occurring. Within a few nights of our opening, a man who'd come to the Comedy Store paid me £100 to voice an ad for a car dealer who'd got stuck with a load of little Honda Acty vans that he wanted to shift quickly. After that I'd frequently lend my voice to a range of products.

To my mind voice-overs were just the sort of journeyman work that any actor would undertake and were therefore ethically justifiable. Though appearing in ads for TV or cinema was another matter. If you appeared in a commercial and were a well-known performer then you did seem to cross some sort of line into endorsing the product being advertised, which in turn made you look venal and unprincipled. Of course this was not the point of view of the majority of the public, who were perfectly happy to see their favourite stars in commercials, but rather this was the attitude I thought my particular audience would take, since these were my own feelings.

I also liked working in voice-over studios. In many ways it was the most uncomplicated and enjoyable part of what I did. When making a radio ad the people in charge, the creatives from the ad agency and the production company, needed to get you in and out as quickly as possible because they were being charged by the hour for the studio and the mixing time. This meant they really appreciated it if you got on with the job without any actorish messing about, and this in turn led to a no-nonsense air of all of us being professionals simply involved in getting on with the work in hand.

And I was good at it. I seemed to have this clock running in my head so if the engineer said, 'Alexei, can you take a quarter of a second off the end and give the words "wheaty goodness" a sense of infinite longing?' I could do it on the first take. In the reception area of the voice-over studios there was always a nice bowl of fresh fruit and another full of chocolate bars and toffees with which I often used to gum up my mouth just before a recording, and a pretty young boy or girl would ask you if you wanted a coffee.

Although he would later change his mind, at that time Rik was dead set against either appearing in adverts or doing voice-overs and there was an early rupture between him and Adrian when his performing partner starred in a number of commercials for a bank playing a 'Vyvyan'-type character. It was odd in some ways that Rik wouldn't do commercials because of all of us he had the strangest relationship with money. Quite early on me, Linda, Rik and Lise tried to start a production company together. The Oxford and Cambridge University boys had already begun to found businesses such as Talkback – Mel Smith and Griff Rhys Jones, and Hat Trick – Jimmy Mulville, Rory McGrath and Denise O'Donoghue, which gave them much greater control of their output and a much larger share of the profits. The only thing that came out of our plan was the name of our production company which was Sunken Fence. This was a humorous title for anybody who could be bothered to figure it out because another word for 'sunken fence' is 'ha-ha'.

We had only one meeting at Rik and Lise's flat but as soon as we started to talk Rik said, 'Right, so this is where you rob me of all my money,' a weird expression on his face, so then we had to spend the rest of the meeting persuading him that this wasn't some elaborate scam designed to defraud him of his earnings. We never tried again.

I had always wanted a social circle who all knew each other, who didn't need to be seen one at a time in distant corners of London, and through being friends with Dawn and Jennifer, Rik and Lise, Adrian, Peter and Nigel and their partners I had finally achieved it. There was a club called Zanzibar in Covent Garden, a prototype of all the other members' clubs that came later where we would all go. The designer of the club, which was long and narrow, said that his greatest achievement was putting the toilets at the far end so that everybody got to see everybody else as they went backwards and forwards to the lavs to snort cocaine. Keith Allen would later serve a stretch in Pentonville Prison for smashing the large mirror behind the bar. I never paid to be a member of the Zanzibar but Simon Oakes, the smooth young man who'd taken me and Tony to Edinburgh, had told me to always tell the girl on the door that I was 'meeting Rock Sandford', a man I did not know at all. This continued to work even after Rock Sandford was jailed for a jewellery robbery. Lise Mayer on the other hand discovered after an overdue examination of some neglected bank statements that she'd been paying for her membership of the Zanzibar for five years after it had closed down and become a hamburger restaurant.

It was Rik and Lise that me and Linda spent the most time with. Lise was, like Linda for mine, a vital part of Rik's career, co-writing both *The Young Ones* and Rik's character Kevin Turvey as well as trying with varying degrees of success to keep him out of the pub. A lot of the time we would simply hang around. They would come to our flat or we would go to theirs and hours would pass, but what Rik liked to do most, once he'd built up a body of work, was to watch tapes of himself on TV. He did not watch these tapes in any sort of analytical way but rather he viewed them as a devoted fan of Rik Mayall, some ordinary person who had encountered the comic at the beginning of his career and couldn't get enough of these extraordinary performances. As Rik watched Rik he would laugh with the wholehearted enjoyment of somebody who had not seen the material before, thrilled and stunned at the comedic brilliance that he was witnessing. With anybody else this could have seemed narcissistic but with Rik the pleasure he took in seeing himself on TV seemed so innocent that it was charming.

And I actually helped expand the circle. In between making *The Young Ones* and its transmission I played a supporting role in an LWT sitcom all about nuclear war entitled *Whoops Apocalypse* written by David Renwick and Andrew Marshall. Lenny Henry came along to one of the recordings. I had been friends with Len since *OTT*. Before I met him I'd had a fantasy that I would introduce this young, black, mainstream comic to the work of innovative comedians such as Lenny Bruce, Steve Martin and Richard Pryor and he'd be incredibly grateful. When we met filming a sketch for the pilot on a snow-covered tennis court in a Birmingham suburb it turned out he knew a lot more about the work of Lenny Bruce and Richard Pryor and every other interesting comedian than I did, possessing hundreds of tapes, scripts and vinyl recordings of their work, whereas my knowledge of these comics was largely based on seeing one film or on something a bloke had told me once.

Dawn French came to see me recording the sitcom too and it was here she met Lenny for the second time (having not taken to him on the first occasion). Afterwards they went off together to a jazz club, the electricity of sexual attraction crackling between them. My comedy writing friend Dennis Berson tried to go along too but they ran away from him.

I was excited that Lenny might become close to Dawn because from what I knew of his life it seemed quite hard. Shipped off at the age of sixteen to work the Variety circuit, travelling on a Sunday night to spend the week in terrible digs in Yarmouth or Inverness, doing twelve shows a week alongside all those awful hack comedians. Even when we were making *OTT* Lenny would often leave rehearsals early because he was booked to do a show on an RAF base or at a rugby club. And as well as trying to make his way in the difficult world of comedy he was also expected by many to carry alone the burden of black consciousness in the entertainment business. That evening in the foyer of LWT when I'd gone to meet my friend he was in the midst of being harangued by the black African boyfriend of one of the station's executives who maintained that Lenny's African comedian persona Joshua Yarlog (Yarlog being a play on Yarwood, after Mike Yarwood the popular TV impressionist) was a stereotypical portrayal of Africans. While this bit might not have been to the man's taste it was genial and popular and there was no malice in it.

In fact the only controversial aspect of Joshua Yarlog was his catchphrase and Lenny blamed me for that. He insists that he told me during rehearsals that he was having difficulty finding an authentically African-sounding hook for this creation and I suggested he shout out the word 'Katanga!' from time to time.

This he did and it seemed to go down well with the audience in the studio. It was only after he and Central TV received a number of anguished and disappointed letters and phone calls that Lenny learnt that Katanga was the place where Patrice Lumumba the charismatic and popular Congolese independence leader and the first democratically elected Prime Minister of the Republic of the Congo had been tortured and murdered at the behest of Belgian mining interests, the CIA and MI6. I denied all responsibility and certainly had no memory of ever mentioning Katanga. Linda had a third explanation which was that I had done it subconsciously to make trouble.

Knowing all these interconnected people did not make my social life any less frantic though because I remained friends with all the bitter single men and women who I'd known before TV success and *The Young Ones*. This meant that I continued to have to travel to remote parts of Clapham and Walthamstow to spend time with them. Except that now they'd grown more bitter and resentful because by contrast with their lives I was doing so well. In the saloon bar of some bleak, smoky pub, having paid for all the drinks, I would be on the receiving end of a long monologue during which they told me how difficult my success had been for them. Afterwards they'd make me buy them dinner in an Indian restaurant where they would sometimes start crying. Then I'd be forced to cycle miles to get home because if I took a taxi they'd roll their eyes at my extravagance and that would invite another angry monologue.

Me carrying on seeing these individuals was not self-laceration but rather part of an effort to maintain my authenticity. I'd noticed that whenever I spent any time with a big star, a dinner party at their home to which I was only invited once or the launch of a movie, they never seemed to have any old friends. Everybody there was a celebrity of exactly the same or slightly lesser status than them. It dawned on me that as soon as these people became famous they'd got rid of anybody who'd known them before that time. After all you couldn't act like a demi-god if there was some bloke around who knew you when the big kids stuck your head down the toilet at school.

I was certain that that celebrity life wasn't for me and I didn't want to be thought of as somebody who had dumped his old mates so this was part of the price I paid. Sitting in grim Indian restaurants while bitter men wept over the frustrations of their lives across the stained tablecloth.

Perhaps that was where a lot of my money went, buying presents of bicycle accessories, alcohol and ponies for these ungrateful friends.

A Blow to the Head in Helsinki

Just after the turn of the year, me and Linda, Rik and Lise, Nigel and Roberta and Lise's older sister Cassie went on a skiing holiday to Austria. Three-fifths of *The Young Ones* going on a trip together was a sign of how close we were. I don't think there were many TV series where most of the cast would vacation together. Of course *The Young Ones* going on holiday together did mean we had to make sure that the dynamic of the boys' house didn't repeat itself outside the studio. Me and Linda had to be particularly vigilant to ensure that Rik didn't bully Nigel in the same way that the fictional Rik bullied Neil in the show.

After the fortnight was over, Linda and I caught a train to Munich and from there, with me tranquillised, we flew to Helsinki in Finland. In terms of money and fame the next big step up if you could make it was to appear in movies and late in 1983 I'd been offered a part in the film *Gorky Park*. I was familiar with the work on which it was based and as a fan of books such as Ed McBain's 87th Precinct novels, I thought the idea of setting a police procedural within the

Moscow detective force was genius. I was to play the part of Fyodor Golodkin the black marketeer. My first task as a movie actor had been to visit a voice coach in Twickenham in order to flatten out my accent and give me a neutral sort of voice. I had to do this because there was a dilemma at the heart of the film which didn't exist in the novel. How were people to speak? The solution might have been to have the Russians speak in 'Russian' accents but that often sounded crass. The more upmarket answer would have been to have those playing the Russians speak 'English' English and for the Americans to speak 'American' English but then they hired a Polish actress called Joanna Pacula for the female lead who, whilst possessing the right kind of wispy beauty, also spoke with a strong Polish intonation, and then William Hurt as Arkady Renko decided to give himself an accent which, though striking, came from nowhere on the planet so the accents were all over the place.

The movie was to be shot in Helsinki, since permission had been refused for filming in Moscow. After a few days Linda left me in the Intercontinental Hotel and flew back to London meaning I had to entertain myself.

The problem was that the stand-up comedian is the lone wolf of the entertainment tundra; we want all the attention for ourselves. We are not prepared to share any of the audience's gaze with other performers, writers or even a set, it's just us and a microphone and this shapes our personalities. By contrast a movie is very much a collective enterprise. Even a main actor is only one of maybe a thousand people on whom the success of the project depends. Because I was a member of the supporting cast my schedule was fitted around that of the main performers, leaving me with a lot of time on my hands, time which I found hard to fill. To cope with these spells of inactivity actors come to see the entire film unit, both the cast and the crew, as a surrogate family which provides them with sustenance and diversion while I just sat around waiting for Kenny Smith to somehow magically appear and sort everything out.

In the end if I wasn't filming I hardly went out, because in January the city was a cold and confusing place. All around were forbidding Scandi-fascist buildings, the bay was frozen over and the city's streets were covered in a sheet of ice. When one of our drivers wanted to turn a corner they didn't use the steering wheel, they just pulled on the handbrake and slid round the bend.

The one restaurant that served decent food and wasn't too expensive seemed to be the Finnair Terminal in the centre of the city, a large canteen-like place. The only problem was that you had to know what you wanted to eat, without recourse to a menu, before you could order and pay. Once you'd had a stab at what was available you then gave your choice to a grim Soviet-faced woman who issued you with a chit. This you gave to another woman who dished up the sardines, cream crackers and yoghurt you'd ordered.

The sole places where you could purchase extraordinarily expensive alcohol were government-owned shops, which only opened a few hours a day and whose walls were lined with large posters of cirrhotic livers, the corpses of drinkers found frozen in the snow and beaten-up women.

The only time I went for a walk it merely increased my sense of dislocation. The parliament building which was near our hotel and overlooked a big railway siding from where dark green trains decorated with Cyrillic script departed for Leningrad had, ranged across the front of it, three statues of recent Finnish prime ministers. The first statue was a conventional bronze in the pre-war heroic style, the second from the 1950s was slightly less representational, though still recognisably a human figure, but the third was two large polished granite pebbles, one about two metres high and the other slightly smaller, which made me wonder if the last prime minister of Finland had been a pair of pebbles.

Generally I just hung around the bar of the hotel marvelling at how much they could charge for a beer. One night before filming began I was sitting by myself in a corner when William Hurt and the British actor who played his sidekick, Michael Elphick, came in. Hurt had insisted that since he and Michael were buddies in the film they should go out and get drunk together. What he hadn't realised was that Elphick could be an unpredictable and unpleasant drunk with a particular dislike of a certain kind of self-indulgent American actor. As they entered they were already in the middle of a drunken argument, which centred around me. There was a scene where, during my interrogation, they were supposed to pick me up and hang me out of a window, except Bill Hurt complained he had a bad back and wouldn't be able to do it. Finally Elphick, tired of Hurt's whining, said, 'Bill, take your glasses off.' Which Bill did, unhooking them from his ears with the fumbling concentration of the very inebriated. Once he'd done that the star of the movie raised his head and Michael punched him very hard once in the face.

It was a sign of how unpopular William Hurt had made himself on the movie even before principal photography had begun that Michael wasn't immediately fired.

Helsinki at that time served the same purpose for the Soviet Union as Hong Kong did for Communist China, a handy place where they could do deals with the capitalist West. The bar of the Intercontinental was one of the places where these deals were done. Armenian political commissars knocked back endless vodkas with sad-faced Finnish timber merchants; beautiful Estonian prostitutes with hair the colour of butter solicited Israeli arms dealers into honey traps over cloudberry liquor from beyond the Arctic circle; and Texan oil men exchanged beers with copper-skinned Tajik fur traders; yet the bar possessed absolutely no atmosphere whatsoever. It was quite remarkable how dull it was and how slowly time passed there.

Things weren't much better when I was filming. A proper big Hollywood movie is like a huge demented circus that takes hours and hours to set up its camp, erect scenery, flood the area with light, then has its performers in costume and make-up put on a show that lasts perhaps a minute and a half. There was a kind of actor who passed the long empty hours by telling stories. Richard Griffiths was one of these. He would relate endless anecdotes that seemed to flow into each other so there was never a gap for anybody else to get in, and though you remembered laughing it was impossible to recall afterwards what they had been about.

Richard Griffiths' US counterpart on the film was an actor called Brian Dennehy. Perhaps because they were outside my experience I found his tales more fascinating. I would listen entranced as he told stories about how he'd been married to the dancer Twyla Tharp and the time he'd once shared a prison cell with Lenny Bruce. The only tales he told that gave me pause were his recollections of fighting in Vietnam, since I had been a supporter of his enemy – the Vietcong. I found out later that my discomfort was misplaced after a book was published called *Stolen Valor* in which the author revealed that Brian Dennehy, though he had been in the Marines, never served overseas and his tales of fighting in Vietnam were all completely untrue.

Elphick's method for passing the empty hours was to be drunk all the time. As an experiment I tried going on one bender with him which began at lunchtime on a Friday in the hotel bar and then progressed into the centre of town. I finally bailed out at about 9.30 that night while Michael didn't reappear until the following Tuesday, following an incident involving ice skating pair Torvill and Dean, a bunch of flowers and a horse.

Making a movie also turned out to be as dangerous as *The Young Ones* but this time the person in danger was me. The special-effects guy is the technician in charge of all explosives and pyrotechnics. I should have suspected there was something wrong with the one on *Gorky Park* since he was missing three fingers on his right hand and possessed only one watery bloodshot eye that worked, the other being covered by a large black patch. My character Golodkin ends up being shot in the head and, to achieve a particularly spectacular splatter effect, they made me a false latex forehead underneath which sat a fingernail sized explosive charge taped to a pack of fake blood.

At a signal I was to set off the explosive charge myself with a small plunger attached to a wire that ran under my clothes. What I didn't know was that the special-effects guy had failed to put a protective plate behind the explosive squib so that when I set it off, rather than blowing outwards it exploded backwards into my head. It felt like I'd been hit square in the brain by a large glass ashtray. After that I can remember very little, though the wardrobe mistress, Sue Wain, said I fell backwards onto the stairs and my eyeballs were vibrating in their sockets so they all thought they'd killed me. Once they were sure they hadn't, the bastards made me do it all again.

In between these two takes I was sitting in a chair in the make-up wagon shaking uncontrollably. Before we'd started shooting, knowing there'd be explosions on my head, the make-up woman had inserted large earplugs in my ears and then tinted them so they would not be noticeable on camera. Allied with the ringing in my head this meant that I was completely deaf when possibly the greatest film actor of his generation sat down in the chair opposite me and began chatting.

Lee Marvin was playing the role of the main villain in the movie – Jack Osborne. During his long career he had starred opposite Brando in *The Wild One,* Spencer Tracy in *Bad Day at Black Rock*, shown a surprising gift for comedy and won an Academy Award for *Cat Ballou*. He had also made *The Dirty Dozen* and *Point Blank*. Compared to a lot of action stars he was quite left-wing and, unlike Brian Dennehy, he had actually seen action as a Marine during the Second World War. In fact he was wounded during the Battle of Saipan and had been awarded the Purple Heart. He was a famously private man who rarely gave interviews and was sparing with his views even on set. Yet there must have been something about me that he found sympathetic since he sat and spoke to me for nearly half an hour. Unfortunately because of the high-pitched screaming in my head and the earplugs I was unable to hear a single word he was saying and my side of the conversation was confined to affable grunting, enthusiastic nods and encouraging smiling.

Afterwards I asked the make-up woman what had been said but, not wanting to intrude into a private conversation between two actors, she deliberately hadn't listened. All she could tell me was that she'd got the impression there had been some really insightful tips concerning the business of movie acting and a long description of what it was like working with Clint Eastwood on *Paint Your Wagon*.

After that Lee Marvin would nod at me affably but we never spoke again.

When the movie came out it didn't do that well at the box office but I actually got singled out for some good reviews. My assumption was that from this point I would go on to do more films and they would get better and better and my performances too would continue to endlessly improve but in some ways that first film is as good as I ever got.

The only person I got on with and stayed in touch with after filming had finished was the wardrobe mistress, Sue Wain, the one who'd worried that they'd killed me. Her husband John Wain also worked in the film industry as a first assistant director on commercials and when he came out to visit we had a meal one night. A while later when she was working on a film being made in Liverpool, an adaptation of a Beryl Bainbridge novel called *The Dressmaker*, Sue thought it would be nice to get Molly a day or two's work as an extra on the movie.

Wardrobe mistress is without doubt the hardest and most demanding job on a film: the costume department are required to have the clothes for that day's shoot ready and prepared long before the cast arrive and then, after filming has finished for the day, they have to wash and clean and store those same clothes, which means they work very long hours and those hours tend to be even longer on a period film such as this was, since it was set in the 1950s.

During her first day of employment as an extra, Molly, who should have remained on the set at all times, kept appearing in the wardrobe wagon saying to Sue, 'Oh Sue, do come on and sit down and have a nice chat to me.' When she was rebuffed, Molly attempted to organise a strike amongst the supporting artists demanding more pay. After that my mother was told by the assistant director that she shouldn't come back following lunch, so once she'd got her two free meals, barging in front of Billie Whitelaw, Jane Horrocks and Joan Plowright in the queue at the catering wagon, Molly went home still wearing her vintage 1950s costume, which was worth a lot more than the ordinary, shabby clothes she had left behind.

The Secret Life of 'Ullo John! Gotta New Motor?'

For some time the neighbours when we shared the lift with them in Lannoy Point had been saying pointedly, 'Saw you on the telly last night. I bet that's well paid, that is, appearing on the telly.' The implication being that as a fabulously wealthy show-business couple, almost on a par with Richard Burton and Elizabeth Taylor, or at least Mr and Mrs Val Doonican, we no longer belonged in a subsidised council flat. They had a point. It did feel slightly odd when the string of taxis and limousines would turn up at our flats to take me to film shoots and studio recordings. This strange situation reached a peak when in March 1984 I was on *Top of the Pops*.

I appeared on the world's number one pop music show as my hit single got to number fourteen in the BBC Chart, or number twelve in the rival Pepsi Chart, which I consider frankly to be the more authoritative.

The earliest prototype of what became my chart-topping song 'Ullo John! Gotta New Motor?' appeared as far back as the days of me, Cliff and Bill Monks. It was inspired to some extent by Ian Dury's 'Reasons to Be Cheerful' and partly it was a tribute to the Cockney drinkers in the Bedford Arms. The mod poet character who performed it in his pork-pie hat was derived from bands involved in the two-tone mod revival such as Madness and performance poets like Linton Kwesi Johnson as well as again the Cockney drinkers in the Bedford. At first I would just do it unaccompanied and it was merely a few repeated couplets but gradually it grew and got mixed in with the whole 'Mr Sweary' bit until it was my big finish every night at the Comic Strip.

One of the unexpected side effects of this association of me, Cockneys and motors led the people behind the BBC's arts documentary series *Arena* to contact me to ask if I'd like to present a film they were making about Britain's most popular car, the Ford Cortina. The idea of making a serious documentary about a mass-market car was at that time a radical one. Arts documentaries were supposed to concentrate on earnest high-minded subjects such as Nobel Prize-winning novels or expressionist painters, but the *Arena* crowd had always been different. The group of producer/directors, Mary Dickinson, Anthony Wall, Alan Yentob and Nigel Finch, occupied their own little enclave in Kensington House, Shepherd's Bush, away from the main buildings and interference of the BBC bureaucracy, and their films had a dreamy style, often with no voice-over. Nigel Finch and Anthony Wall had already made *My Way*, which dealt with that song in a very postmodernist way and now they wanted to give the Cortina the same treatment.

In the film I did a *Mastermind* piece in which the answer to all the questions is 'Cortina', then I conducted an interview with former bank robber and one-time Britain's most wanted man John McVicar, who endorsed the Cortina's credentials as a getaway car, and I wrote and performed a rather embarrassing song called 'Rogue Rep'. One stroke of luck we had was that the news that the Cortina was going to cease production and be replaced by the Sierra came out before the film was edited so the director Nigel Finch quickly got a film crew together and I improvised a eulogy on the demise of the car in the Cortina Sandwich Bar in Holborn, during which I falsely claimed that the car's name had been inspired by the good-value sandwiches available in the shop.

The Cortina documentary is still the most watched arts documentary ever shown on BBC 2, or something.

One of the *Arena* directors, Mary Dickinson, then asked me if I'd like to be featured in a documentary series called *Comic Roots*. This series looked at the comedic influences of various comedy performers. There is a particularly bizarre edition featuring Kenneth Williams singing music-hall songs in a pub to some very uncomfortable-looking drinkers. Since my career was only four years long I thought it was a bit early to be having a retrospective so I decided to give my film a narrative structure by making it about my obsession to get a drink outside licensing hours and convert it into a pub crawl. In making this film I devised a technique which I would use in all my own later TV series, which was me talking to camera walking along while doing what was essentially stand-up comedy.

My song 'Ullo John! Gotta New Motor?' was recorded at Island Records' Basing Street studios, round the corner from

Tony Allen's house. I went in there about nine at night to find that the producers Clive Langer and Alan Winstanley had already put down a basic guide track. I then spent the time until midnight improvising more couplets: 'What's that switch over there for? What's that switch over there for? Ow ow ow ow ow! Ow ow ow ow ow!' and singing the chorus. We also did a version that was just me swearing over and over which was pressed as a twelve-inch and later became a big hit in German discos. After that I left them to it and I guess that through the night they chose the best bits, which in those days must have meant them physically cutting up bits of tape and sticking them back together again.

The video was shot later and the cover photo is of me and John McVicar posed during the *Arena* documentary.

The song was first released in 1982 with me performing it on *OTT* and flopped completely. I thought that was it, but at the end of 1983, Island Records bought a half-share of Stiff Records, and the founder of Stiff, Dave Robinson, was brought in to run both labels. Robinson had had great success over the years: he'd signed Madness, and Ian Dury's 'Hit Me With Your Rhythm Stick' had been an enormous hit all around the world for the label. On taking over he went through the back catalogue of Island looking for records that the previous management had failed to make hits. He was going to prove that he could make almost anything a hit and one of the records he chose was 'Ullo John! Gotta New Motor?'

During my first meeting with Dave he said to me, 'People really hate you.'

'Yes,' I replied.

I think it was a surprise to him, he had never before encountered another entertainer who so polarised people, and this was somebody who'd signed Shane MacGowan and the Pogues to his label. With Dave's help the record was forced into the charts. None of the radio stations or MTV would play it, so Dave arranged to have a TV and a VHS machine placed in two hundred and fifty record shops and for my video to be on constant play. He also had thousands of Cortina-shaped twelve-inch picture discs pressed, which people bought as collector's items even if they didn't want to listen to the song.

You found out your chart position on the Tuesday which also meant if it was high enough you were then guaranteed *Top of the Pops*. When the call came saying the record was creeping up the charts it was a moment of tremendous exhilaration. It felt like such a massive thing having a hit record. Marie Curie might have conducted pioneering research on radioactivity, been the first woman to win a Nobel Prize and be the only person to win twice in multiple sciences but she never had a song in the charts – I did.

Top of the Pops was recorded in the same studio as *The Young Ones* and many of the crew, floor assistants, camera and make-up were the same, yet it was still a wholly different experience. It felt like one of those dreams where all your free will has been taken from you. The music industry with all its massive wealth, glamour and power was present, each band surrounded by a retinue of girlfriends, publicists and record company executives. At one point for a camera rehearsal I was standing on the podium on which I would perform and around me were several other acts also on little stages. On the studio floor I could see all the record pluggers from the different labels chatting together about their charges going, 'What's yours like?'

'Oh he's a bit of an arse, he made me buy him a shirt before he'd rehearse . . .'

'Mine thinks he's funny but he's just weird.'

I felt like a racehorse being surveyed by its owners and it struck me that those guys were the unchanging substance of the music business; we, the performers, were interchangeable.

While I was recording *Top of the Pops* I should also have been on stage at the Warwick Arts Centre in Coventry, since I was in the middle of a tour. To do both was clearly impossible but there was no way we would pass up 'The Pops' so Dave Robinson had a big Mercedes saloon waiting on the curving forecourt outside TV Centre, driver at the wheel, its big engine running. Once my bit had finished and I was cleared, me and Linda ran to the Mercedes and we accelerated away.

To get me there as swiftly as possible the driver had been told that the record company would pick up any speeding tickets. It felt like an appropriate end to what turned out to be my one true day of being a pop star, to race hectically up the M1 disregarding the laws which applied to the ordinary populace, then to go on stage over an hour late and for nobody to be able to hear me because I hadn't done a sound check. I imagined that to live every day like this, as so many in the music business did, would quickly send you mad.

Island Records, the label I was signed to, was far and away the most interesting and innovative record company on the planet. Founded by heir to the Branston Pickle millions Chris Blackwell, a posh Englishman living in Jamaica and in love with reggae music, the company had their first hit with 'My Boy Lollipop', sung by Millie Small. Now amongst my fellow signees were Irish band U2, Bob Marley and the Wailers, Robert Palmer, the B52s, Grace Jones, Tom Waits and Marianne Faithfull. In 1982, Paul Morley and producer Trevor Horn started the ZTT label which was allied to Island and whose biggest band were Frankie Goes to Hollywood. Also part of the Island family were ZE Records founded by Michael Zilkha, heir to the Mothercare clothing empire. Zilkha termed his label's music 'Mutant Disco', and signed bands such as Was (Not Was), John Cale and Suicide, The Waitresses, Bill Laswell's Material, Tom Tom Club and Kid Creole and the Coconuts. ZE was described by John Peel in *Melody Maker* as 'the best independent record label in the world'.

I had nothing to do with any of these people.

THE WORKERS UNITED WILL FREQUENTLY BE DEFEATED

At the age of thirty I'd finally learned to drive. Before taking my test, to practise I'd bought an ancient blue Fiat 124 from a farmer in Oxfordshire. Rob, a friend who lived in Banbury, brought it to London for us. Rob was the owner of a very badly behaved dog called Trin and when he got up to our flat he said, 'Just to say that Trin's damaged some of the back seat of your car a tiny bit.' Looking down at the little square box of a vehicle twelve floors below we could clearly see the huge chunks of white foam that had been ripped out of the rear bench.

The next day, looking at it just sitting there, I decided that I'd move the car a few yards for a bit of practice. Usually I took Harry with me but on this occasion I figured I would be able to drive the short distance, from one side of the road to the other, by myself. So getting into the Fiat which smelt of foam and dog slobber I started the engine and jerkily pulled away from the kerb, managing to get it up into second gear. Unfortunately just as I was about to park again another car came up behind me so I panicked, floored the accelerator and shot off up the road. Unable to stop or turn round I reasoned my only hope was to get to the big traffic roundabout at Hammersmith a mile away, circumnavigate it and return in the direction of home. This I managed to do, travelling at about five miles an hour, and causing a huge angry queue of vehicles behind me. By the time I got back, Linda was in tears thinking I'd been killed in a crash.

After I'd passed the driving test Kenny Smith sold me his old car, a 2.5 litre Triumph with big fat tyres and no power steering, which meant it took substantial effort to change direction. One of the main reasons I bought this particular car was so I could say to Linda as I drove past my old school, 'Look, they said in there that I'd amount to nothing but I'm driving past my old school in Triumph.'

In it I would take long drives that didn't require much steering, up to Edinburgh for instance just for the pleasure of being on the move, unfettered and free, and as I regarded the torrent of other vehicles on the motorway I would think to myself: Probably up to twenty-one per cent of the people in those cars are vaguely aware of who I am.

Then after the success of 'Ullo John! Gotta New Motor?' I bought myself what I thought of as a luxury car although it was not a top-of-the-range BMW, Jaguar or Mercedes such as some other comedian might buy, and my car was only a luxury car if you thought that Harold Wilson was still the Prime Minister. In choosing what to drive I'd decided I did not want to be seen at the wheel of some rich man's limousine which I thought would be bad for my image but rather I required something enigmatic and cool and British-made but outside the hierarchy of executive cars. So I purchased a 1970 Rover P5B coupé, a car I'd desired since seeing a black example driven by James Fox in the psychedelic gangster film *Performance*. Styled by Spen King and David Bache who also created the Range Rover, the P5B coupé was based on the Rover 3.5 litre saloon as driven by the Queen and Mrs Thatcher and as crashed by Princess Grace of Monaco but unlike other coupés, two-door versions of their four-door relatives, this car retained all the doors and was of the same width and length as the saloon. The main difference being that the roofline had been lowered by two and a half inches along with thinner central pillars and the addition of custom Rostyle alloy wheels, all of which gave it a sinister and sleek appearance. I bought my coupé for £5,000 from a posh Buddhist squatter called Quintus who lived in Somers Town, a dilapidated 1930s housing estate behind St Pancras Station. Then I had it sprayed black.

The first long drive I took in the Rover was up to South Yorkshire to do some shows for the striking miners. It was clear from the start of the Miners' Strike in 1984 that this was a climactic moment. An opportunity for the Conservative government to begin the process of destroying the power of the trade unions. It also seemed clear that this strike was going to be a tougher fight than the ones that had gone before in the 1970s.

There was a girl I was friendly with at Chelsea called Nicola Clarke. Her flat was opposite the Bellman Bookshop and sometimes she'd cook me my tea after the meetings. Nicola's father Tom wrote a brilliant Play for Today called *Stocker's Copper*, broadcast in 1972, and based on events during a strike of clay miners in Cornwall in the early part of the twentieth century when a large number of specially trained Welsh policemen were billeted in the homes of the strikers. One of the coppers Herbert Griffith is sent to stay with the Stocker family and after an uneasy period Griffith and Manuel Stocker become friends.

Yet when the confrontation between the miners on the picket line and the police finally arrives the policeman Griffith, despite their friendship, batters Stocker to the ground.

The trade unions did not realise that the long golden post-war summer when they had been able to strike whenever they wanted, to stop the trains and the factories and the mines, had been the exception and we were about to return to sterner times.

To take on the miners the right changed the employment laws, co-opted the police and unleashed the reactionary press while the left deployed me and Billy Bragg. There were many large benefits I took part in including a concert over several nights at the Royal Festival Hall featuring regulars of the left-wing fund-raiser circuit such as me, Billy Bragg and The Style Council but also Wham! who were then at the height of their teen fame and unlike the rest of us taking a bit of a risk by appearing at such a political event. A section of the audience booed Wham! when they appeared, ostensibly due to the fact that during their songs George and Andrew mimed to a backing track but really I thought because they were uncomfortable with somebody so mainstream appearing at the show.

Off my own bat I organised a tour of miners' clubs in South Yorkshire.

Cruising through those mining villages, street after street of neat yellow brick terraces, my Rover, low, black and sinister, gave the impression that the Kray brothers were visiting Grimethorpe to attend a concert given by the famous colliery brass band.

Perhaps because the cars were cheap or maybe out of some left-wing sentiment the miners seemed to have bought a lot of cars made in Eastern Europe or the Soviet Union. Brown Ladas, pale white Moskvitches and rear-engined Skodas in the most depressing shade of pale blue usually reserved for the walls of a TB ward lined the roads. All these cars reminded me of some of the industrial villages I'd visited with my parents when we used to holiday in the Eastern Bloc, a feeling that was further enhanced by the police road blocks on every road in, at several of which we were aggressively questioned about our movements, and the raw feeling of tension, resentment and fear in the air.

Because of our politics and our family's odd attitudes I had always felt like a bit of an outsider but part of me yearned to have what the miners had (at least for the moment) – they were part of a community that had known who it was and what it was for hundreds of years.

When some of the women from Armthorpe stayed with us in London they noticed in the kitchen the large jars that Linda kept lentils, split peas, beans, oats and barley in to make soups and her famous five-bean salad but they had no idea what they were or what these pulses and grains could be used for and were vaguely horrified when Linda told them. In return when we stayed with the miners in South Yorkshire they served us what they called a 'proper miner's meal' which turned out to be Bird's Eye Ranch Burgers and instant oven chips. Though I stayed silent what struck me was how thoroughly these women had been robbed of their traditional food culture. You'd have thought given that the miners were behaving as perfect consumers in enthusiastically embracing the idea that this manufactured garbage was more 'modern' and 'convenient' than proper food that capitalism might give them a break and not crush them under its iron heel but that wasn't how it worked.

Yet a few of these women seemed to be the only ones who were getting something positive out of the strike. Because the men were not allowed to travel it fell to the wives, girl-friends and daughters to organise political lobbying and food distribution so that they began to be aware of a world outside their pit villages and to develop a real sense of purpose. It just seemed a pity that in Britain it had required such a cata-strophic upheaval for these women to achieve some feelings of self-worth though I wondered if they would one day find themselves as a result of their efforts like me isolated in some kind of limbo eating five-bean salad, no longer authentic-ally working class but not anything else either. I left South Yorkshire with a mournful sense that the strikers were likely to be beaten and that would mark the beginning of a big reduction in the power of the left.

A little while after the conflict had ended in complete defeat one of the women rang me and asked if I could come up to South Yorkshire again to do a benefit for their local rugby club which needed a new clubhouse. I felt both saddened and affronted. I wanted to say to her, 'Don't you understand, I was only up there because I was trying to play my part in the war between the right and the left, between oppression and freedom, between evil and good. You don't get a big star like

Alexei Sayle turning out to do a benefit for your poxy rugby club!' But I didn't say any of that, I just told her I was busy.

During 1984 in an era before people regularly attended big theatres to see comedians, I sold out the massive Dominion Theatre in London and returned to the Edinburgh Fringe Festival for two late-night shows at the Playhouse Theatre in front of six thousand drunken, overexcited and hysterical fans. And though I felt defeated at the vanquishing of the miners I consoled myself with the thought that I was part of something profound with *The Young Ones*, all of us of one mind, united on a joint mission to revolutionise comedy, to kick out the old ways and build something new.

Then there was a moment during the making of series two in 1984, in the episode entitled 'Bambi', the one where the boys appear on *University Challenge*. In many ways it is my favourite episode.

I don't play any part in the central storyline of that particular show. My role, as the train driver giving a speech to some Mexican bandits about the revolutionary biscuits of Italy, had been shot earlier in the summer in Bristol so I was not involved in the live studio that week but that didn't stop me calling in to TV Centre to hang around during the pre-record.

They told me that Paul was off shooting some scenes around TV Centre and it took me some time to track them down. When I located the camera crew they were just inside a side entrance of the main building. Going closer I was surprised to see Mel Smith from *Not the Nine O'Clock News* acting the part of a BBC security guard. Then the next day in the studio his partner Griff Rhys Jones was on the set playing the role of question master Bamber Gascoigne while Stephen Fry, Hugh Laurie and Emma Thompson had been cast as the team from Footlights College.

After the recording I sought out Rik, Lise and Ben in the bar. Agitated, I said to them, 'What are all those people doing in our show? I seem to remember we agreed that all these public school Oxford and Cambridge types are the enemy, they represent systemic class oppression and the dominance of bourgeois ideology in popular culture which we have made it our mission to destroy.'

The writers all looked surprised. 'No, that was just you. We never agreed any such thing. That was all just in your head. Didn't you notice that we never subscribed to your demented class-war ravings? We think Mel and Griff, Hugh and Stephen and Emma are all just absolutely lovely. Mel's going to give us a ride in his gold Rolls-Royce later, Hugh's made us a cake and Griff's been shouting at people to make us laugh.'

A Life Told in Preserved Meat

That first summer of the Miners' Strike, as well as travelling to South Yorkshire and back I was making my second movie, in the South of France. The film was called *The Bride,* a quasi-feminist retelling of the black-and-white James Whale classic *Bride of Frankenstein.* My old friend Sting, who I hadn't seen since I'd dropped in on him the night before *OTT* began, appeared in the role of Baron Frankenstein; after fashioning a clumsy male monster played by US actor Clancy Brown, he succeeds the second time around by creating a beautiful female in the shape of *Flashdance* star Jennifer Beals.

The production was based in the medieval walled Languedoc town of Carcassonne. Linda was with me and the South of France in summer was a much nicer place to be than Finland in winter. On our first night we went for a drink with Sting and Jennifer Beals in a local bar but when we got there the owner told us it was closed even though it was only about nine. 'Fucking buy the place,' I said to Sting, but he wouldn't because he was pretending to be ordinary. Maybe he would have bought it if the bar had once been owned by Voltaire.

The director Franc Roddam had previously made the mod movie *Quadrophenia* and there were several young British actors from that film on *The Bride*, most notably Phil Daniels who played sidekick to my evil circus owner, and Gary Shail, both of whom were very keen on a party. One night despite my best efforts everybody ended up in our hotel room where they drank and ate all the contents of the minibar. Old habits died hard and not realising we could easily afford it the next morning Linda and I were appalled at how much the hotel was likely to charge to restock the fridge. So while I kept the room-service people at bay, Linda set off into town to try and find replacements. The trouble with minibar stuff is that they deliberately buy odd sizes precisely so you can't easily restock, therefore it took her all morning to track down four 23.5 gram packs of peanuts, six 8.2 ml bottles of champagne and a four-sided Toblerone bar.

Unfortunately *The Bride* was a movie that rapidly fell behind schedule (my role was supposed to be completed by mid-August but in fact my last day of work was Christmas Eve) which meant the lesser cast members such as myself and Phil had many days when we weren't used. Held on 'standby', we would lie around the pool of our hotel, the Hôtel Cité, a rambling place with a suit of armour in every corridor, basking in the hot summer sun.

One of the producers of *The Bride* had another movie on his slate which had just finished shooting in Los Angeles entitled *The Woman in Red*. He approached us as we flopped sweating beside the Pool carrying a battered cassette player which he'd borrowed from the hotel reception. The producer obviously just wanted to talk to somebody and we were the only ones around. Excitedly he said, 'Hey, you guys. Stevie Wonder agreed to write a song for our other movie and I've just been sent the first demo copy by courier.' Then he pushed the button on the cheap tape machine and we were some of the first people in the world to hear 'I Just Called to Say I Love You' as it rolled out across the glittering blue water towards the ancient stone walls and the cypress trees lining the hotel's drive.

I had a tendency sometimes to regard the time before I was in show business as a prelapsarian idyll. An era free from responsibility, criticism, compromise and anxiety. I needed to remind myself occasionally that perfect, unique moments of happiness such as this – listening to a new track from Stevie Wonder played to me by a man I didn't like much beside a glistening pool in the South of France – were only possible because I had succeeded as an entertainer.

While some of us were under-used the principals were working far longer than had been envisaged. Clancy Brown as the monster was required to have a complex latex skin built up on his face, done by the same woman who'd created the Elephant Man's head. This meant he had to be in the make-up trailer at 4.30 a.m. Because of his early call he was supposed to only work every other day for a maximum of eight hours but instead he was on set more or less all the time. Actors by and large do not complain but after a few weeks, one evening his real skin came away with the latex. Clancy was immediately put on a private jet to London and filming suspended.

That day as we waited for news of what was going to happen next there was a slightly hysterical carnival atmosphere amongst the cast and crew. To pass the time the actors decided to have a football match in the baking sun. One of the principal cast members of *The Bride* was David Rappaport, star of *Time Bandits,* and David's stand-in, like himself, was a dwarf so each side chose one person of restricted stature each. I played in defence and discovered that dwarves are surprisingly difficult to play football against; because of their low centre of gravity they are very hard to foul. I tried repeatedly to knock David over but he would be round me in a flash. Then a second assistant came and told us that filming wouldn't begin again for at least two weeks.

Me and Linda got the TGV to Paris then travelled onwards to London. We hung about at home for a few days then got in the Rover and headed back to France. To drive over eight hundred miles in a car built fourteen years before but with engineering that was a decade and a half older was taking quite a gamble and indeed all the electrics failed just as we were about to board the hovercraft across the Channel. The RAC got me going again in one of our many assignations, part of a liaison that would go on almost weekly for as long as I owned the coupé. In some ways the second or third most profound relationship in my life was between me, my car and the RAC.

Taking the hovercraft was like traversing the Channel in a demented wind farm. The noise from the engines was phenomenal and even on the calmest of days the ride was so bumpy that you arrived in Calais just a few moments before you threw up. But if you were patriotic the hovercraft made you feel proud because the technology was more or less entirely British. The French tried to build their own version which they called an *aéroglisseur*. It was much more elegant in appearance than ours but it hardly worked at all and you would often see it there on the concrete ramp in Calais lying tilted sideways, its skirt all rumpled and dishevelled, like a drunken girl after a night out in Warrington as you vomited proudly on European soil.

After the initial glitch the Rover behaved itself and motored back across France, the big Buick-derived 3.5 litre V8 engine burbling away as we sped down the autoroutes into the heat of the South. When we reached Carcassonne filming had still not resumed so not wishing to hang around we headed off again, driving further south, finally crossing into Spain. Needing fuel I stopped the coupé at a shabby little town right on the Spanish side of the border. Pulling into the petrol station provoked a sudden and unexpected tug of memory. Looking around at the tiled roofs, the faded antique shops and dusty bodegas I said to Linda, 'I know this place.'

While the fascist dictator General Francisco Franco had ruled Spain we had felt unable to visit. When he died Linda and I felt it was our anti-fascist duty to have a holiday there so a couple of years later, in 1977, in the time we were still poor, we took a ten-day package tour to the Costa Brava. It was a cheap holiday with four of the ten days spent on the coach that took us from London to the Catalan resort of Calella. We left Victoria Coach Station in the early morning, crossed the Channel on the ferry and by lunchtime were in a weird French modernist new town where most of the passengers ate at a branch of a café chain called something like Restaurant Flunchy. Not me and Linda though. To save money we had brought our own food with us, fruit, tomatoes, bread and tinned pâté, along with a metal plate and a small knife. We ate this sitting outside the restaurant on a bench.

In the late morning of the next day, tired and sticky, we swapped coaches to a Spanish bus at a petrol station in the shabby border town of La Jonquera. Before departure I sat on a stone wall at the petrol station to consume the last of our supplies. The wall was only about three feet high on our side but on the other dropped down perhaps twelve feet to an impenetrable tangle of cactus and weeds. Clumsy from lack of sleep I managed to knock the plate, the last tin of pâté and the knife off the wall and down into the cactus. Peering over the side we could see it but there was no way our food could be retrieved. So without breakfast we got on to the Spanish bus and proceeded to spend a week at the ill-named Hotel Relax.

On the way back to the UK all that could be seen from the rear of the coach was rows and rows of straw donkey ears poking above the seat backs, gently swaying along with the rhythm of the road, all belonging to the large souvenir animals everybody apart from us had bought.

Now sitting at the wheel of my Rover in 1984, I realised we were once more in that same petrol station in La Jonquera. I said to Linda, 'I wonder if our pâté is still here?'

With great excitement I approached the wall. Leaning over the drop, I was eventually able to discern, nestled amongst the cactus, the metal plate now rusty and corroded, the knife, its wooden handle rotted away, and beside it the mottled tin of pâté.

It lay there visible but inaccessible like the past. From then on whenever we were in the South of France or Northern Spain we would go and visit our pâté and when

I told Peter Richardson who holidayed every year with his kids at a resort on the Costa Brava about it, they started visiting our pâté too.

Over the years this tin of pâté, the knife and the metal plate seemed to me to become a sort of monument to my career and my life. Every time I looked down at the slowly decomposing metal I reflected on how far I had come, who I had been when I lost my pâté and who I was now.

A Note on the Author

Born in Liverpool, the only child of Communist parents, Alexei moved to London in 1971 to attend Chelsea School of Art. He became the first MC of the Comedy Store and later the Comic Strip. After years of stand-up, television, sitcoms, films and even a hit single, he published his first highly acclaimed collection of short stories. *Barcelona Plates* was followed by *The Dog Catcher*, two novels: *Overtaken* and *The Weeping Women Hotel* and a novella, *Mister Roberts*. The first volume of Alexei's memoirs was *Stalin Ate My Homework*.